Th lture of Burnout

WHY YOUR EXHAUSTION IS NOT YOUR FAULT

Kristen Donnelly, PhD
Erin Hinson, PhD

kardia
WRITING & PUBLISHING

For permissions, contact:

Abbey Color Incorporated
400 E. Tioga Street
Philadelphia, PA 19134

Cover design by: Maggie M. Griffin

ISBN: 979-8-9874696-7-5

Kindle ISBN: 979-8-9874696-6-8

Table of Contents

Section Four: Solutions

In Conclusion...

Dedication:

To all the folks lying on the floor like crumpled up pieces of paper wishing they could actually take a nap. To all the workers who know they should be treated better, and to all the employers who agree but don't know how to do it. To all the students who have taught us so much, and to everyone who has said "oh my god you're right" when we've summarized this book for them over the past five years. To our families, framilies, friends, and colleagues that love us, teach us, listen to us, and support us.

Author Note:

Hello. It's us, Erin and Kristen. We like context, and we want to state a few things up front quickly so we're all on the same proverbial page.

> — We're recovering academics, and you're going to find a lot of citations in this book. We've tried to back up everything we argue with receipts but also keep it more readable than either of our PhDs. Thanks to Eleanor, Laura, Josh, and Sharyl for keeping us honest in our attempts.
>
> —You'll notice we capitalize "White" in this book when talking about race. This is because we want to emphasize that "white" is not the default way to be a human and should, instead, be a proper noun just like style guides have recommended the capitalization of other racial groups.
>
> — There are statements in this book that will make you uncomfortable, and some will make you angry. We know. They made us angry, too. We're all learning together. Thanks for your trust as you traverse these pages.

A very important first step in moving this from a presentation to a book was Kristen's talk at the Belief and Belonging Festival 2022. To see it for yourself, please head to: https://bit.ly/BBFburnout.

Section One:

What is Burnout?

This book is about how we can all human better.

And we, The Good Doctors, have long felt that the answer to how to human better is a simple one: ask more questions, make fewer assumptions. But that's easier said than done.

Humans are really, really good at making assumptions; our brains love to group people, find patterns, jump to conclusions. When pattern recognition is helping you tell the difference between a branch and a deadly snake, it can save your life! But when you jump to conclusions about how other people feel, why they're reacting to a situation a certain way, or how they might react to something in the future, you put yourself at risk of misunderstanding the people around you. And when people are misunderstood in a relationship—be it at work, at home, at school, at church, while volunteering—those relationships erode, they disconnect, they struggle, they may even burnout.

America has a culture of burnout. This country is built-on and continues to perpetuate the ideas that a person's worth comes only from hard work, that rest is a wasteful indulgence, that exhaustion is a personal failure instead of a cultural inevitability, and that good health starts and stops with physical fitness. We are also inundated with the message that there is only "one right way" to find well-being (and it'll cost you just three easy payments of $19.99!).

In the immortal words of our favorite infomercials: there's got to be a better way. And there is. We can build a culture of *balance*. A culture where everyone is valued as a human being with inherent worth, emotions, individual life experiences, and something to contribute.

So, this book is actually about a lot of things. It's about how to prevent burnout in your organization. It's about how to better relate to your kids. It's about how to strengthen the relationships in your life, and it's also about how to better understand *yourself* and why you might be the way you are.

So, it's about how to human better, and we believe that in that regard there is always room to grow.

What is this book not about?

Up until now, the vast majority of the focus on burnout recovery and care has revolved entirely around helping a burnt out individual build coping skills and find a path to healing. That's awesome! If you're feeling burnt out, or like the environment you're in is leading towards burnout, then there are so many amazing resources to help you deal with that. If you flip to the endnotes, you'll find a link to a list of those resources for you to peruse at your leisure.

This book will still be helpful for you if you're feeling burnt out, exhausted, overworked, and misunderstood, but we won't be listing out therapy exercises or self-care routines. Instead, we'll be talking about the root causes of burnout, as well as the trunks, branches, and leaves that have grown from that root.

We're going to talk about something new here. We're going to look at the types of cultures that create environments where people burn out. We're going to examine the factors that contribute to exhaustion, misunderstandings, and interpersonal conflict in a workplace, family, or organization. We're going to ask: how can we build spaces where *everyone* is humaning better, together? So, this book is not going to be about personal healing. At its core, it's going to be about cultural healing.

Our hope is that understanding the culture of burnout better will not only help those who are burnt out find ways to feel better, but will also help prevent that kind of suffering in the future. We have the power to reshape the broken parts of organizational systems, and that empowerment starts with understanding.

Have questions? Fantastic. You're already halfway there.

Why should I read *another book* about burnout?

Because we're trying to look at *why* we're all so exhausted and why so many of us are burned out from a different angle. We're looking at culture. Because without addressing the culture that we're all living in, a lot of the current recommendations for healing can be Band-Aids on bullet holes.

For folks in *deep burnout*, we definitely recommend turning to some of the resources listed in that link at the back of the book.

There are absolutely excellent resources for doing the work that focuses entirely on your journey back to personal balance.

The more we researched and talked to people—and lived our own lives—though, we noticed that the individual answers weren't enough for most folks we talked to about burnout. They couldn't understand why different things didn't work for them, and then, they either blew off a self-care routine entirely or they felt the weight of shame for having to try so many different ones.

As social scientists, we love seeing cultural patterns and, then, investigating the why behind them. If you're looking at a river and there are a lot of people drowning in it, we are grateful for the folks throwing life preservers, but we're also going to hike up the stream to find out why everyone is in that dangerous situation in the first place.

This book is our hike up the river.

Who are you, anyway?

We're Erin and Kristen, two best friends who are giant nerds and passionate about helping people understand themselves and the world around them. We also happen to have training from some of the world's top universities in how to study cultures and do so professionally.

In both of our PhD documents, we wrote personal disclosures so that our readers would understand the perspective of who they're reading. We feel pretty strongly we should do that here as well.

Kristen:

I'm a cishet, White, middle class American from suburban Philadelphia who really, really wishes I traveled less so I could have a dog. My family has owned our own manufacturing business since I was 7, and I now co-own that with my younger brother. I'm married to a man who grew up in Northern Ireland during the Troubles, who I met when I was living there for my PhD work. We're intentionally not having children, but adore spoiling our nieces and nephews. I grew up and lived most of my life on traditional Lenni-Lenape lands, but I did not recognize that until my 30s.

Academically, I hold a Masters of Social Work in International Community Planning and a Masters of Divinity in Cross-Cultural Religious Anthropology—both from Baylor University—and I have a PhD in Sociology from Queen's University Belfast. I've studied the treatment of women in Protestant religious spaces for about 20 years, and I tend to focus that research in cultures that have experienced armed conflict (Rwanda, Colombia, South Africa, Northern Ireland).

Professionally, I've done everything from being an amusement park employee, to teaching sex-ed in Northern Irish high schools, to helping start non-profits in both the United States and various African nations. I've worked on music festivals, argued with politicians about expanding care coverage for contraception, and held students as they cried over their parents' divorces. Currently, my title is Chief Operating Officer of Abbey Companies—and through that I get to be the Founder of Abbey Research and work with two of my best friends on the planet to help everyone in the world get along just a little bit better.

In terms of what we're going to talk about here, I've been exhausted since I was ten, and probably flirted with burnout a few times. I've got some mental health diagnoses of my own that come with medication and therapy, and I had an accident as a child that means I'm in chronic pain now as an adult. I've tried a lot of the things Instagram promises me will cure my burnout, and none of them have stuck. I can't meditate, yoga doesn't do it for me, candles are fine but my allergies mean scents aren't super helpful, and the idea of daily exercise makes me break out in hives.

The main thesis of this book started about two decades ago when I moved to Northern Ireland for the first time and realized that life could move at a different pace than I was used to in America. As someone in my early 20s, I absolutely assumed the way the world worked was how it worked for me, and I'm sure I was completely jagweed to a lot of my colleagues at the time (so sorry, guys!) because I couldn't understand why we stopped to drink tea together three times a day. What the hell was a year off of work for maternity leave? What do you mean that people don't take work home with them at the end of the day?

Over the year of living there, I realized that maybe hyper-productivity wasn't the only way to human. Maybe breaks were essential, vacations were good, and spending an entire afternoon with your friends just hanging out wasn't a waste of anyone's time.

Then, I moved *back* to America. All those lessons went out the window, and I flung myself right back into two graduate degrees that fed my need to work 120 hours a week.

And, then, I moved back to Northern Ireland in 2011 to do my PhD and was abruptly reminded of all the things I forgot. You see, while a main cultural value of the United States is productivity, it's probably not in the top five in Northern Ireland. They value family, and memories, and tradition, and loooooonnnngggg pub sessions that may or may not involve inebriation but definitely involve bags of potato chips and live music. If who I was in America was a hyper productive machine who had to schedule time with friends about three weeks out, then who I was in Northern Ireland was someone available to pop round to someone's house on short notice.

Upon migrating back to the greater Philadelphia area in 2015, I missed Northern Irish Kristen so much I was in physical pain. Only took me about eight years to figure out why.

Erin:

One of the reasons why Kristen and I work so well as a partnership is how different we are as people. I am a cishet, middle class, White, American woman, just like her, but from that point on, we diverge in a lot of ways.

I was born and raised in Colorado, a very different culture from where I live now — Pittsburgh — and Kristen's hometown of Philly. My parents divorced when I was six, and her parents are still married. She is a Christian with deep personal faith, and I am an agnostic.

She grew up a theater kid, and I was a competitive athlete. She is from a small and quiet Danish/Scottish family, and I am from a ridiculously large and loud Irish one. She is married and living with her husband, and I am single and living with and caring for my elderly mother and elderly cat.

Kristen is a stereotypical extrovert, and I am a stereotypical introvert, meaning we have very different needs for social interaction and processing energy. She prefers to talk through ideas and problems, and I need time to process and reflect.

My mother raised me to consider my mental health, always, and she helped me structure breaks when I needed them. Kristen was raised by an entrepreneur who never turned off. We have a lot of different experiences and perspectives that make us who we are, and we bring all of those differences to our work and to the writing of this book.

Lest you think we have nothing in common, that couldn't be further from the truth.

We love sports, reading, Broadway musicals and Taylor Swift. We love to travel and to learn and to try new food. We love animals, awards shows, and being supportive and encouraging friends. We love *American Ninja Warrior, So You Think You Can Dance*, and a bunch of other reality shows.

But the fundamental thing that makes our bond so strong is our shared obsession with being curious. We have both been hyper curious folks for most of our lives. It's one of the reasons we love reading, travel, and any other activity that teaches us something new about ourselves and others.

Curiosity is why we both went all the way to Northern Ireland to get our postgraduate degrees and how we became friends once we got there. Curiosity is why we are social scientists, having always wanted to learn more about different people and cultures. Curiosity is how we learned all the things that make us different and all the things we share.

And, curiosity is a huge part of why we are writing this book. We both have our own experiences with burnout, shaped by our different personalities and experiences, which we will share throughout this book. But, we also know that everyone's experience of burnout is different, and so, rather than write a prescriptive book about solving individual burnout, we wanted to focus on the larger culture issues that got us here in the first place.

If I'm honest, one of the first ways I realized how differently Kristen and I saw the world was the first time I told her that my mom allowed my brother and I to have "mental health days" in Junior High and High School. My mom was a nurse and *never* let us stay home if we weren't sick enough (Once, I tried to convince her I had a fever by sticking the thermometer in my hot tea. She looked at the thermometer, looked at me, and said, "If that was your temperature, you'd be dead. Get ready for school.")

Though she was strict about taking sick days, she knew there were days that school, and life, and sports, and relationships, and stress meant we really just needed to take a break. I remember when I told Kristen that story, she was gobsmacked. She could not conceive of an adolescence where she was given permission to stop, to take a break, to admit that things were hard.

Because of that difference, and many others, we have very different relationships with mental health. But, even with all of that, what we have found throughout our friendship and working relationship is that we both react in pretty predictable ways to the culture of burnout.

Kristen talked about how her experience living in Northern Ireland showed her a different way to exist and to work in the world, and I feel the same. Just because I might be better at slowing down or taking a break, that doesn't mean I wasn't raised in the same culture, with the same toxic work ethics and expectations.

Later on, I'll be sharing my journey through caregiver burnout. My experiences with that over the last few years have really fueled my passion to write this book. We hope that all the stories we share in these pages help you understand that if you are burned out, it is not your fault. It is not you that is broken, it is the culture of burnout that is disordered. We can't fix our own burnout until we see the whole picture, so we're going to Bob Ross the shit out of burnout—let's start painting.

Chapter 1:
What is Burnout?

Before we get into the technicalities of what is and what is not burnout, let's start with the reality that no one can actually agree on this. One of the problems with current research and data on burnout is that there isn't one unified definition that we universally measure against.

The World Health Organization (WHO) maintains a resource called the International Classification of Diseases (ICD), designed to be a "global standard for diagnostic health information." In 2019, they added burnout to the ICD-11, and they define burnout like this:

> Burn-out is a syndrome conceptualized as resulting from chronic workplace stress that has not been successfully managed. It is characterized by three dimensions:
> 1) feelings of energy depletion or exhaustion;
> 2) increased mental distance from one's job, or feelings of negativism or cynicism related to one's job; and
> 3) a sense of ineffectiveness and lack of accomplishment.
> Burn-out refers specifically to phenomena in the occupational context and should not be applied to describe experiences in other areas of life.[1]

At this point, you might be asking if this means that burnout is a disease a doctor can diagnose, and the answer is, no, not in the U.S. (we're going to get into why we feel that's not a bad thing in a moment). In this 11th revision of the ICD, the WHO has put burnout under "Factors influencing health status or contact with health services," which specifically means it's *not* a disease or a disorder. It's a factor that might lead someone to seek out healthcare services. According to the WHO, experiencing burnout makes a person feel like something is *wrong*. And, that person is right. Something *is* wrong. But, it's not something wrong with *them*.

To reference yet another mysterious acronym, the DSM-5 (Diagnostic and Statistical Manual of Mental Disorders) defines a mental health disorder like this:

> A mental disorder is a syndrome characterized by clinically significant disturbance in an individual's cognition, emotion regulation, or behavior that reflects a dysfunction in the psychological, biological, or development processes underlying mental functioning. Mental disorders are usually associated with significant distress or disability in social, occupational, or other important activities. An expectable or culturally approved response to a common stressor or loss, such as the death of a loved one, is not a mental disorder.[2]

It's important to note that a critical part of a mental health disorder is that it involves behavior or patterns of thinking that are, themselves, *disordered*. "An expectable [...] response to a common stressor [...] is not a mental disorder," and that's what burnout is. It's an expectable response to an environment where instead of peaking and subsiding, stress is never-relenting.

A stress cycle response to stressors is normal, expected, and, a lot of the time, healthy, but burnout is a stress cycle hyperloop. Our reaction to stress is supposed to be, by its very nature, a *cycle*. One that completes and restarts, as needed, to protect us in times of stress by activating the core self-protective measures: fight, flight, and freeze. In burnout, the cycle does what it's supposed to do, but the stressor never wanes and the cycle never completes.

In their book, *Burnout: The Secret to Unlocking the Stress Cycle*, Emily and Amelia Nagoski explore how burnout involves being perpetually stuck in a stress cycle for so long and to such an intense degree that it becomes your base state of being. In a "forced swim test," rats who were made to swim, without hope of shore, to the end of their physical ability, simply gave up. Not just in the water, but even after being removed. They were exhausted, not just physically, but emotionally and mentally too. Their stress cycle was pushed to the limit, and it's the same when we experience burnout.[3]

You're probably flipping back to where we said that not classifying burnout as a disorder wasn't a bad thing and getting skeptical right about now, but here's why that's the case: because it appropriately places the root cause not on a disordered pattern of thinking in the sufferer, but on the situation that is causing the suffering in the first place.

The rats in the swim test aren't wrong to give up. Their situation is hopeless! They're out of energy with no land in sight! Their best hope for survival is to float as long as they can and maybe be rescued. And, when someone is immersed in an environment of extreme stress for a long time, it makes perfect sense for them to be exhausted, done, disconnected, and give in to the urge to float listlessly until rescue comes—which, in cases of burnout, it often never does.

You are not the disordered one, your environment is.

A culture of pushing workers, volunteers, or family members to the limits of their stress cycle over and over until they give up turns an office, or a school, or a non-profit into a forced swim test. This is a perspective that is so pervasive in the U.S., that we Americans actually live in a culture of burnout.

By that, we do not mean that everyone in the U.S. *is* burned out. We mean that everyone has the *potential* to burn out. We also mean that burnout is permissible, even admirable, and celebrated. Workplaces that are in and of themselves forced swim tests aren't rarities. They're the gold standard and supported not just by our cultural perspective but by employment law, healthcare structures, social services, and economic measures of success.

Some practiced swimmers, or those with a bigger toolkit of coping skills, might last a little longer before floating. The most inexperienced swimmers might think this is just what rat life is like and they just need to power through. But, most people will hit that point of burnout sooner rather than later, and whether you're floating without hope or still frantically doggy-paddling, this cultural environment is harmful to us all.

Wait, go back, what's an "occupational context?"

Caught that in the WHO's definition, did you?

> Burn-out refers specifically to phenomena in the occupational context and should not be applied to describe experiences in other areas of life.

We see this kind of language a lot in discussions about burnout: it's all about work. But, even though we could argue that an "occupational context" still includes volunteer positions, there's still a lot that it doesn't include, and it does put the emphasis on burnout being something that is inherently tied to being paid.

When researchers ask people about their level of burnout, they're usually asking people to self-identify if they feel burnt out or have experienced burnout. No shortage of ink is spilled speculating on whether or not burnout is real (it is), what causes it (we'll get into that), and what to do about it (please see Section Four). What no one seems able to agree on is what it actually *is*.

What is the history of burnout?

In 1974, Herbert Freudenberger, one of the first scholars to study burnout, defined burnout as "failure or exhaustion because of excessive demands on energy, strength, or resources." His definition doesn't specifically *exclude* non traditional and unpaid work settings, it just doesn't explore them. His perspective was based on the personal experiences of his and his colleagues at a free clinic in New York City, and his arguments for the causes and contributory factors for burnout leaned heavily on how the work made his colleagues *feel*. They were burnt out because they were over-invested, overworked, and under-appreciated.[4]

In the late 1970s, Christine Maslach took the baton and, with a few colleagues, continued to examine this syndrome, ultimately developing the MBI (Maslach Burnout Inventory), which is a questionnaire designed to evaluate a person's level of burnout. This inventory remains the most widely used quantitative measure of the condition.

Over the next 30 years, research expanded to consider other occupations besides healthcare workers—like teachers and athletes—but at the same time, it became codified into the general understanding that burnout was an occupational condition. Consideration for the other ways that stress can manifest were largely ignored. For a long time, Maslach's research, while critical and informative, was such a gold-standard, that burnout was only studied within the framework that had already been set by her work:

> The MBI appeared to provide a common understanding of the concept, suggested that it was a coherent phenomenon, and made it possible to measure burnout without the necessity of questioning or reflecting on the basic assumptions relating to this mental condition and its societal implications.[5]

This feeling persisted that responsibilities which don't involve monetary compensation are simply, inherently, not as stressful as those that do. From not only data we've read, but from being humans in the world, we know this is a glaring oversight.

Maslach isn't the only person to try defining an index or inventory with her MBI. Pines and Aronson developed *The Burnout Measure*, which focuses on "the aspect of physical, emotional, and mental exhaustion in response to prolonged exposure to emotionally challenging situations." Kristensen et al. proposed the Copenhagen Burnout Inventory. Halbesleben and Demerouti published the Oldenburg Burnout Inventory, and we have the Bergen Burnout Inventory from Salmela-Aro *et al.*[6]

The issue is that we're not fully sure a measurable scale is going to cut it.

How does burnout happen?

When Kristen was in youth ministry, the anecdotal wisdom was that youth pastors only lasted an average of 18 months in their jobs. In the intervening decades, there has been little empirical evidence gathered as to why that is, but the general consensus remains.[7] To be completely frank, one of the reasons for this is that, in many churches, they are treated as poorly compensated volunteers. There is little institutional support for youth pastors, the hours are erratic and don't lend themselves to a traditional family life, and many enter the profession directly out of college. Much like other religious volunteers, they may see their work as a calling from God. This adds additional pressure to work as much as possible and to ignore exhaustion due to theological framings of religious leadership.

We highlight this idea of "calling" because the emotions around work are just as important to this conversation as physical manifestations. If you feel that you must do this work to gain favor with your deity, or because you are put on this planet to do this work—be it paid or unpaid— the risk for burnout is even higher than someone for whom work is not attached to emotional labor.[8]

And, it's not limited to outside-of-the-home workplaces! The first research on parental burnout in the United States actually took place in the 1980s, but it wasn't until 2018 when someone developed an actual diagnostic rubric for psychologists to use. Belgian researchers Isabelle Roskam and Moïra Mikolajczak "theorized that while severe situations such as a sick child can contribute to burnout, any parent can experience it."[9] Their four dimensions of parental burnout may sound familiar to anyone in the role (or anyone who remembers the WHO's definition above).

1. Exhaustion at one's parental role
2. Contrast with previous parental self
3. Feelings of being fed up with one's parental role
4. Emotional distancing from one's children

So, we propose a new definition of workplace (to replace "occupational context") that includes: any organization or group of humans that you have a commitment to providing your time, energy, and expertise to.

It's the sense of obligation, the feeling of being trapped—for one reason or another—that creates the potential for stress. Then, it's disordered expectations, either from others or that our culture prescribes you to put on yourself, that locks that stress cycle in. And, that can happen anywhere that you have an obligation to someone else, whether money is involved or not, or whether the obligation is to your boss, your congregation, your best friend, or your own child.

There's a compounding factor, too. If you work 9-5, volunteer at the food bank on Saturday mornings, and have two kids you parent during all of this, then the stresses from each of those situations aren't completely compartmentalized in your mind; they build. If work wants you to produce twelve hours of work in eight hours, the food bank wants you to start doing Sunday mornings too, and one of your kids is getting bullied at a school that doesn't seem to care, then that all adds up! And, each of these groups has expectations of you—that you contribute your time, your knowledge, your caring, your investment, day in and day out.

Or, maybe you're one of the people holding those expectations for others and wondering why you're seeing a decline in their well-being.

We're going to use "organization" a lot in this book, and sometimes "workplace" too, but since burnout is a reaction to relentless, excessive stressors—and those can pile up in way more than just a paid, occupational setting—know that when we use these words, we're referring to our new definition and that burnout can happen when expectations are disordered and compounded in so many different places. This allows us to explore the cultures that create burnout in a holistic way, instead of just blaming "bad workplaces" and wiping our hands and marching off, proud of a job well done. There's a lot more going on here, and that makes it more complicated to unpack.

What is the difference between stress and burnout?

Clearly, stress and burnout are inextricably linked, but they're also not one and the same. It's common to refer to a heightened period of stress as "feeling burnt out," but true burnout is living in a pervasive state of stress, regardless of the fluctuations of outside stressors.

Think of it this way. We experience stress on a scale. As stressors enter and leave our lives, the level of stress we have and the amount of time we spend in the stress cycle goes up and down like the gain level on a microphone as we speak.

When life is in balance and stressors are low, the stress level is low.

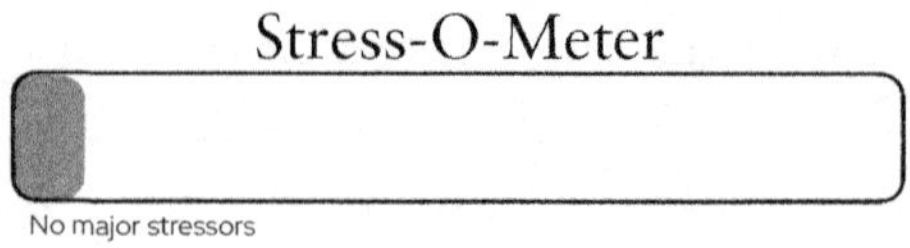

When something stressful happens, such as when work piles on an extra project or your elderly mother gets sick, the stress spikes.

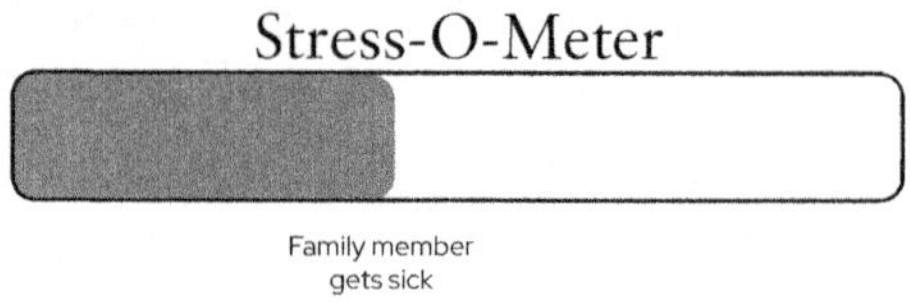

At the high end of the meter is the burnout area. Peaks of high stress will pop you into it, but with a normal cycle, you'll be able to process the stress and return to normal levels. If you can't process that stress, however, you become locked in that burnout zone perpetually. This requires being pushed into that heightened state of stress over and over for a long time without access to the skills or environment you need to complete the stress cycle and return to baseline.

Everyone's "long time," everyone's "heightened state," and everyone's "being pushed" is going to look different, but we all have the capacity to end up locked in the burnout zone.

The longer you remain in the burnout zone without an opportunity to cope with your stressors, the more the bottom end of that area becomes a brick wall. Your lowest state of stress becomes that line. And, then, as stressors continue to come and go, you fluctuate up and down only within that post-burnout space where the lowest possible level of stress is still over halfway up the scale.

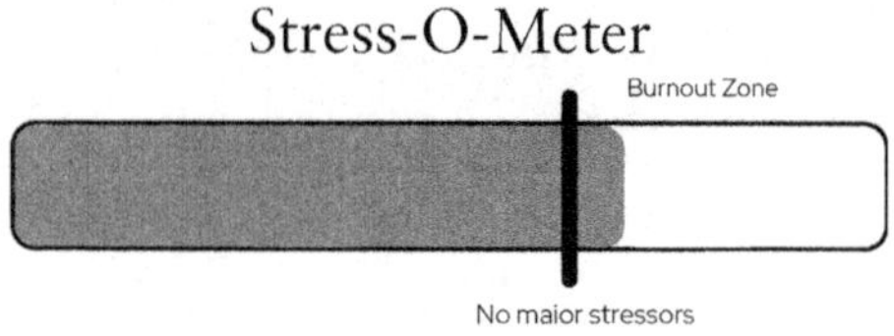

When you're feeling healthy and balanced and you drop your keys in a snowbank, it sucks, maybe even ruins your morning, but by the time you've gotten to work and had your coffee and been distracted by your emails, that feeling fades.

When you're already feeling stressed and you drop your keys in a snowbank, it layers over the other stressors you're already dealing with in your life. You might curse and groan, even stomp your foot. Perhaps, on your drive to work, you need to vent to a friend about how it's barely nine and you're already having a horrible day. But, by the time you come home for dinner, that stress has faded—the baseline might still be a little higher, but maybe you don't even remember you dropped your keys. And, tomorrow is a new day.

When you're burned out and you drop your keys in a snowbank, it probably feels like the end of the world. The relatively small stressor of a minor inconvenience, such as having to get your hand wet as you dig around for your keys, stacks on top of a base state of being that is characterized by a never-ending stress cycle.

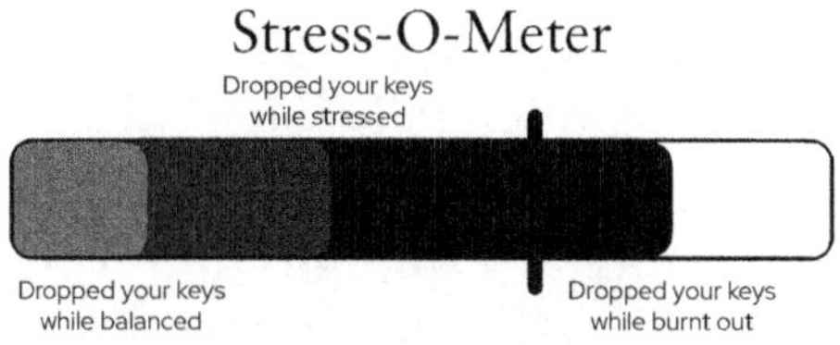

To an outsider, your reaction might look like a major overreaction, but to someone in burnout, dropping your keys has absolutely blown the lid off your stress scale because there was so little space left to manage stressors. Someone who is living with a normal stress baseline can't understand why you dropped your keys and then burst into inconsolable tears. Or, how dropping your keys made you just turn around, walk back inside, and crawl into bed, keys be damned.

Burnout is a trauma that holds you in a constant, pervasive place of stress. It rewrites your relationship to stressors and rebuilds your baseline state into one of perpetual stress. And, it can be impossibly difficult to escape from this cycle of trauma.

Chapter 2:
The Effects of Burnout

What does burnout feel like? What does it look like?

Like your bed is made of sticky molasses that doesn't want to let you go, but once you get out of bed, the whole world is made of quicksand.

Like nothing's worth doing and your hard work will never be recognized, so you might as well give up and do nothing.

Like your brain is simultaneously a wall everything bounces off of so you can't retain any information and a ping pong ball that won't rest anywhere.

Like you'd give *anything* to get to take a break that actually feels like a break, to the point of fantasizing about a small accident putting you in the hospital for a few days or joking that needing surgery would be a good way to finally snag a decent nap.

Like everything that happens to you is personally designed to ruin your day, every day.

Some days, it might feel like everything's fine and you're killing it, and other days, it feels like if your phone rings *one more time* you're going to throw it through a window.

Everyone's experiences of burnout are a little bit different because everyone's responses to stress are a little bit different. Some people shut down. Some people get angry, and some people panic. There are so many factors that affect how being burnt out makes us feel: age, gender, past traumas, compounding stressors, even the way you learned to express your emotions as a child.

Stress is directly tied into our hormonal system as well. So, in addition to the toll on our mental health, burnout can present with physical symptoms and comorbidities such as chronic pain, anxiety, digestive issues, headaches, and insomnia.[10]

Since burnout isn't in and of itself a diagnosis of a disorder, we can't easily have a checklist of symptoms or experiences that mark someone's suffering as being burnt out, but as the WHO said above, three commonly agreed upon characteristics of burnout are:

1) feelings of energy depletion or exhaustion;
2) increased mental distance from one's job, or feelings of negativism or cynicism related to one's job; and
3) a sense of ineffectiveness and lack of accomplishment

These might seem wishy-washy to you, or too vague, or even way too common. Certainly, we've all experienced feelings of energy depletion or exhaustion in our lives. In a culture where a person's value is placed on what they do, produce, or accomplish, being tired is often worn as a badge of honor. Being tired just means you're working hard, right? And, working hard means you're a good person (And, don't worry, we'll get into *why* Americans believe this soon).

We're challenging a culturally embedded belief when we say that being tired, disengaged, or feeling like a failure are *bad things* that are a sign of a problem. In fact, this statement, in and of itself, makes burnout difficult to define and to measure.

We've also found that gender has a significant role to play in how burnout and stress are experienced. We'll really dig into gender in Section Three, but a few of the key differences in how men and women experience burnout are:

- Men are more likely to experience depersonalization—including "apathy" and "numbness"—and women are more likely to experience burnout through emotional exhaustion.[11]
- For women, one of the most significant effects of burnout is the "tiredness and the constancy of doing something at any given time, without time or rest to recuperate."[12]

- For men, gender roles play a very limiting role in male burnout. Our perceptions of masculinity and associated characteristics make it harder to identify burnout in men, especially since they tend more toward cynicism (depersonalization) than exhaustion. Since we already tend to have "emotional distancing" as a masculine gender norm, it's harder to see burnout in men.[13]

This means that women usually have emotional breakdowns when they are burned out while men emotionally withdraw—usually from their life and relationships away from work.

There's much more to unpack about the impact of gender roles on American burnout culture, but we'll leave it for now. For the moment, just know that gender only adds to burnout being so hard to define and even harder to measure.

The real test of burnout should be: has your baseline stress level been pushed past a point of no return? But, this is, of course, difficult to test for in any given situation. It's difficult because if you ask someone who is experiencing burnout if they feel like they've been pushed past the point of no return, then they might say no, but this also may have been their reality for so long that they can't recognize it in themselves. On the flipside, someone in a period of normal but acute stress, like a sick loved one or an unusually difficult work project, may correctly identify the feeling that they've been pushed past the point of no return, and yet, when the stressor resolves, so does that feeling.

But, we're not here to try and make a list of criteria for burnout—clearly, others before us have tried and perhaps others after us will succeed. Instead, the takeaway should be that burnout occurs when a person's environment locks them in a stress cycle from which they can't escape. Different people are different (something you'll hear from us a lot in this book), and so, burnout is not going to look and feel the same for everyone.

It's important to remember that we can't determine if a person is going to burn out, or is already burnt out, based only on examining their situation from the outside. While toxic work environments and pervasive hustle culture are certainly part of the recipe for burnout, each individual person's experience is going to be different. After all, if you expose a group of ten people to a flu virus, some will be very sick, some may only be mildly sick, some may pass the virus on to others without appearing sick themselves, and some may not catch it all.

In the same way, a culture of burnout doesn't mean that everyone will become burnt out, but the rates will be higher, recovery will be harder, and, perhaps most importantly, burnt out folks won't be able to find social or structural support for that healing.

What does burnout do to the body and brain?

A stress response is designed to get us out of a dangerous situation ASAP. You see a tiger, and your body is flooded with adrenaline and other chemicals that give you the extra boost you need to book it back to safety.

The trick, here, is that this response is supposed to be quick, intense, and then *over*. When the danger passes, we are able to complete the stress cycle and find balance again. However, in the culture we live in now, there are few tigers that are easily escaped. Stress haunts us, stalks us, and new stressors are often piled on before old ones are halfway out the door. And, that takes a toll on our bodies.

The Canadian Centre for Occupational Health and Safety lists the following as possible symptoms of prolonged stress:

- headache
- muscle tension or pain
- chest pains
- increased heart rate and blood pressure
- weakened immune system
- fatigue / insomnia
- stomach and digestive issues
- high blood sugar
- increased cholesterol and fatty acids in blood for energy production systems
- increasing forgetfulness, anxiety, restlessness, irritability, defensiveness, mood swings, hypersensitivity, anger, etc.

- decreasing ability to think clearly or focus
- chronic anxiety
- chronic insomnia
- muscle pain
- heart disease
- depression
- obesity

Did any of these symptoms ring true for you? We could have checked a few off, for sure.

In addition, lack of sleep, anxiety, depression, mood swings, and self- or over-medicating in an attempt to find relief can lead to damaged interpersonal relationships, distraction to dangerous levels, errors in judgment, poor reaction time, and a higher likelihood of physical stress like strains and sprains.[14]

But, the damage done to a body isn't just what we can measure from the outside. Research is currently exploring changes to the brain caused by burnout and chronic stress, and the results are… not great. A study by Michel, for instance, tells us:

> Emerging research shows that the chronic psychosocial stress that characterizes burnout not only impairs people's personal and social functioning, it also can overwhelm their cognitive skills and neuroendocrine systems—eventually leading to distinctive changes in the anatomy and functioning of the brain.[15]

MRI studies show that people currently experiencing burnout have real and lasting damage to their brain. The area that handles emotional reactions, for example, is over-large or swollen, and the connections to the areas allowing us logical reasoning are damaged. As a result, participants in the study mentioned above found it more difficult to process negative emotional reactions and return to a balanced emotional state after a startle reflex.[16]

And, if all that weren't horrible enough, living like this can also increase mortality. A study by Gonzalez-Mulé & Cockburn found that those who worked jobs with high demands but low control (a perfect pot for burnout to brew in) showed a 15.4% increase in the odds of death versus those in positions with low job demands.[17]

Burnout is hurting us, even killing us. It's doing damage to our brains and disrupting our brain chemistry. We are not creatures designed to live in a never-ending torrent of stress, with a lion always over our shoulder, activating a stress response that only has a short-lived benefit and a lot of long-lasting harm. As Michel's study warns us:

> Mounting scientific evidence shows that burnout takes a profound physical toll that cascades well beyond our professional lives [...] Integrative research teams are demonstrating that burnout is not just a state of mind, but a condition that leaves its mark on the brain as well as the body.[18]

What does the mark of burnout look like for you? For your loved ones? Burnout goes so far beyond affecting our professional lives—it touches every part of who we are, how we think, and what we do about our exhaustion. But, before we can start to address this effect, we have to know the larger context, the how and the why of our culture of burnout.

Chapter 3: A Culture of Burnout

In the spirit of asking questions, you might be asking: why should I care? Or, if you do already care (because you're reading this book, after all), you might ask: why should the organizations I work for care? And, honestly, those are both fair questions!

On a human level, you should care because the toxic expectations our culture promotes don't just hurt people who are actively in burnout, they hurt everyone. Shifting expectations to protect your friends, family, neighbors, kids, grandkids, co-workers, and community from mass-scale burnout helps everyone.

On a personal level, you should care because you might think you're personally safe from experiencing burnout, but when unhealthy behavior is written so deeply into our culture, no one is safe. All it might take is a new unexpected stressor—a sick family member, a new boss, layoffs, a health issue—to send your stress levels sky-high. And, if the environment you are in doesn't provide enough support to survive that stressor, then you could get stuck there, right in the middle of high stress and quickly sliding into full burnout.

On a cultural, communal, and organizational level, leaders and decision makers should care because burnout is incredibly expensive and destructive. Harvard Business Review estimates that burnout costs the U.S. $125-$190 billion dollars in healthcare spending annually. That's right: billion.

According to the WHO, burnt out employees are tired and cynical, and they lack a sense of accomplishment. It's not difficult to imagine the negative impact that attitude and feeling of exhaustion will have on performance. Burnt out employees take more sick days—for both their mental and physical health—raise insurance costs, are more likely to quit and turnover quickly, and are less productive, even when they're working as hard as they can. Happy employees see a 12% boost in their productivity while unhappy ones see a 10% drop.[19] That spread can mean a world of difference for an organization, especially a small one.

A 2021 study by Headspace found that almost half of Americans took a sick day that year due to stress, anxiety, or mental health. 45% of people surveyed also admitted that stress caused up to a two-hour hit on their daily productivity.[20] At an average hourly wage of a salaried employee clocking in at about $30, that means a loss of $14,700 per year, per employee, for nearly half of a company's entire staff. Stress-related sick days are estimated to cost U.S. companies $30 billion a year.[21]

Companies want solutions to this problem. Even if the cynic in all of us finds it hard to believe that big organizations want happier employees, we can confidently say that they do want lower turnover rates and lower insurance and healthcare costs.[22] High stress workers are 30% more likely to have accidents than those with low stress. 60% to 80% of on-the-job accidents are attributed to stress,[23] and insurance claims for stress related industrial accidents cost, on average, nearly twice as much as non stress-related accidents.[24]

Burnout also damages relationships with customers. Customers who interact with employees who are experiencing depersonalization and demonstrating emotional disconnection, which you might remember was the WHO's second sign of burnout, are more likely to rank the service from both the employee and the organization as worse.[25]

Unhappy employees (or volunteers, or parents or, or...) simply don't perform as well, on any front. Reflect on the last bad day you had—did you get a lot checked off your to-do list? Now, imagine that every day's baseline is a bad day and all you can hope for is for things to be slightly less bad than the day before. A burnt out staff is expensive in time, money, productivity, and loss of goodwill. If the damage burn out does to an individual's health and well-being isn't enough to spur organizations into action, then hopefully profit loss and decreased productivity will motivate organizations to change their cultures of burnout.

So what's the takeaway of all of this?

The short and short of it is that burnout is a normal stress response pushed too far. A human body designed to handle brief, intense periods of stress, such as the threat of a tiger attack, is instead plunged into a constant state of tiger-stalking until every ringing phone, crying child, or project request feels like another tiger added to the ever-growing, never-shrinking ambush of tigers.

While burnout is often defined as being a workplace issue, a workplace is more than the place you show up to from 9-5 to earn money, and burnout isn't the same for everyone. There are many compounding factors for how we experience burnout individually, and a singular list of signs or symptoms doesn't serve us all that well.

Burnout is destructive, both to individuals and to organizations. The approach in the past has largely been that burnout is an individual problem with individual solutions, but we need to examine the cultural environment that is cultivating more experiences of burnout in record numbers.

So what do we do about it?

Our culture of burnout means that we are all, collectively, fostering an environment that breeds exhaustion, disconnection, and a sense of personal failure. If we can, instead, move to a culture of balance, then we can foster an environment that supports growth, comfort, safety, and community

We think the first step to that is understanding.

There are a lot of resources out there for building a personal toolkit of coping skills. Books, such as the Nagoskis's, *Unf*ck Your Brain* by Faith G. Harper, and *The Bouncebackability Factor* by Caitlin Donovan,[26] have a plethora of ways to help you understand why you're feeling exhausted and disconnected and how you can cope with it.

But, it's absolutely mission critical to start building organizations—and a wider American culture—that fundamentally believe in an environment where people are allowed to thrive instead of asking them simply to cope. We need everyone—not just those who are already burnt out—to build an understanding of what burnout is and how to prevent it so we can begin to develop preventative and mitigating practices to address our disastrous cultures of burnout. We must stop forcing exhausted individuals to wade through a sea of expensive "healing" products in an effort to fix themselves. We need to examine how we got to where we are and why we believe the things we believe. We need to do the difficult and challenging work of moving forward with empathy, understanding, and a true desire to make things better for everyone.

Research is lacking when it comes to the cultural context of burnout. Studies look at what burnout looks like, the organizational contexts that can create it, and how to heal from it, but as Linda and Tosten Heinemann explain, "The social and societal context of burnout is not taken into account systematically."[27] Up until now, this statement is true, but we'd like to change that unfortunate reality. And, together, we will.

In the next section of this book we're going to explore the important question, "How did we get here?" We will answer this question by looking at the cultural foundations that have built America into what it is today.

In the third section, we're going to talk about where we are now and the current factors that create environments that force people to doggy-paddle for their lives.

But, know that it *doesn't have to be like that.* Humans are perfectly capable of being productive, attentive, and useful employees (or volunteers, or stay-at-home-parents) and, at the same time, being respected, understood, and supported at work, home, and everywhere they offer their time and expertise. So, in the fourth section, we're going to talk about solutions to the problem on a cultural and organizational scale.

The fourth section is also where we're going to share some action items, approaches, and reflections that can help you move away from a default mindset of contributing to a culture of burnout and can help you be a part of shifting our culture from burnout to balance.

This is a problem that's fixable, but fixing the core issue isn't the purview of the people who are suffering from burnout. The responsibility of change falls to organizers, leaders, managers, lawmakers, and mentors who can reshape our perspective on a healthy organizational structure, engage with others on a deeper level, and be willing to fight to break cultural conditioning that's hundreds of years old.

Section Two:

The Soup We Swim In

Why soup?

Well, this might seem like a strange title for our second section, and truly, by the time you finish reading this book, you'll be damn tired of our soup metaphor. But, you'll also have a solid understanding of all the parts of our American culture of burnout. So, why are we talking about soup?

As two social scientists, we are trained to look at the world around us and to study the history, context, and meaning behind it all. In fact, we've talked about these elements of the human experience for years—whether through our corporate trainings or for videos on our YouTube channel. As obnoxiously curious people, we are constantly asking the same questions over and over. "Why does this happen?" "Why do people behave this way?" "What are the origins of this piece of culture?"

For quite a number of those years, Kristen used the phrase "the soup we swim in" to talk about any element of cultural understanding. When we talked about the culture of gun violence for our podcast, for example, we talked about Americans' relationship to gun ownership as "the soup we swim in." The phrase means, any part of a culture or society that can be a cause of a particular problem, an explanation for a particular behavior—basically, it is any reason for why things are the way they are and it's inescapable.

Therefore, for this section to make sense, we need to unpack what we mean when we say "the soup we swim in" in relation to America's culture of burnout. This section is where we hop in a time machine and go back to the origins of American work culture. We will also break down other elements of American culture that are an essential part of our burnout culture.

Questions we will consider include: What are the key ingredients that make up this soup? What is the broth made of? How long has it been simmering before we started to add other ingredients? How did we get to the version of the recipe that we have now?

The Good Doctors' American Burnout Soup

TIME TO COOK: *403 years*
SERVES: *Entire US population*

INGREDIENTS

- The stock of Puritanical beliefs (broth)
- 1 spoonful of dried US history and culture
- 2 tbsps intersections spice mix
- 1/4 cup each of generations (finely chopped)
- Season to taste with the stories we tell (collective & individual)
- 2 cans of chunky gender roles
- 3 lbs. of ground Wellness Industrial Complex

DIRECTIONS

1. Simmer the stock of Puritanical beliefs for 400 + years
2. Slowly stir in the US history and culture, intersections, gender roles, and finely chopped generations.
3. Season to taste with the stories we tell
4. Brown the Wellness Industrial Complex in a skillet, then add, stirring regularly
5. Serve with fresh capitalism and don't enjoy!

To cover our questions thoroughly, we're going to cover a bit of American history. We're going to explain why generations shape our understanding of work and burnout, and we're going to talk about other ways to be human that can influence how we live and work—such as gender, race, and ability. Then, we're going to spend a little time talking about the relationship between storytelling, trauma, and burnout, and finally, we're going to wrap it all up by talking about the big C—not cancer, COVID.

Chapter 4:
I'll Sleep When I'm Dead, or Why the Puritans are to Blame

Why is America's culture of burnout so darn special?

The expectations we have of our working population didn't just pop up out of the ground in the last ten years, American culture was built on the foundational premise that good people are hard workers. If you'll allow us a brief foray into socio-religious historical ponderings, we'll explain why.

Even though America is not a Christian nation, the first non-Indigenous settlers were English Protestant Christians fleeing persecution for their separatists beliefs. The first group of these settlers to land and stick and truly establish themselves as an enduring culture were the Puritans.[28]

To be clear, the Puritans are not to be confused with the Pilgrims who participated in the fabled "First Thanksgiving." A good way to keep those two groups distinct in your mind is to remember that the Pilgrims arrived first, came over on the Mayflower, and packed beer on their ships to the New World. The Puritans, on the other hand, arrived second, landed elsewhere in Massachusetts Bay, and packed Bibles. What they had in common, though, was 1) their fashion sense (they were both apparently into black clothing and those funky hats) and 2) they were both, ultimately, chased out of Europe for their opposition to the Church of England.

The Puritans believed firmly that the Bible was the inerrant word of God (meaning it was word-for-word dictated from God's mouth by the hands of man to the page). They also believed that their calling in the New World was to create a "City on a Hill" (literally what their leader, John Winthrop, preached), which they described as a city that ran entirely on Biblical principles as determined by God's providential will. They also believed that this "City on a Hill" would serve as the manifestation of the Kingdom of God on Earth.

Or, in non-Christian terms, they took what they thought the Bible was teaching, decided it would be best if everyone agreed with their interpretation of it, and set up shop to create a culture that was centered around their faith practices (but, just to note as a fun fact, this wasn't a full theocracy the way we think of the word).

Before we get any further, we should pause on that last point—they did not establish a theocracy. These folks did not have the modern concept of the separation of Church and State, but they'd just fled a monarchical theocracy and weren't interested in recreating one. To them, Church and State were symbiotic. That is, while there were parts of society they thought should be governed by the civic state (taxes, permits, who collects the garbage), they believed that all civic policies should be informed by the state church.[29] This is an important evolution from England's reality—where the monarch is the head of State and the Church—to what America enjoys today through the religious freedom protections provided in the Constitution.[30]

So, back to our pals who landed in Massachusetts and founded the Massachusetts Bay Colony. They were the first group of White folks to have economic success in North America, and so, they determined what success meant, what survival meant, and every group that came after them followed their model.

The New England Puritans were the original purveyors of the "American Dream." How did they achieve this? Through three very important pieces of their theological system:

1. To be a pious person—which to them meant you

were a *good* person—you had to work really hard. Laziness was a sin.
2. Part of working really hard was the belief that—with a few exceptions like barn raisings—asking for help was a weakness.
3. Working really hard on Earth was to earn your heavenly reward: entrance into heaven and an afterlife of joy and rest.[31]

The idea of working really hard and then being rewarded for it is also a basic tenet of capitalism, and so, of course, they achieved financial success[32]—as soon as the Indigenous folks taught them what corn was and how to cook it. Capitalism works if you measure success by resource accumulation.

Over time, the idea of working hard for reward and financial (material) success became simplified down and distilled, and it solidified, moving from an opinion into an absolute fact that hard workers and good people are the same thing. Add in the Puritans' strong sense of individualism (only your faith and your works affected your reward), and you can probably see some of the ways these ideas are still influencing us today.

So, the beginning of America—when she was but a seed of an idea—was that you were a good person if you worked hard, and you were supposed to do it alone.

Rest is for later.

Or: I'll sleep when I'm dead.

We've probably all heard, or made, that joke, but how much of a joke is it, really? American culture continued to develop and the civic religion did alongside it.

And, yes, our culture has evolved, and there are many more influences than just the Puritans. But, a core seed was planted, and this vine has curled into the way that we think, relate to others, and most importantly, the way we view work, productivity, and rest.

In other words, the Puritans were the people who first decided who got to be and what it meant to be American. They are the folks who picked the original broth flavor, if you will. So, we've expanded their idea of "who" gets to be American, but we need to check the "what" and "how" of it all because America has just kind of accepted the "what" and the "how" without double checking to make sure this is actually what and how we want to be.

And, it's not just the "people who work hard are good people" aspect we need to explore. There are larger ramifications at play as well. For example, we often assume that if you are a good person, then you'll work hard, and capitalism declares that working hard will earn you lots of money. Therefore, if you're poor, then you must not be working hard. And, we also often assume that those who don't work hard are bad people, and they deserve to struggle and suffer.

We get infected with the idea that everyone is able to pull themselves up by their bootstraps, that the *only* thing standing between *any* American and success is more hard work. It's too uncomfortable for most of us to consider that sometimes hard work is not rewarded with success because we are so conditioned to believe the opposite is true. We struggle to understand that sometimes good people do not or cannot work hard and that sometimes success comes to those who have not worked hard. It is even more confusing for us to stop and to examine what success really means and why we're striving so hard for it.

Chapter 5:
A Little Bit Salty

All right. Now, we've got the base of our broth made from Puritan beliefs, but before we move on to the meat and potatoes of this soup, it needs a little seasoning. Returning to our recipe card, next on the ingredients list is a healthy spoonful of U.S. history and culture.

That might seem like a tiny amount of a pretty big ingredient, and perhaps it is, but if you've ever had unsalted broth, you might see what we're getting at. Truthfully, each of the seasonings we're about to discuss could be their own book on burnout, but we don't have the time or the space to dive deep with all of them here. So, instead, this chapter is going to be a light touch on a few critical aspects that shaped the way American culture grew and changed over the years: individualization and privatization of American home life, pharmaceutical companies, and the 24-hour news cycle.

Why is American culture so individualistic?

One of the most significant ingredients that helps flavor our broth and turn it into Burnout Soup, is the hyper-individualistic nature of American culture and society. In social science research, we talk a lot about cultural values and norms (we'll be talking about gender norms and roles a lot in the next two sections). Perhaps the most widely debated cultural value is the spectrum between individualism and collectivism. America is one of the most individualistic cultures in the world, and a lot of that individualism can be traced back to our friendly Puritans.[33]

Let's begin with those key tenets of Puritan belief:

1. Being a good person means working hard
2. Being a good person means doing it alone
3. Being a good person means not resting until you are six feet under

We can easily see how they would reinforce ideas of individualism. Individualistic cultures tend to have a big emphasis on independence and have strong feelings of autonomy. Ava Rosenbaum describes the difference between individualistic and collectivist cultures like this: "People in individualistic cultures view themselves separately from the group, whereas people in collectivist cultures view themselves as part of the group."[34]

Taking that a step further, Claire Andre and Manuel Velasquez define individualism as "the belief that 'the good society' is one in which individuals are left free to pursue their private satisfactions independently of others, a pattern of thinking that emphasizes individual achievement and self-fulfillment."[35] The Puritans started us on the path to hyper-individualism, and each successive group of cultural and political leaders followed that path.

Andre and Velasquez argue for the impact of the writings of John Locke for our uniquely American understanding of individual freedom.[36] But, in his book on the roots of American individualism, Alex Zakaras contends that we have the Jacksonian era (1820-1850) to thank for the real calcification of some of our biggest national ideas.

This period was the era of mass democracy. Combining those democratic changes with the expansion of print culture and the availability of cheap newspapers within American homes, we see the creation and practice of several "foundational myths" that shaped our national identity.[37]

Zakaras defines foundational myths as ones that tell "a story of the national origins that explain who its people are and who they are meant to be."[38] One of the key foundational myths from this period in American history was the myth of the "self-made man." As these myths about our country's founding and origins began to propagate through the widespread use of print media, such as newspapers and pamphlets, we evolved into a country that "celebrated the freedom and self-reliance of the ordinary white farmer, settler, and craftsman."[39]

We'll be talking about race and gender a bit later on in this section, but it is important to point out here that racial and gender discrimination play a big part in American individualism. Zakaras writes, "[In] Jacksonian America, the free individual celebrated in the nation's mythology was almost always a white man, and the broad freedom he asserted included the freedom to subordinate women, to expropriate Native American lands, and to enslave and oppress Black Americans."[40]

In examining the creation of this foundational myth, we can certainly see how "the American Dream" became just a re-framing of the individualistic impulse within American culture, which found its popular expression in the phrase "self-made man."

How did American home life become so private?

You might think it odd to include a section about the history of porches on American homes, but trust us, it's not the strangest Google search we did for this book. In reality, the evolution of home architecture has a lot to say about our current culture of individualism and burnout.

Porches reached their height of popularity in the second half of the 19th century. They were important to American culture because they helped to evolve social norms by becoming an extension of the house, an "outdoor parlor" where people could socialize with their friends and neighbors.[41]

Incorporating the rapid growth of what became the American middle class, the Industrial Revolution helped ensure that front porches were an important architectural feature that indicated status and wealth. However, this all began to change after the Great Depression and World War II. At that point, if Americans could afford homes at all, they were moving away from urban centers and toward suburban developments that featured prefabricated houses with simpler styles.[42] By the middle of the 20th century, front porches were few and far between.

These changes meant that American's home lives became more private and isolated, especially in the suburbs where neighbors lived farther apart, and socializing turned inward to activities inside the home. Following WWII, the next great shift in American culture came from the start of the Cold War and the increasing fear of communism across the country. As Senator Joseph McCarthy and the American media focused on which famous celebrities could possibly be secret communists, Americans learned to be afraid and distrustful of their neighbors.[43] Within that context, at least for the American middle class, the front porch began to become a fading memory as seeds of distrust were continually being sown into American culture.

Have you ever wondered what true crime has to do with burnout?

Neither had we, but we found a connection!

Another pivotal shift in the privatization of American home life was the 1959 murder of a family in the small town of Holcomb, Kansas. The story of the Clutter family became the subject of Truman Capote's blockbuster novel *In Cold Blood*, and through his painstaking reconstruction of the murder and subsequent investigation, Capote describes how a sense of fear, vulnerability, and distrust spread through the rural community. Where once they never locked their doors and never hesitated to help a stranger, the effect of this case changed the way the town of Holcomb, and a lot of Americans, thought about their home and their home life.

At this stage, we wouldn't blame you for being confused as to how all these ingredients belong in our soup recipe. But, it is important to remember how each of these changes were viewed through the lens of American individualism. If you already believed, for instance, that you were supposed to achieve success and happiness through your own individual achievements, then each of these examples—from the changing of home architecture to the rise of anti-communist sentiment and the media coverage of American violence—was a subconscious reiteration that it's just better to go it alone.

And, what is one of the biggest factors of the high rates of burnout in America? Our hyper-individualistic culture that raises people to turn inward to solve their problems and not outward to build a community that can help figure out collective solutions. Our culture of distrust that is perpetuated by the mass distribution of fear through the media, from accusations of communism, which we still see happening today, to true crime murder that also continues to gain in popularity each year.

Why do American pharmaceutical companies have so much power?

One of the biggest ways that Americans have bought and sold the idea that we have to solve our problems alone is the uniquely American power that pharmaceutical companies have in determining how any of us are going to achieve "wellness."

It might sound strange, but one of The Good Doctors' similar experiences with culture shock came the first time we returned home after traveling abroad and turned on the television. We have no memory of what we were watching, or why, but we both remember being shocked by the frequency and the duration of commercials for pharmaceuticals.

Why was that so shocking? Because they don't have ads for pharmaceuticals where we previously traveled and lived. In fact, aside from the U.S. and New Zealand, they don't have them anywhere else in the world.

"But how do people know what medicines or treatments to take?" you may ask.

They speak to a medical professional before they decide what medical intervention they need. But, in the Land of Private Healthcare and Big Pharma, that is not the desired course of action.

So, how did we get to this place? How did pharmaceutical companies get so much power over ordinary Americans? Why are we the only developed nation in the world to have astronomically high costs for private healthcare? These are all great questions, but first, we want to add a short disclaimer:

The pharmaceutical industry is *always* driven by demand, which is driven by marketing rather than truly being driven by science. Drugs are *always* released before fully adequate testing on potential side effects. We're fully ready to admit that the industry is a shitshow right now, but in its defense, it's always been a shitshow.

Before we can understand how this particular shitshow has such an impact on our culture of burnout, we need to take a stab at answering those questions.

Why do we have privatized insurance?

We cannot understand the full impact of the massive and overreaching pharmaceutical companies unless we start with the concept of private insurance. Most of the big changes in American healthcare started to take place in the middle of the 20th century.

We really have President Franklin D. Roosevelt to thank for privatized healthcare. During his tenure in the White House, he froze wages and created a specific tax that allowed employers to provide private insurance as a perk to employees. The tax allowed anything they spent on employee health care to be tax deductible. When this new tax benefit was combined with the need to be competitive for new talent, America saw a dramatic rise in the significance of private health care.

The labor boom following the end of WWII saw increasing demand for high quality healthcare, and by 1951, Aetna and Cigna became the first for-profit insurers in the market.[44] These companies essentially opened the floodgates on the market of private insurance, and by 1959, "70% of all Americans had health insurance plans that covered the most widely prescribed drugs."[45]

When did we get mass produced, widely available medicine?

The entire pharmaceutical industry started from the idea that it was helping to "cure" pain and started long before there was any thought of government regulation. While penicillin was the first wonder drug for the masses, Americans understood drugs as a solution to their pain for nearly a century before that wonder drug hit the market.

There are lots of stories of how Civil War and Mexican-American War vets needed relief, and tiny pills or tonics or smoke gave it to them. When you think about it, it's not a far leap from the idea of penicillin to early mental health medications, which were ineffective and numbing, to what we have now.

So, how did the first "wonder drug" of penicillin come to be? Believe it or not, it was the last global pandemic. It was the Spanish Flu of 1918 that "spurred academic and private researchers to redouble their efforts to find treatments for contagious infections" because pharmaceutical companies "had nothing to slow or treat the pandemic."[46] In 1928, Alexander Flemming invented penicillin while working in his Scottish lab, and by 1942, it was ready to be mass produced for the world. And, mass produced it was.

What came after penicillin?

As penicillin flooded the market, the general public believed that it was a miracle drug for all ailments, but the medical and pharmaceutical communities knew that it wasn't. However, in order to keep their profit share, they had to keep convincing Americans that one pill was truly all they needed for any ailment.

Post-War American culture was marked by the attitude that Americans believed they were powerful and they could defeat anything—both facism and bacteria. We already had pain pills to help with suffering, and now, we needed pills to fix our bodies. Early pain medication combined with several antibiotics fed into that need and started to reinforce the idea that any problem could be solved with the right pill or shot.

Remember, the Puritans gave us the belief that to be a good person, you had to do it alone. America took that belief and molded itself into a highly individualistic society, and now, all of a sudden, individuals could solve their own medical problems by taking a pill.

At this point in our history tour, you might be wondering how the FDA fits into all this. Our good friend FDR introduced the first regulations into American pharmaceuticals with the Food, Drug, and Cosmetic Act of 1938, which led to the creation of the Food and Drug Administration (FDA).[47] American pharma was not pleased with this new regulatory body. As an industry, they hated any attempt at regulation and had "always operated in an industry built on the inviolable rights of consumers to self-medicate."[48]

Shocking that an industry making money hand over fist wouldn't want regulation, eh?

How did Pfizer and Arthur Sackler ruin everything?

You might think that question a bit confrontational, but if you've seen our YouTube coverage of Hulu's smash mini-series *Dopesick*,[49] then you know we have pretty strong feelings about the Sackler's and the carnage they wrought on the American people.

We have yet to talk about the role of medical advertising in all this, and that's where the Sacklers and Pfizer come into the story. Following the boom production of penicillin and other antibiotics, some pharma leaders argued that all medicine should be put in a public trust, as they'd all made their money off the boom, and shouldn't continue to make obscene profits off the health of the American people.

As every good story needs a villain, Jack McKeen—the then CEO of Pfizer—decided that they would rather continue to make obscene levels of profit. Pfizer went on to create a massive marketing campaign for their broad spectrum antibiotic, terramycin (invented in 1950). The marketing of terramycin marked a real sea change in American pharma, as it was the first time there wasn't even the pretense of public good motivating the production and distribution of the drug.[50] They made the drug purely for profit, and the American pharma industry never looked back.

Who was the evil genius behind this marketing campaign? None other than Arthur Sackler, the man who invented medical advertising at Pfizer in the 1950s.[51] Operating on the principle that you should be able to make your own healthcare decisions, they set out to convince Americans that they shouldn't trust their doctors, because they don't know what's right for you. Our culture of distrust is now adding mistrust to the mix.

Why would American pharma want you to believe that? Because the more you believe that your doctor can't help you, the more you are desperate to find a solution to your health problems, at any cost. This basically created all the space American pharma needed to flood the market with one pill after another.

Arthur Sackler's legacy in the industry was that he always chose what would make Pfizer the most money over advertising that was medically truthful or transparent.[52] He found loopholes in federal regulations by advertising directly in medical journals, which was not subject to government oversight. He basically created the blueprint for how big Pharma companies operate to this day.

What does all this history have to do with burnout? How many times have you thought to yourself, or heard a friend say, "God, I wish I could just take a pill and feel better?" Or, "It would be so much easier if there was a quick fix for this?"

We have these thoughts, and we make these wishes, because of the stranglehold that American pharma has on American society and on the idea of physical health and well-being. We've been living under the influence of medical advertising for so long, that our first instinct when something is wrong with our bodies is to find a pill to treat it with—entirely on our own because, remember our Puritan lessons, we don't need anyone's help. Distrust of each other and mistrust of our healthcare professionals is a potent recipe for American individualism.

And, this is especially true for how we approach burnout. The power of American pharma is a huge reason why American burnout culture is so darn special. But, how did these toxic messages and advertisements get beamed into our homes, our hands, and our brains day in and day out?

Through mass communication such 24-hour news networks, the internet, social media and smartphones. So, before we move on to talk about other larger ingredients of our burnout soup, we're going to spend a little time talking about what OJ Simpson has to do with all this.

Do we know the lasting impacts of the 24-hour news cycle?

Well, we do know one lasting impact of the 24-hour news cycle: fear. Fear that is mass distributed to sow the seeds of distrust and mistrust and enhance the American version of individualistic ideas. Some call it freedom, but it sure sounds a lot like fear to us. And, perpetual fear only leads to burnout.

When we deliver training on generations to members of Gen Z (13 to 28 years old as of this writing), we often talk about the white Bronco car chase from the coverage of the OJ Simpson murder case and trial. We're usually talking to young people who weren't alive when that happened, so we explain that it was a seminal moment in American media history because it was the first time that daytime programming was interrupted for breaking news.[53]

Can we even imagine a time before breaking news banners were a part of our daily life? These kids *can't*, and it's one of the ways that we teach them that the America they know is very different from what previous generations ever experienced.

What the media frenzy over the Simpson case created was the world of 24-hour news media coverage, another uniquely American invention. Even though CNN, the first 24-hour news network, was launched way back in 1980, they didn't grow in popularity and reach until their coverage of the Gulf War in the early 1990s and the Branch Davidian/FBI standoff in Waco, TX in 1993.[54]

But, it was the constant media coverage of the Simpson trial that forever altered the media and news landscape. If you lived through this time, then you might remember that every aspect of the trial was covered by Court TV and CNN, "an unprecedented standard for the 16 months of legal developments—and people followed along."[55] With this coverage, the trial and the live televised verdict became one of the most influential media events of all time. It "created some of the most intense early demand for the current 24-hour news cycle and sowed the seeds for the reality television boom to follow."[56]

This singular moment in American TV history is, in large part, responsible for the mass information and 24-hour news cycle we now cannot escape. When we lived abroad in Northern Ireland, we quickly realized that folks outside of America were not inundated with sensational and sensationalized news stories day in and day out. As we fast forward to present day America (2023 at the time of writing), many scholars of this phenomenon are writing about the impact of this coverage on our mental health.

Since we've had almost 30 years of post-Simpson 24-hour news, and added to that mix the internet, smartphones, and social media, there is a growing interest in understanding the impact that the constant stream of information has on our ability to process and recover from the stress this can cause.

If you think back to the early few months of the COVID-19 pandemic, then you can remember the fear, the uncertainty, and the constant stream of news and information, which had a significant impact on our ability to deal with the stressors of the pandemic.

So, why is this an ingredient in our burnout soup that we need to explain? Because we are living through this era of information overload, and the more we study it, the more we learn about how it's impacting our mental health and stress responses.

Why is the 24-hour news cycle so stressful?

"Headline stress disorder" was coined by Dr. Steven Stosny in the wake of the 2016 presidential election.[57] This concept references the high levels of stress that Americans experience when they are tuned into the 24-hour news cycle. The disorder can lead to feeling overwhelmed and powerless, as well as experiencing stress over the news being consumed.[58]

When medical professionals began to study this heightened stress they found that "subjecting ourselves to an endless barrage of tragedies and trauma can foster a real sense of being out of control."[59] In relation to burnout, think about how much more difficult it can be to recover from the stress of your everyday life or a particularly stressful event when you feel as though you can't recover from this "barrage of tragedies and trauma" surrounding your everyday life.

If you are experiencing almost constant stress from the impact of the 24-hour news cycle—and it doesn't matter if you consume that news from the TV, from social media, or from the news app on your phone—then you may start to develop self-protective measures against the high level of stress. One of these self-protective measures gaining in popularity is the concept of "compassion fatigue."

We'll talk more about compassion fatigue in our Section Four discussion of boundary setting, but we feel it is important to get you familiar with the concept here, first. You may have heard it mentioned during the worst times of the pandemic, or even following another string of mass shootings.

Compassion fatigue is defined as "a state of exhaustion and dysfunction, biologically, physiologically and emotionally, as a result of prolonged exposure to compassion stress."[60] While many people only associate it with caregiving professions, it was not long after it emerged as a concept in healthcare that "a similar concept began to appear in media studies—the idea that overexposure to horrific images, from news reports in particular, could cause viewers to shut down emotionally, rejecting information instead of responding to it."[61]

Basically, what compassion fatigue is asking is if it is possible to experience burnout from the news? From the research we conducted, there seems to be a growing perspective that compassion fatigue is a natural response to feeling overwhelmed by the number of traumatic events consumers of 24-hour news coverage are exposed to on a regular basis.

To connect this back to burnout, let's revisit the WHO's three characteristics of burnout:

> 1) feelings of energy depletion or exhaustion;
> 2) increased mental distance from one's job, or feelings of negativism or cynicism related to one's job; and
> 3) a sense of ineffectiveness and lack of accomplishment

All these characteristics can be found in how Americans respond to the daily bombardment of breaking news, catastrophes, crises, and traumatic events that comprises our uniquely invasive and pervasive 24-hour news cycle.

Both of us cycle through compassion fatigue regularly in order to strike a balance between staying informed and taking care of ourselves, but we wanted to highlight what is uniquely American about how we consume news and information and how it contributes to our culture of burnout—it overloads and overwhelms us.

We'll have plenty of tips and solutions in Section Four for how to set and maintain healthy boundaries, which is a huge part of living in the world today, but for now, it's time to head back to our trusty recipe.

We've taken our Puritan broth and added American individualism, which is carefully crafted from the privatization of homes (distrust), the power of pharmaceutical companies (mistrust), and the era of mass information (fear and overload). The soup is now starting to smell strongly of the base of American burnout culture.

The next big ingredient we have to add is the importance of understanding generational differences when it comes to burnout. We've all heard the jokes about Boomers never retiring, and Millennials being too poor to have a mortgage, and now, it's time to unpack what that all means for how each generation handles the stress and expectations of the workplace, and how they handle burnout.

Chapter 6: When You Were Born Matters: Generational Differences

What are generations and why are we talking about them?

When it comes to values and expectations, we're currently witnessing massive shifts between the generational cohorts active in the American workplace. To talk about burnout, we have to talk about generations because Millennials and Gen Z—the two youngest generations in the workforce—are dramatically altering the way we look at a work-life and a home-life balance, the way we reprioritize what a workplace looks like, and the way we talk about burnout.

We like to say we've studied generations since before it was cool, but we've certainly studied generations since before COVID. For the last three or four years, we've been spending a lot of time looking at generations: what they are and how they impact the way we work. Undoubtedly, COVID had a big part in this, which we will get to as well, but let's start with the basics. What are generations?

A generation is a 15 to 20 year period we use to describe a cohort of humans. These groups are marked by their world views and the social, political, economic, and technological changes that all happened within that 15 to 20 year time period. Each generation is usually influenced by larger sociological changes. For example, Baby Boomers were largely impacted by changes in U.S. foreign policy after World War II, the Civil Rights Movement, and the large-scale cultural changes of the 1960s.

Because of these influences, each generation represents its own culture, and there are even subcultures within those larger cohorts.

We'll be breaking down elements of each generation, but it's important to remember that these are generalizations. Within each age group there will, of course, be differences, and none of the age cut-offs are hard lines—the edges of every generational group will always be fuzzy. Using averages and aggregate data can be an amazing way to study groups of humans, but when generalizations become stereotypes applied to individuals, that can be harmful.

These different groups and subgroups bring different beliefs, values, and expectations into the workplace. Since we're living through a significant shift in how we think about work, life, rest, and burnout, we're going to start by looking at generational differences through the lens of this shift and the effects of its magnitude.

What current generations are shaping the workplace?

Currently, there are four generations active in the global workforce:

- Baby Boomers (born between 1946-1964): 59 to 77 years old
- Generation X (1965-1980): 43 to 58 years old
- Millennials (1981-1995): 28 to 42 years old
- Generation Z (1995-2010): 13 to 28 years old

You might be wondering who decides on these generational names and timespans? As fun as it would be, there is not a yearly convention where all us generation scholars sit around a table and vote on names and dates.[62]

If you read up on generational differences, then you'll see different time spans for some groups, and even a few folks holding on to the descriptor "Gen Y" for Millenials. Having a small difference in years between these groups is fine because there is a lot of cultural overlap for people born in, say, the early 1980s or in the mid 1960s.

However, there is one generational timespan that we have relatively strong feelings about: Gen Z. In generational research, you'll see a lot of people start Gen Z in 1997, but we, along with a few select others, feel that 1995 is a much more relevant year to mark the division.

1995 is, generally, the year in which the internet became broadly available in American homes, and so, it makes sense for us that Gen Z begins at the start of that colossal technological change. When you then add in all of the other extensive technological changes occurring since 1995, it means that this group *only* knows the world through the lens of rapid technological change. For this and for other reasons, we are witnessing the largest generation gap in modern history between Gen Z and the three other generations in the workplace. What this means, essentially, is that Gen Z lives in a world that is almost entirely different from all the other generations. So, that big gap can, at times, create a big disconnect.

What about generational stereotypes?

Let's take a minute to consider the current ages of both Millennials and Gen Z. One of the biggest issues with how we talk about generations is that we tend to judge folks based on stereotypes, and we don't develop a realistic perspective on these different age groups, especially as time passes and each generation ages.

We are both Elder Millennials (born 6 months apart in 1983), and we remember being the butt of workplace jokes in our 20s. If we had a dollar for every article claiming we were ruining the workplace because we wanted bean bag chairs and fancy coffee machines, then we would be two very wealthy women. What we've noticed is that because we spent so much time talking about how the twenty-something Millennial was changing the American workplace, we've frozen Millennials in their 20s.

Culturally, we have a hard time accepting that this group is not just out of college but has been working for twenty-odd years and is raising the next generation. We still prefer avocado toast over mortgages, but that's because we're in so much debt we can't afford a mortgage, not because we're too immature to value them.[63]

As a culture, we also treat Gen Z like teenagers. When we teach about generations, we always specifically mention the age ranges because we want people to know that Gen Z are graduating and entering the workforce at high rates. By the time you read this book, some of them are likely even approaching their 30th birthdays. It's important to know that we've got a good number of Gen Z in the workforce now, and a lot of the changes that we're going to be talking about in this section are influenced by the increasing number of members of Gen Z who are demanding them.

What do you need to know about each generation in the workplace?

Generations Timeline	Information Courtesy of: Seemiller and Grace (2019) *Generation Z: A Century in the Making* & Stillman and Stillman (2017) *Gen Z @ Work: How the Next Generation Is Transforming the Workplace.*
GENERATION X **(1964-1980)** Key Events and Context: Watergate, Cold War, AIDS epidemic, high divorce rates Key Traits: Cynical, independent, family focused Generation Connection: Raised by Silent, raised(ing) Gen Z	**BABY BOOMER** **(1946-1964)** Key Events and Context: Civil Rights Movement, Vietnam War, Cold War, Space Race Key Traits: Individualistic, strong work ethic, competitive Generation Connection: Raised by Greatest, raised Millennials
MILLENNIALS **(1981-1995)** Key Events and Context: 9/11, 2008 recession, Columbine school shooting, high loan debt, climate change Key Traits: Digitally connected, more diverse and progressive, focused on personal experiences Generation Connection: Raised by Baby Boomers (helicopter parents), raising Generation Alpha (Zoomer)	**GENERATION Z** **(1995-2010)** Key Events and Context: 2008 recession, 2016 election, COVID-19 pandemic, shoot/mass shootings, climate change Key Traits: Digital natives, hyper customized, independent, driven, more diverse Generation Connection: Raised by Gen X (lawnmower parents)

In order to understand each generation, we need key pieces of information that help give context to the characteristics of each group. We won't waste your time, or ours, by going over this graphic in detail, but we do want you to get a sense for why when you were born matters when we look at burnout.

We've included three categories on our graphic: Key Events and Context, Key Traits, and Generation Connection. The Key Events and Context are necessary to understand how each age group views the world and the big issues facing them, such as equality, civil rights, justice, and global politics. Considering the Key Events for Gen Z, such as mass shootings and the COVID-19 pandemic, can teach us why they tend to be more risk-averse, why they prefer in-person work environments, and why they struggle to make low stakes decisions.

The Key Traits section can help us understand what each age cohort will value and how those values will impact the places they work. Members of Gen X, for example, tend to be more family focused and also tend to be supervisors who are more flexible with work from home arrangements than their Baby Boomer counterparts. Likewise, because Millennials grew up during significant digital change, they are adept at straddling the lines between analog and digital office spaces, while their younger counterparts in Gen Z might struggle.

We find the Generation Connection section to be one of the most insightful. Knowing more about how each generation approaches parenting is essential to understand how they are shaping the next generation entering the workforce.

When we're training Gen Z college students, we always ask them how many of their parents choose their college classes for them. Every time we ask the question, more than half the room of students raises their hands. Neither one of us can imagine our parents being that involved in our classes after high school, but that is the reality for a lot of Gen Z students and their Gen X parents.

If Boomer parents were called "helicopter" parents for always hovering over their children, Gen X parents are now called "lawnmower" parents because they "try to remove all the difficulties that their children might have to deal with."[64] The term first originated in a 2018 post on a teacher support forum. The anonymous writer, speaking from their own experiences as a middle school teacher, warned that lawnmower parenting is causing problems because "instead of preparing children for challenges, they mow obstacles down so kids won't experience them in the first place."[65]

We've found that this deep relationship between parents and child impacts Gen Z's ability to make decisions for themselves and to think independently and critically about new information. Just with this example alone, it's easy to see how parenting styles might influence the type of employee Gen Zers will be in the workplace.

So, when we were born matters. What events we experienced, especially as adolescents before our brains fully developed, matters to how we see the world, how we see ourselves, and how we feel about work.

This means that each generation, and even subgroups within those age cohorts, is shaped by these unique experiences. All these larger context clues become part of the burnout soup we're all swimming in, and members of each age group will react to them differently. Every person you work with is the combination of a "unique constellation of attributes."[66] Those constellations inform *how* we work together *and how* we build workplace cultures around those sometimes shared, sometimes contrasting, traits and values.

What are key generational workplace-related values?

Obviously, there are lots of elements of workplace culture that are going to be affected by shifts in generations. When we were in our late twenties the national conversation was all about how Millennials wanted pool tables and bean bag chairs in their office spaces, and because of our weird and outlandish demands, we were ruining the workplace.

These claims were never backed up by hard data, but it was a deep belief among the workplace zeitgeist. We remember drowning in all the *Forbes* think pieces, speculating about why we wanted pool tables and what it said about our workplace values. While we didn't actually want outlandish perks, Millennials were seeking a movement away from deeply held beliefs about what the workplace had to be.

As each younger generation enters the workforce, they bring with them their different worldviews and values, and this changes the ways we all think about certain staples of the American workplace.

There are a lot of specific elements of the workplace that we could focus on, but the two that consistently come up in our research with the most stark differences are: 1) changes younger people want in the physical environment they work in and 2) various generations' adaptation to rapid technological changes.

Physical Office Environment

Millennials are now the largest generation in the American workforce and because of that influx of employees, there are a lot of rapid changes taking place.[67] We've already established that we weren't all secretly wishing for napping pods and arcade games, but Millennials did make their mark on the physical office environment. In the last 15 years, we've seen a big push for open office plans with lots of space for collaboration, as well as an expressed need for private spaces to hold sensitive meetings.

With the rise in entrepreneurship and the gig economy, we also saw the explosion of coworking spaces across the country.[68] This led to a lot of innovative ways to reimagine the physical office environment, and the impetus for this shift came from younger generations.

Way back in 2018, we supervised a research project that asked newly graduated students to describe their expectations for the physical work environment. The research gave us significant insights into what new hires might expect, but it also gave us a surprising revelation. Until we had the data from students about the diverse and flexible options they wanted in work environments, we hadn't realized the direct impact of study environments at college campuses on their workplace expectations.

College students are trained to work in a range of physical spaces. They have traditional classroom/collaborative learning, but most college libraries now have small study rooms, conference rooms with technical support, different styles of furniture, different lighting options, etc. This teaches students that a work environment should provide a variety of styles and structures because humans have a diverse range of learning styles and therefore, need a diverse range of environments.

After graduation, when these students arrive at their first job and are told that the entire office must be cubicles or must be open plan, they simply don't understand why it cannot adapt to the different needs of its newest employees. Older generations might view their suggestions as the complaints of spoiled kids, but what did they expect after the culture showed the emerging adults what was possible?

In the years before COVID, we saw demands for the greater recognition of accommodation and inclusion when it came to office design. Offices created breastfeeding rooms, began to move away from using overhead lights, and made a host of other changes. Then, when the pandemic hit, we had another workplace revolution.[69] This time it was about the possibility of remote work or work from home.

The pandemic forced most industries (education, manufacturing, medical, and service industries excluded) to rethink the point and purpose of a physical office space. Are they needed to be productive? Are they necessary to build company culture? We haven't answered any of these questions yet because we're still figuring out what a post-COVID pandemic workplace really looks like. And, as more and more Gen Z enter the workforce, we're seeing another generational shift in their desire to have jobs with a large on-site component.[70]

A lot of these changes in physical office spaces can also directly affect the rate of burnout in a particular workplace. If leadership is willing to be flexible about office design and remote work, then they are more likely to recognize that their employees have a diverse range of needs and personal situations that dictate not only how and when they work, but how they feel about workplace flexibility and productivity.

Technological Changes

Technological change is a rather obvious one, right? In our generations graphic, we describe Gen Z as "digital natives."[71] This means that they *do not* know a world without smart devices, social media, widely accessible internet, and endless supplies of entertainment and information. Millennials are adept in both analog and digital devices, since we came of age during that transition. And, we've all heard the jokes about old folks, Boomers especially, struggling to understand how technology works.

Through our work with the Community Research Institute (CRI)[72], we supervised a research project that asked if Gen Z college students expected to be the default tech support in their post-college workplaces. We have fond memories of running that research project, mostly because one of the students claimed early on that Millennials were horrible at adapting to technological change.

The results of the research were surprising, showing that Millennials didn't experience as much pressure to provide technical support for older folks in their lives as we thought. Turns out that Millennials are much more likely to be the technology translators because of their ability to straddle the analog and digital divide.

The technological divide between Gen Z and the three other generations in the workplace is currently one of the biggest challenges facing multigenerational workplaces.[73] It's certainly the area we get the most queries about because the gap is so striking. Without question, the biggest complaint we get from older generations is in regards to Gen Z's problem with answering emails.[74]

For many decades, email was the standard communication practice within the American workplace. However, in talking to all of our colleagues at universities and experiencing this ourselves, Gen Z is generally allergic to emails.

But, what their older bosses failed to consider was that no one had actually ever taught them the importance of sending emails. This revelation is quite startling to most of us because we tend to assume that because Gen Z live on their phones they use them the same way that everybody else does. This is a dangerous assumption when you're talking about how to all work together.

Inter-generational teams need to find a balance between educating new employees on workplace standards and evolving with the times. Young people entering the workforce doesn't just mean potential conflict, it also means a chance to grow and to learn for older workers as well. Perhaps the age of email is over and programs such as Slack and Discord will continue to take over when it comes to office communication. But, what we do know is that all of this change leads to one thing when we do not learn to adapt to it—burnout.

Technology use has a huge impact on our culture of burnout. Too many people take the availability that technology brings and use it to overwork themselves and others. But, just because you *can* be reached 24 hours a day, doesn't mean you *should* be reached 24 hours a day.

Yet, some of our assumptions about technology use are also likely wrong. We're learning that just because Gen Z has spent their lives with smart devices doesn't make them bad at boundaries. In fact, it's quite the opposite. We're seeing more and more research that indicates they are actually more deliberate than other generations about when they use these digital tools and when they don't.[75]

But, setting boundaries is still an uphill battle for everyone when it comes to technology and access.

And, why is that?

Say it with us now: because boundary setting is countercultural.

As you can imagine with some of the differences in these core workplace values, we are left with a lot of challenges for our multigenerational workplaces.

What are the biggest challenges to the multigenerational workplace?

Communication

Different generations have different expectations for how and when teams communicate about work, but it goes beyond whether or not an employee replies to emails. From ellipses and emoji use to slang and memes, there will always be differences in communication styles among different generational groups.

How We Practice What We Preach:

> Team Abbey Research has set out to model the inclusive workplaces we're always telling others about by incorporating many different methods of communication. All three members of our team are Millennials, so we have that innate adaptability to new platforms, but we are also super communicative about how we each need to send and receive information.
>
> We use Slack for almost everything because it allows Kristen to talk things out, it allows Erin to visualize what Kristen's talking about, and it allows Eleanor to see potential problems and ways to create more effective structures. We've learned to love the power of Google sheets, and we are

always considering the next adaptation to make our fully remote team more effective and efficient, while also creating and maintaining space for our three very different work styles and home lives.

Having three people work on the same Google doc or page for the website has presented its own challenges. We have a lot of conversations about how each of us needs to work, how we can support each other, how we can work on strengths and weaknesses, and how we need to communicate about it. One of our most used mottos is "clear communication is kind communication" (thanks, Brené Brown!), and it can certainly help bridge some pretty large generational gaps.

Methods of communication also need to come into workplace flexibility conversations. We need to be prepared to ask ourselves and others how we can communicate with each other to maintain the boundaries that need to be set. How can we create systems that allow people to have more control over their own time while still keeping team members connected?

There are many technological and communication apps that can support those changes. However, there are just as many that continually violate those kinds of boundaries. Good leadership involves exploring options, soliciting feedback from team members on how well the current system works, and making changes when necessary.

Leadership Styles

Another immense challenge faced in today's workplace is leadership and management styles. Boomer management style tends to be what we refer to as "pound the table." It's dictatorial. It is the "my way or the highway" approach. Boomers were raised by parents who went to war, and their lives were also shaped by war and high rates of military service. This leadership style made sense then. It does not make sense now, and it is often viewed as abusive or at least damaging and unproductive.

For Millennials and Gen Z, research tells us that the preferred leadership style is much more collaborative.[76] It's much more interesting to figure out what works for everybody than dictating from the top what work should look like. This style is a lot more work for management and middle management, but all the data shows us that this will be significantly more effective in the post-COVID American workplace.

Conflict Management

When Kristen and her brother took over leadership of our parent company from their father, there were a lot of things they wanted to keep the same. There were also quite a few things that needed to evolve. One of those was how disciplinary meetings were handled and the intentional shift from starting by telling someone where they went wrong to asking them for their version of events first. Here's a quick story from Kristen:

> The idea to shift how we started meetings didn't come from out of nowhere—we have learned from a lot of people along the way. Our VP often conducted highly emotional meetings by asking people to tell him their version of what happened, and we noticed that by doing that, he could diffuse some of the intensity of the situation. Combine that with training in creating a trauma-informed culture, and we decided to implement a practice that all meetings which might end up in disciplinary or corrective action—or any situation we simply need to get to the bottom of—begin with "tell me what happened."
>
> By doing this, we get to accomplish a few things. One, our folks know that we don't have omnipotent knowledge and that we need to learn what happened in order to make any decision. Two, they are reminded that we value them and their experiences. Three, we actually can accomplish

> more to fix whatever happened because the solution is collaborative. Our turnover rate is always low, yes, because of other benefits we've offered, but this policy helps keep it that way.

Global Connectivity

Lastly, a challenge you're going to continually face is that different generations have different relationships with global cultures and global economies. As we said earlier on, a lot of this difference has to do with the big social and cultural events they experienced in their adolescence. But, another substantial factor is that the longer we have all of these smart devices, the more we're able to know what life looks like everywhere else. You cannot tell people that this is the only way it goes when they can look on TikTok and see that there are other options and other approaches.

We live in a global society, and that's not going to change; it's only going to increase. Additionally, your workforce is also probably its own global society. Dominant culture used to be able to pretend that everybody was a White Anglo-Saxon Protestant. It was never true then, and it certainly is not true now.

A more inclusive workplace culture means that there are going to be different religions in the workplace who need time off for different religious holidays. You may have language barriers between speakers of different languages. Or, there may be cultural barriers contributing to inter-office miscommunications when it comes to sense of humor, slang, expressions of respect, and in-office relationships.

Global connectivity is exciting for all its opportunities of growth and innovation, but it also presents a lot of challenges. This is especially true when it comes to workplace environments, benefits, policies, and leadership styles, which are requiring more innovation and change that not everyone appreciates. But, we are more connected than ever to different ways of working and living, and it's getting more difficult to convince people that change isn't possible.

There needs to be a lot more intentionality around leadership now than there ever was before. Not only because we have four very different generations in the workforce, but because the world is culturally richer than it's ever been, and we can no longer ignore—and it's actually not healthy to—all the ways these changes are shifting our workplace expectations.

How do generational perspectives on all these things affect our culture of burnout?

It may sound simple to say that how you were raised to see the world and what you experienced in that world impacts how you think about work and rest and boundaries. But, in all our research into burnout conversations, generations are often left out of the mix.

Generations shape what each age group thinks about being an American and what it means specifically in the workplace. Therefore, they also shape what each group thinks about burnout.

Even though Millennials are the largest generation in the workforce, they still aren't in enough positions of leadership and power to enact all the changes they'd like to see. Our culture of burnout persists, in part, because older generations are resistant to changing the way we think about work and life.

Each generation that enters the workforce changes it because they bring with them their own worldviews and values. We have yet to fully see how Millennials and Gen Z will permanently change the workplace, but we do know that they are the two most progressive generations when it comes to understanding mental health and prioritizing its treatment and support.[77]

We're on the brink of a major societal shift when it comes to workplace flexibility and culture, and it's part of the reason we wanted to write this book. We want our book to provide the cultural context that many folks of all ages are missing, so that they can understand the full picture of why Americans are overworked, exhausted, burnt out, and demanding change.

Now that we've added our ¼ cup generations to the broth, it's time to start chopping the other bits of humanity that get added next. Not in a *Dexter* way, though. We promise.

Chapter 7: Different People are Different (and That's Okay)

The next ingredient we'd like to add to the soup is...basically, all the other things that make up your life. "Different people are different" was a phrase that we started using shortly into our friendship. It was a short and simple phrase that we used when talking about something different, or surprising, about another person. It became our equivalent of "you do you" or "all God's children."[78]

As we quite naturally transitioned from best friends to business partners, we kept using the phrase, especially as it came up in our work as corporate trainers, in our analysis on our YouTube channel, and in any conversation where we were attempting to explain differences that people found perplexing, or frustrating, or fascinating.

We've already established that, regardless of what else goes into your burnout soup, Puritan-flavored capitalism is in everyone's well-seasoned broth. When you were born and how old you were when you experienced international events are some of the main ingredients. Other ingredients include the individual and communal traumas you've experienced and how often you've engaged with the Wellness Industrial Complex.[79] However, that isn't the fullness of you. You are those things and so, so much more. Because, different people are different.

When burnout hits us, there are a lot of ways that who we are, how we see the world, and how the world sees us can create a unique burnout experience. That's what this section is all about. The bowl we each get our soup poured into is a little bit different, and the shape and size of our spoon is, too, which changes the serving we get and the way that soup tastes.

At Abbey Research, we spend a lot of time teaching and training about diversity and inclusion, which is really the nuts and bolts of the idea that different people are different.

Diversity, Equity, & Inclusion is one of the biggest topics and, at times, biggest challenges facing the American workforce, and it plays a primary role in how folks experience burnout. But, before we get to the meat of this ingredient—our innate diversity—we have some prep work to do in the kitchen, and part of that work is exploring what diversity and inclusion really mean.

Diversity means people of different races, right?

One of the main problems with how a lot of folks talk about diversity is that they pretend the only diversity that matters is racial, and most of the time, they also reduce this to Black people and White people.

Is there massive and systemic racial inequity in America between Black and White folks? 100%. But, that is not the only racial inequity that exists, nor is it the only one that exists in your workplace culture. When we have conversations that only address the structural inequalities between Black and White folks, we aren't having conversations about including more Asian, Latino, or Indigenous populations. Or, people who are mixed race. Or, people who are a different race than their parents. Or, people who are the same race from different parts of the world whose understanding of race may be radically different. We also can't reduce DEI down to this one, single way that different people can be different.

In 2020, when law enforcement officers murdered Breonna Taylor and George Floyd, a very quick reaction by a lot of companies was to hire DEI experts and assure the public that they were going to grow their diversity. We wailed at our screens that they were missing the point.

Wait, why shouldn't we try to grow diversity?

Because, we can't. We can't grow diversity because diversity already exists. What we *can* grow is inclusivity.

Regardless of the racial or gender makeup of your organization, it is already diverse. Every single organization is that way because every single human is diverse. Remember when we talked about each person being a "unique constellation of attributes?" Well, they bring that unique constellation to your office every day, whether they look visibly different to you or not.

Diversity is the reality, so *inclusion* is the goal.

Inclusion means you take an honest look at your level of racial or gender (or other forms of) diversity and ask how you can be more inclusive. Inclusivity means creating spaces where any aspect of humanity can be seen and valued. It means that we represent the breadth of humanity, not just the folks who look like us, talk like us, pray like us, or love like us. Inclusivity means going beyond what you can visibly see as different, thinking about it as a divider between people, and getting to know the person in front of you.

Maybe they have a transgender child, or maybe they lost a family member to addiction, or maybe they love baking macarons as stress relief. All of these things make up who a person is. But, they may not bring all these things to work every day. They might not because they don't feel like it, but they also might not because they don't feel safe or included.

Your workplace is already diverse, but we guarantee that there are people who don't feel that it's inclusive. And, a lack of inclusivity has a direct impact on burnout. If people feel they cannot be themselves at work or if they have to hide who they are, who they love, or what is happening in their home life, then that increases stress levels and feelings of isolation.

Burnout doesn't happen because we are working. Burnout happens because we are human and we are not getting enough support (from ourselves and others) to deal with the ordinary and extraordinary stressors in our lives. Being inclusive is burnout prevention.

Let's recap: diversity is reality, inclusion is the goal, and tolerance flattens both to nonsense.

Hold on, tolerance is bad too?

Ask yourself this: has it done any good?

We bet that almost every human reading this book (except maybe The Youths) can close their eyes and picture the Coexist bumper sticker. It was ubiquitous in the 1990s. But, what we've come to realize is that many of us had the sticker, and none of us seemed to stop and think about what that actually meant. What does it mean to coexist? Or, to tolerate someone? As Kristen often quips when she's talking about this on podcasts, all that tolerating someone means is acknowledging that they're alive because it's illegal to kill them.

Where tolerance has gotten us is a society that is completely isolated into groups of people who generally believe the same things, see the world the same way, and usually even look the same. The problem with sameness is that it feeds into our biological instincts to believe that the only people who are safe are people who look and think like us.[80] The world simply does not work like that anymore, and it hasn't for a long, long time.

However, since the COVID lockdowns and the resurgence of the Black Lives Matter movement in the last few years, we feel like this isolation based on tolerance is becoming increasingly toxic. We have all observed that there is a general grumpiness among our fellow humans, higher rates of angry outbursts in public places, and a disturbing rise in violence, particularly gun violence.[81]

We argue that tolerance is never a good thing, but even if it were, or even if it's better than outright hostility, we're certainly not doing a good job of tolerance right now. And we know we can do better. *Much* better.

Being raised to be tolerant instead of inclusive means that many of us did not build the foundations necessary to speak with and be in a relationship with people who are different from us. A good embodiment of that sentiment is the oft-quoted dictum that you never talk about religion or politics. What people really mean is that you don't talk about hard or divisive or emotional things in public, and all that has really done is prevent us from learning how to have all the necessary hard, divisive, and emotional conversations. (Don't get Kristen started on how few of those conversations *need* to be as charged as they are, but humans have rarely been taught the difference between conversations and conversion attempts, but we digress.)

Our inability to view and to interact with diversity in positive and productive ways has very quickly turned into a whole host of "us versus them" ways of being in the world that were counterproductive to a functional society, nevermind building a culture that is truly and authentically inclusive.

So, how do we move from tolerance to inclusivity? Through *understanding*. Understanding is the first step toward building an inclusive anything—culture, relationship, institution. We must begin with understanding what makes "different people different" before we can tackle all the other problems that a tolerant society creates.

For our money, the most helpful concept for learning how to understand difference is the concept of intersectionality.

What is this "intersectionality" word I keep hearing about?

Well, we are so glad you asked.

In the 1980s, Dr. Kimberly Crenshaw coined the term intersectionality to describe the phenomenon that not all women experience the world the same way.[82] Dr. Crenshaw was observing the particular phenomenon of the experience of Black women versus White women; however, since then, social scientists expanded the use of her term to mean any way in which we differ from other people that could affect how we move through the world. That might sound a little bit confusing so allow us to break it down even further.

No matter your gender, you are never *just* your gender. You are also always your race, ethnicity, socioeconomic status, educational level, and more. All these things affect not only how you see the world and move through the world, but how other people perceive and treat you. From a sociology perspective, we can study the generalizations of larger groups, but an individual person can never be reduced to just one aspect because we don't experience each piece of ourselves in a vacuum.

Understanding intersectionality means understanding all the things you can *and* cannot see that make you different from others, and often, the best way to do that is to learn about other people. Let's take the two of us as an example. We already talked about our differences and similarities back in our introduction, but let's revisit anyway.

We are both White women. We are both middle class, over educated nerds who have close family ties to our biological family. If you look at a picture of us, as you can feel free to do on the back cover, then you'll see that we look a lot alike. We both have dark hair, we both dress very similarly, and we both are very conscious of our posture.

However, what you can't see from our picture, and what you may not know unless we tell you, are some of our other intersections. For example, Kristen was raised in a vibrant and communal Church environment, while Erin was raised in a vibrant and communal Irish-American environment. Erin's parents divorced when she was a child, but the divorce was amicable and she was still actively raised by both parents. Kristen's parents are still married.

While we both have brothers, Erin's is older and Kristen's is younger. In terms of bodies, Erin has always been a body size that fits into most elements of society, i.e., she fits in plane seats and doesn't have to think about the size of chairs at restaurants. This is in contrast to Kristen whose body has always been larger than society is okay with. This has come with additional baggage for her, due to her feelings about her body and her participation in diet culture for most of her childhood.

Erin has hypoglycemia, which means her blood sugar can plummet and require an immediate snack to rebalance, while Kristen has a strong sensitivity to fluorescent lights, which can give her migraines. Kristen was raised in Philadelphia and has a very strong relationship to the early history of the United States, and Erin was raised in Colorado with a much stronger relationship to pre-colonial history and the Indigenous inhabitants of our country.

We carry many differences within us that affect how we move through and see the world. Now that we've been such close friends for over a decade, we are each used to thinking about how the other person would perceive or handle a given situation, but it takes a lot of communication, a lot of vulnerability, and a lot of curiosity to get to this place.

So, while two people might look similar and sound like they come from similar backgrounds, we are all a lot of things all at once. We are *all* a lot of things that other people can see and can't see, and we are a lot of things that we may not even be aware of ourselves. Some of these things make it easy for us to fit into the cultures we live in, and some of those things make it more difficult.

That is intersectionality at its core. There is no singular "normal" human. Difference is baked into humanity, and we can't ignore, reject, or merely tolerate those differences if we want to build a culture of balance. We need to embrace and include everyone's individual intersections.

What does it mean to be "normal" anyway?

We deeply believe that normal is only a setting on a tumble dryer. There is no such thing as being "normal." What we mean when we talk about normal is, in fact, shared elements, values, or experiences within a culture. If you share those things, then you are perhaps in the center of that culture, meaning you are important and you feel accepted. If you don't share those things, then you are perhaps on the outside of that culture, meaning that you are not important and you don't feel accepted.

It is important to remember that cultures can be all shapes and sizes. We have American culture, which is massive, but each state, city, town, region, neighborhood can also have their own cultures. Families have cultures, and so do ethnic groups, religions, sports fandoms, and book clubs. You can be centered in all cultures you live in, some cultures, or no cultures. That is a key part of intersectionality—where each of your differences intersect might mean you have a different experience of a culture, and therefore, a different experience of burnout.

In order to keep our language as simple as possible, we are going to refer to the things that are centered within a culture as "normal."

For example, in both Philadelphia and Pittsburgh it is considered normal to be fans of sports and particularly fans of American football. The football season in both cities is dominated by the narrative of that sport. If you are somebody who doesn't like football, or perhaps even actively hates it, then there are parts of the city life that you will not participate in, and you will be "othered." When you are othered, you are the opposite of normal—you are not accepted, you are not included, because you are different from what the culture decides is normal.

Being othered can be simple—you don't go to games and have never been to a tailgate. It can also be more difficult. Let's say you work in an office where *everyone else* actively follows the team. Not doing so could mean you are on the outside of that group, that you are something other than normal in that context.

Being othered is awkward at best and harmful at worst.

It's normal for most people in their 30s in the United States to be married with children. For those dealing with infertility, any question about "starting a family" or having children can be incredibly painful. As such, questions like these are seen as small talk. They're asked with regularity, and few seem to see it as the personal topic that it really is.

Kristen and her husband have consciously chosen not to have children, and she's come up with all sorts of creative ways to answer the question that gets inevitably posed in every social situation where she meets new people. But, honestly? There are better questions to ask, things that include more people in their answers and don't cause pain for those who are othered in that social category.

One of the ways that Erin is constantly othered is because she is an introvert. Being an introvert in corporate spaces can be challenging and frustrating. People assume because she is sociable, she is extraverted, and this leads to a lot of other assumptions about her personality and work style. She has to fake extraversion in many situations because different personality types are not alway considered "normal." She often feels like she has to use a lot of energy to pretend to be something she is not in order to be included in many circumstances.

While some normal versus other situations are pretty low stakes—what bands you like, what hobbies you enjoy, which university you went to—others are really high stakes.

In most of the world, when we say "human" the default assumption is an individual who is a White, cisgendered man, usually middle-aged and middle class, definitely heterosexual and married with children. He's probably 6'1" or thereabouts, able-bodied, and with an average body size and muscle strength.[83]

Sure, there are a load of folks who fit all those categories, but there's also a whole load who don't. Infrastructure, education, medical, legal, and engineering decisions are made every day based on this generic assumption, without even considering it. This means that—in terms of global social participation—any way in which you line up with those categories means you are privileged, and any ways in which you do not mean you are oppressed.

And, every system around the world—economic, educational, political—is built on and within other systems of oppression and privilege. There is no escaping them, and they're there whether you realize it or not. A lot of White folks in the United States were educated about structural racism in 2020, but structural racism has been here from the minute the Jamestown settlement was established in the 1600s.[84]

Okay, we know that's a lot. We got some more though, so take a deep breath. Perhaps obtain a snack if you need one, and let's keep on going.

Why can't you have privilege without oppression?

There are a variety of levels within the broad categories of "privileged" and "oppressed." We want to start broadly, so you can understand your own life in these terms.

Let's start first with emotional reactions to being othered. We've all felt them! As we said above, it's awkward or even painful to feel on the outside of the group. It's one of the reasons we love platforms like Discord and TikTok, where people can find other people who love the same things they love and not feel so alone.

Here's a quick list of some social categories. Take an inventory of yourself, have you ever felt othered because of cultural norms or oppressed by historic systems because of:

- Your race
- Your sex

- Your gender
- Your sexuality
- Your educational degrees/certifications
- Your bank account and access to financial wealth
- Your marital status
- Your military service
- Your faith or religion
- Your ethnicity

Think about what emotions you felt at that time. Those emotions are valid.

They are also not the whole story.

In the immortal words of the *Mean Girls* musical, "That's a feeling, not a fact."

Just because you feel oppressed or persecuted, in terms of societal power, does not mean that you are. Social power shifts, but there are some general constants.

The two of us will always hold social power because we are White. Always. In some places, we will hold social power because we are women, and in other spaces that won't be the case (Ask us sometime about academic conferences. Yikes on bikes, y'all.). If you are a Christian in the United States, then you have social power. If you eat meat, if you are physically fit, if you have post-graduate degrees, if you make more than six figures, then you have social power and privilege within our systems.

The first step to understanding yourself and the world around you is to acknowledge the areas in which you do have privilege.

Do you have a brain that works the way society wants it to? Privileged.

What about a job that allows you to pay for childcare without government assistance? Privileged.

Being *privileged* does not make you a bad person or a good person, it just makes you a person.

Being *oppressed* does not make you a bad person or a good person, it just makes you a person.

Let's go back to that inventory again. If you've felt othered, then take a minute to ask yourself if that was a feeling related to that moment in time, or if it's a reality of the systems in which we live.

An individual can be privileged in some ways and in some contexts, othered in some ways and in some contexts, and oppressed in some ways and in some contexts.

All of the parts of who we are influence how we experience the world, the workplace, and our own intersections with privilege and oppression. Our goal in this section is to get you to see that diversity goes beyond visible differences such as race, ethnicity, or ability, and to understand that inclusivity means building a culture where all differences and diversities can thrive.

Finally, as a note, not all experiences of oppression are equal throughout the world. Historical and systemic oppression of people of color across North America since the moment settlers landed on the continent, for example, shaped our governmental and cultural systems into barriers to equity. We recognize that this book does not even *begin* to scratch the surface of any of those realities and also want to acknowledge that a lot of other wise and learned people have covered this ably.

How individuals experience burnout is impacted by the various intersections they exist in. So now that we've explained why intersections matter and what effect they may have on someone's lived experience, let's dig a little deeper into the junction of intersectionality and burnout.

What about intersectionality and burnout?

As a culture, we're getting better about recognizing different intersections when it comes to burnout. You can find a whole list of articles explaining why burnout rates are higher in women, or healthcare professionals, or neurodiverse folks.

Before we move onto the next section, we want to expand on how a few of these different intersections can influence how you experience burnout. We've already covered generations, and we'll do a deep dive into gender a little later on, but those are obviously not the only ways that different people are different.

Don't take this section as a comprehensive exploration of all the research out there on burnout and intersections. We've just hand-selected a few specific ones to showcase. On that same note, there is still so much more research that needs to be done.

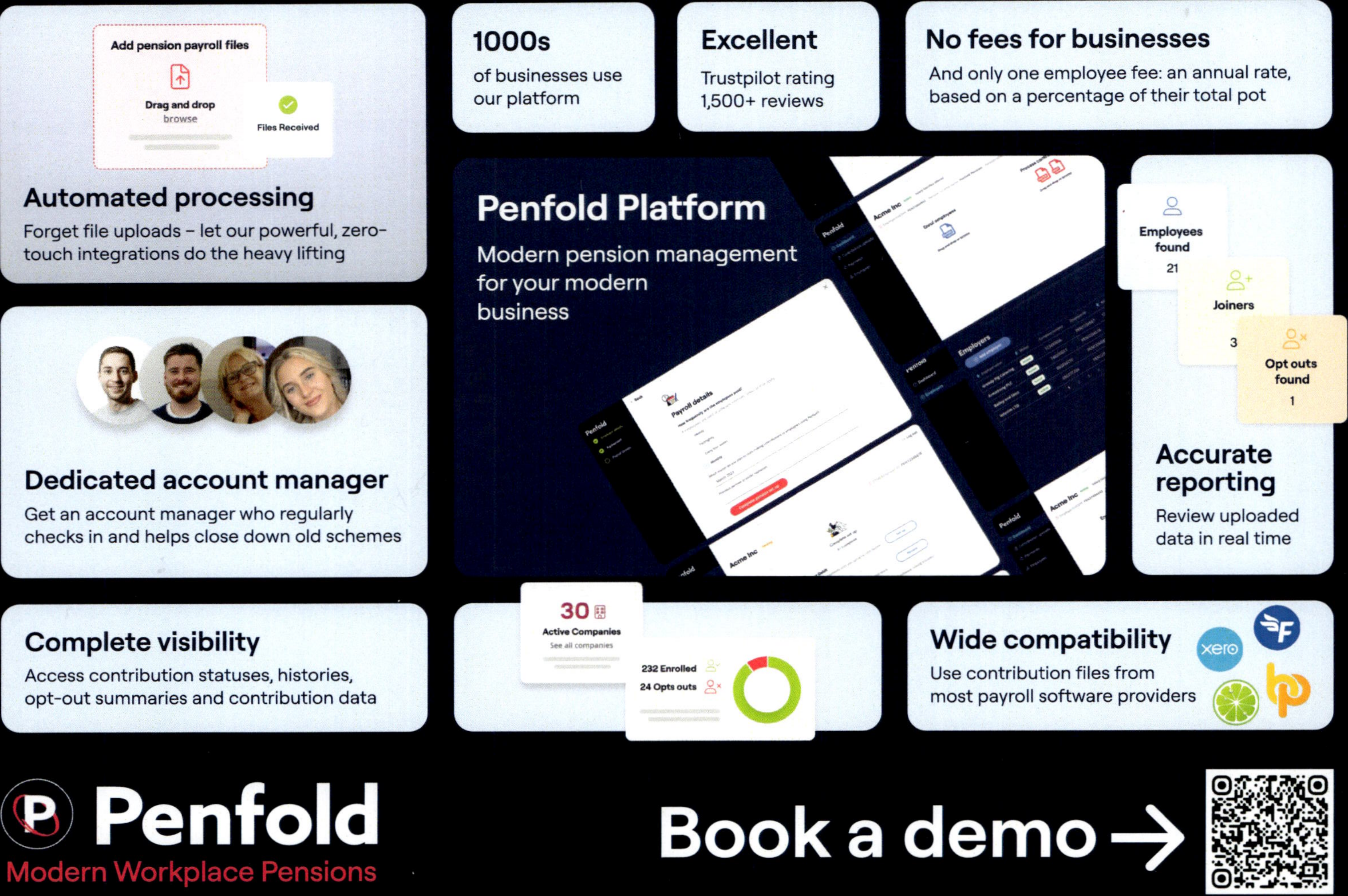
Add pension payroll files
Drag and drop
browse
Files Received
Automated processing
Forget file uploads – let our powerful, zero-touch integrations do the heavy lifting
1000s
of businesses use our platform
Excellent
Trustpilot rating
1,500+ reviews
No fees for businesses
And only one employee fee: an annual rate, based on a percentage of their total pot
Penfold Platform
Modern pension management for your modern business
Employees found
21
Joiners
3
Opt outs found
1
Accurate reporting
Review uploaded data in real time
Dedicated account manager
Get an account manager who regularly checks in and helps close down old schemes
Complete visibility
Access contribution statuses, histories, opt-out summaries and contribution data
30
Active Companies
See all companies
232 Enrolled
24 Opts outs
Wide compatibility
Use contribution files from most payroll software providers
Penfold
Modern Workplace Pensions
Book a demo →

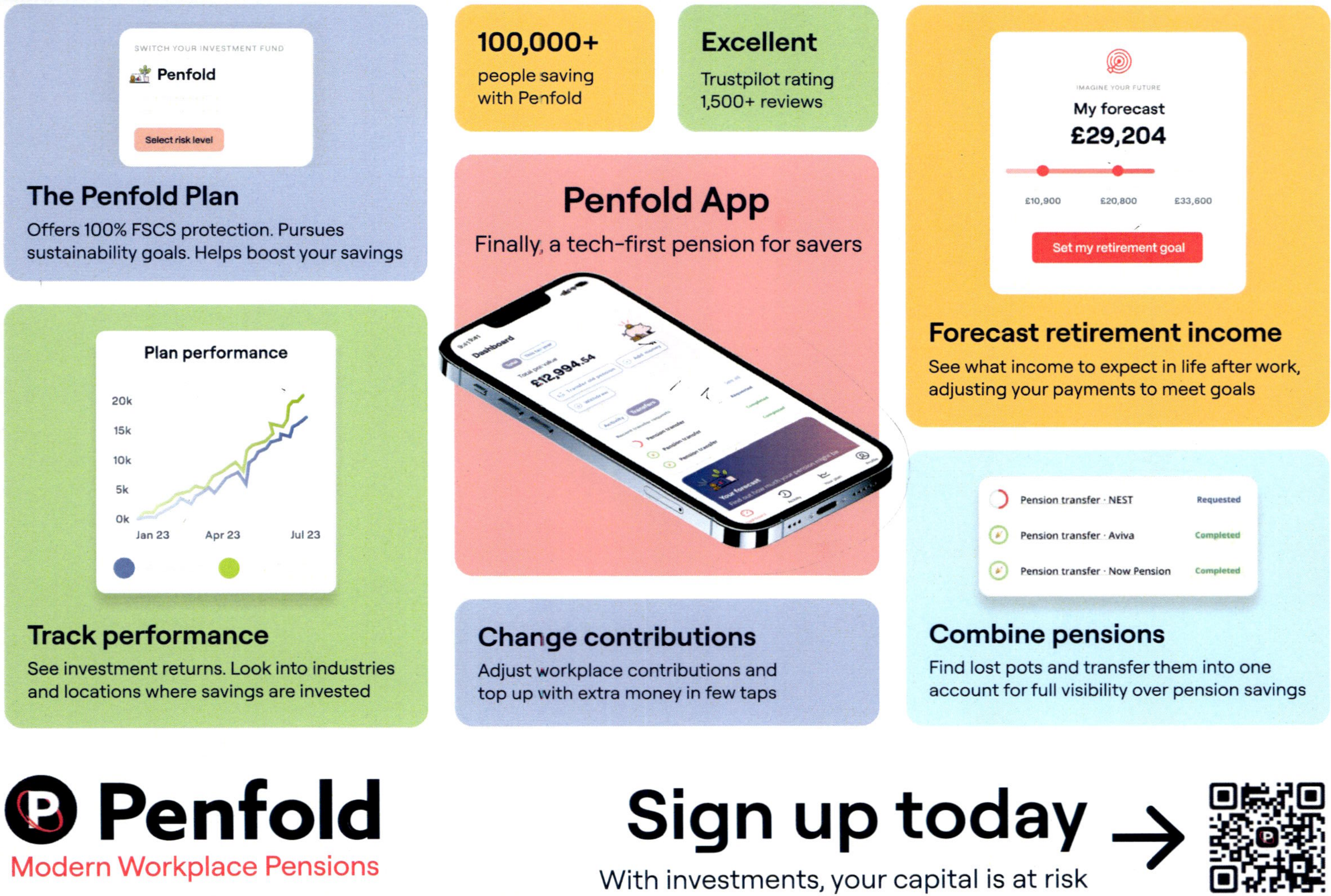
SWITCH YOUR INVESTMENT FUND
Penfold
Select risk level
The Penfold Plan
Offers 100% FSCS protection. Pursues sustainability goals. Helps boost your savings
100,000+
people saving with Penfold
Excellent
Trustpilot rating
1,500+ reviews
IMAGINE YOUR FUTURE
My forecast
£29,204
£10,900
£20,800
£33,600
Set my retirement goal
Penfold App
Finally, a tech-first pension for savers
Dashboard
£12,994.54
Forecast retirement income
See what income to expect in life after work, adjusting your payments to meet goals
Plan performance
20k
15k
10k
5k
0k
Jan 23
Apr 23
Jul 23
Track performance
See investment returns. Look into industries and locations where savings are invested
Change contributions
Adjust workplace contributions and top up with extra money in few taps
Pension transfer · NEST
Requested
Pension transfer · Aviva
Completed
Pension transfer · Now Pension
Completed
Combine pensions
Find lost pots and transfer them into one account for full visibility over pension savings
Penfold
Modern Workplace Pensions
Sign up today
With investments, your capital is at risk

95%	£10M+	4.7/5
Non-agency hires	Recruitment spend saved annually	Hiring manager sentiment score

From Complexity to Simplicity

Hiring the best talent shouldn't be this hard. We help businesses **innovate**, **grow faster**, and **attract top talent** - now and for the future. **We make the complex simple**.

As the talent landscape shifts, we help you stay ahead with a unique combination of **team**, **technology**, and **expertise**.

Our solutions

Full RPO

No talent function? We can manage all your recruitment, from sourcing to onboarding new talent.

Modular RPO

If you've got a strong talent team, you don't need to outsource everything. You need a partner who can amplify what's already working. Use our technology and expertise to elevate your recruitment.

Project RPO

Need to scale fast? We support hiring surges, product launches and market expansions.

Impact X

Need a top leader to drive growth? Our data-led Executive Search finds the best and ensures a fast, seamless start.

Want to Connect?

Scan the QR code to book a meeting and continue the conversation from today's event. Let's connect and explore how **we can make an impact together**!

Recruitment Simplified

www.instant-impact.com

instant impact

impactX

Asian Women & Burnout

Race in America is a massive topic, and the way race influences burnout is deftly covered by other wise scholars.[85] So, instead of trying to get into it all here—and either ending up falling short of a good discussion or doubling the length of this book—we've chosen to highlight research we found specifically about Asian women and burnout culture. The way gender roles affect burnout is also a much larger conversation that we'll be having in Section Three, but it's worth noting here that women experience much higher rates of burnout than men.

Part of the work of understanding that different people are different is understanding how different intersections can mean different levels of oppression, and different levels of burnout. Women of color at work, for example, have to deal with the inequity that comes with being a woman and the inequity that comes from being a person of color from a marginalized group.

Statistically, we know that women of color do more work for less pay, are less recognized, and are less likely to be promoted than White women.[86] What this means is that, for women of color, there are broken rungs on the advancement ladder at every level. When you add on top of that the stress of microaggressions or the experience of being othered because you are the "only" person from your racial or gender category, we know that women of color experience higher rates of work and home related stress, and higher rates of burnout.

To illustrate this point, let's talk about rates of burnout in Asian and Asian-American women. First off, we should note that 2020 saw a 164% rise in anti-Asian hate. We have seen a number of mass shootings in the last few years targeted specifically at Asian-Americans. In a survey from Coqual, 63% of respondents said that the ongoing violence against Asian-American communities negatively impacted their mental health.[87]

Because of this rise in anti-Asian violence, many respondents also said that they don't feel safe doing routine, daily activities—many of which, like exercising or engaging in cultural activities, might be part of their self-care routine or burnout mitigation techniques. Add on top of all this the model minority myth, which perpetuates the idea that because they often outpace and outperform other marginalized groups Asian-Americans need *less* support at work, and you start to get a picture of the potential stressors they face on a daily basis.[88]

Lisa Cheng, a self described "Queer Asian-American," wrote about her experiences with burnout during COVID-19, and her thoughts echoed a lot of the research we found.

> Growing up as a Chinese-American, I was taught that my performance and results depended on my work ethic…To me, my worth was completely dependent on my ability to produce. Even when given the opportunity to rest and pause, I had no clue how to be okay with myself.[89]

Growing up in a Chinese-American family meant that Cheng had to grapple not only with the pressures of Puritanical capitalism and the American culture of work, but the added cultural demands and pressures from her Chinese immigrant culture. We often see that people of color, and then women of color, face an extra pressure to prove their worth and value to their workplace and also society.

Cheng hits the nail on the proverbial head with the description of her specific experience that holds a lot of universal truths for other women of color. Forgive us for the meaty quote, but it was too important to edit:

> American society wants us to earn our living, earn our keep, earn the right to live somewhere rather than acknowledge that we deserve to live even if we are not constantly producing. For many, the pressure of productivity goes deeper than capitalistic tenants. Being a child of immigrants and a victim of the model minority myth is a deadly mix. Ever try to complain about your life when your mom literally survived the Cultural Revolution and used to dig through trash to avoid starvation? Yeah, me neither.[90]

When we add more intersections to our understanding of burnout, it is easier to see how the added stress of your race or ethnicity can create further complications, and be partly responsible for spurring these higher rates of burnout amongst women of color.

Disability, Ableism, and the ADA

As our culture continues to broaden our understanding of burnout, more and more folks are writing about how people with disabilities experience burnout. Disability burnout is defined as "a state of physical or emotional exhaustion caused by or made worse by a disability."[91] It takes the original symptoms of burnout and adds to them the "exacerbation of one's underlying health conditions" and the "creation of new, comorbid health conditions."[92] From this description, it seems pretty clear how work-related and disability-related burnout can significantly affect a disabled person's ability to work and to live.

True workplace inclusivity means that people feel they can bring their whole selves into work. One of the biggest problems we face with disability burnout is the lack of inclusivity at most American work cultures, because over 70% of disabilities are invisible.[93]

For managers et al, this means two things: 1) that you likely have no idea which of your employees have disabilities and 2) those folks are likely facing bigger challenges and barriers to participating fully in your workplace culture. Recent studies from the Harvard Business Review (HBR) found that people hiding their status as a person with a disability are two times more likely to feel anxious and four times more likely to feel isolated at work.[94]

The folks at HBR describe an upsetting reality for people with disabilities: "If you're hiding a disability, the daily grind of early mornings, deadlines, and office politics is compounded into a far heavier burden. You live in fear of being discovered. You work overtime to mask your authentic self."[95]

Providing inclusive work cultures for people with disabilities has to be more than just adhering to government regulations and being in compliance with the ADA. It means creating spaces where people do not feel they have to hide their disabilities, where they can be their authentic selves, and where they receive the most comprehensive care and support from leadership in the organization, regardless of their ability or disability.

Neurodiversity and Autism

When we add the intersection of a person's neurodiversity or autism to our burnout soup, we get a slightly different set of symptoms and causes. Autistic and ADHD burnout is "characterized by pervasive, long-term (typically 3+ months) exhaustion, loss of function, and reduced tolerance to stimulus."[96] The three primary symptoms of neurodivergent burnout include: chronic exhaustion, reduced tolerance to stimulus, and loss of skills such as thinking, remembering, performing basic self-care skills, and activities of daily living.[97]

For neurodivergent folks, some of the most common causes are masking (pretending or appearing to not have autism), not having access to appropriate levels of support and accommodations, and loss of executive functioning due to a high number of stressors.[98] For folks with autism, the cause and effect relationship to burnout is complicated. We know that "autistic traits can amplify the conditions that lead to burnout, and burnout can cause these traits to worsen."[99]

Neurodivergence and autism can often be invisible within the workplace, and therefore, we have to work even harder to ensure an inclusive culture. It's not only the right thing to do, but it's a major factor in burnout mitigation. If your autistic co-workers have the support and accommodations they need, then you can take positive steps toward reducing the potential for burnout.

Immigration Status and Language Access

It may seem rather obvious to say that folks with complicated immigration statuses (whether lawful or not) experience higher rates of fear, uncertainty and stress, but we're going to say it anyway. Immigration-related stress affects tens of millions of Americans every year, but it is an intersection that we don't spend a lot of time on when it comes to burnout.

Because it can be precarious, or even dangerous, to talk about, we don't have a lot of data on immigrants and burnout. But, because it does affect so many people, we knew we needed to highlight it here. Regardless of lawful status, immigrating to another country brings with it the normal stressors of moving, finding housing, jobs, healthcare, childcare, etc., while also adding on acculturative stress, or the stress that stems from adapting to a new culture.[100]

Some of the biggest stressors facing new immigrants are language access issues and language barriers. We know that immigrants with lower English proficiency face issues getting appropriate medical care, accessing government documents, finding employment, and understanding American culture.[101] These language barriers follow them to work where they can be othered and oppressed, as well as socially isolated with limited support networks.

If you take all the potential causes of burnout and add these compounding stressors, then it is not a stretch to imagine that burnout rates among the immigrant population are quite high.

Socioeconomic Status

Similar to our argument about immigration status, we want you to consider how socioeconomic status can impact rates of burnout. To be clear, socioeconomic status includes several key factors such income, educational attainment, financial security, and perceptions of social status and social class.[102]

What we know from studying the intersection of stress and socioeconomic status is that lower wage workers face a number of issues, which can directly affect their rates of burnout. For instance, lower wage workers are more likely to work for small businesses, which means that they are less likely to have access to health insurance, paid vacations, and sick days. Lower wage workers can also have more frequent overtime requirements, little managerial support, and less work flexibility.[103]

The lack of flexibility, stability, and security that comes from working low wage jobs means that people with lower socioeconomic status are more likely to suffer comorbidities such as high blood pressure and weight loss, as well as having a significant impact on their mental health.[104]

Again, we have little data on burnout rates with lower wage earners because the nature of their work—part-time, non-traditional hours, frequent overtime—means that they aren't readily available to take surveys and speak with researchers. But, taking the data that we do have, we can draw enough conclusions to say that it's an area of research that needs much more attention.

What does all this mean for our culture of burnout?

Basically, all these identities intersecting with each other mean that we are all a lot of things, all at once. All these things, or intersections, influence how we see ourselves, how we see the world, how we form relationships, and how we show up to work.

The world is racist, classist, sexist, and ableist. It simply is. It privileges financial wealth, White skin, maleness, and bodies and brains that thrive under Puritanical capitalism. While we're all swimming in our *very* American burnout soup, we each have our own "unique constellation of attributes" or intersections, which means we experience burnout differently. This is one of the primary reasons that we argue against the marketing of individual solutions to burnout as though they are some sort of gospel truth of curing overwhelm.

How can you sell a product that will "fix" burnout if it's targeting a mass audience? How are these products accounting for someone's gender, race, religion, ability or other factors? How can we talk about an individual solution to burnout without talking about the bigger cultural factors?

All of these questions about fixes and marketed solutions are going to be addressed in Section Three, but for now, we'll leave you with this:

Different people are, in fact, different, and we are all complicated creatures who need similar but unique things to navigate through our human experience. We are not only who we have been raised to be, but we are who we tell ourselves we are.

Confused?

Allow us to explain.

Chapter 8: Storytelling

Storytelling is one of the defining aspects of being human. It's part of how we relate to each other and to the world. It's how we process the things happening to us. In addition to the myriad ways we just mentioned how different people are different, another difference is in the stories they've been a part of, told to themselves, or heard from other people.

This might sound like a conscious process—if you're asked to tell a story, maybe you can pull something out of a hat, or at least recount *Little Red Riding Hood*, but there's a little library in our brains that goes so much deeper than that. These are the stories that genuinely alter the way we interact with everything in the world. These are the stories that can make you smile when you smell the same fabric softener your grandmother used or that can make your heart plummet with sadness when a certain song comes on the radio.

These stories are more than just stories to the human brain, they're our framework for processing everything we experience. In the immortal words of one of our personal heroes, Brené Brown:

> In the absence of data, we will always make up stories. It's how we are wired. Meaning making is in our biology, and when we're in struggle, our default is often to come up with a story that makes sense of what's happening and gives our brain information on how best to self-protect.[105]

Remember when we talked about how our response to stress is a normal, self-protective process? So is forming our experiences into stories that we can file on our mental bookshelf and come back to later, especially to answer questions about new things we're confronted with. *"Is this safe,"* we might ask ourselves in a new situation, and our brain can trawl through the library of things we've already processed and pull out the stories that best relate to what's going on to allow us to make a judgment call. Most of the time, this serves us pretty well.

This storytelling is critical to understand when we talk about a culture of burnout for the same reason all the ingredients in our soup are important. There is a unique cultural story we, as Americans, are told and continue to tell ourselves. The story of the Puritans. Stereotypes about people different from us. The story that value and worth are inherently tied to productivity and stress. And, one of the most enduring stories of all—the story that pain, poverty, suffering, exhaustion, and struggle are signs of weakness.

Pain and suffering tell us stories too, stories that stay with us and come back off the shelves, whether it serves us or not. Those stories don't always accurately reflect the facts, either. The part of our brain that handles this story-writing likes simplicity. It likes patterns, and it likes binaries.

We're going to touch on three different kinds of storytelling that all contribute to a culture of burnout that's so difficult to escape: the stories we tell culturally about our past, the stories we tell ourselves, and the stories we tell culturally about our present.

What are the stories we tell culturally about America's past?

Well, one of them we've already discussed: the Puritans. Their belief that hard work was godly is a story that we've re-told so many times, for so long, it's been baked into our cultural heritage.

There's also the one where the Emancipation Proclamation ended slavery. The one where we entered World War II just to save the Jewish people from the Nazis. The one where Indigenous peoples were happy to give up their lands to the Europeans. The one where the KKK went away with the Civil Rights movement. The one where Cinco de Mayo is Mexican Independence Day. The one where everyone has the right to vote. The one where people can be self-made millionaires and we all just need to "pull ourselves up by our bootstraps."

Every one of those statements is attached to a story, and whether true or not, all of those stories combine to help determine how we see ourselves as Americans. Generally, those stories teach us to see ourselves as righteous, victorious, helpful, and better than other cultures.

The issue being, of course, that most of those stories aren't the full truth. The Emancipation Proclamation *did* end slavery—in the Union, where there weren't as many slaves. The final slave was freed from bondage nearly two years after that edict in Gettysburg, and after the Confederacy surrendered. It happened in the South on June 19th, which is why the date is now a federal holiday, by the way.

The United States's citizens *were* concerned about the plight of Jewish people in Nazi-occupied Europe. The United States's government wasn't quite as fussed. Not only did they set up immigration limits so that Jewish refugees could not freely seek refuge on our shores, they only agreed to active military intervention when Japan attacked Pearl Harbor.

Without the nuance, are those stories wrong? Maybe, maybe not. But, they're definitely shallow. And, stories that don't include the full context can lead to harmful choices for ourselves and others.

What are the stories we tell ourselves?

The easiest way to talk about the stories we tell ourselves is to explore the research we have on trauma and its effect on our brains—psychologically and physically. Experiencing a traumatic event actually rewrites the way we see the world.[106]

We are, at our core, animals, and we have an instinctual imperative to avoid experiences that are painful, damaging, or dangerous. So, we have a system designed specifically to make snap decisions about getting us out of those situations. And, it's smart! It's efficient! When we see something potentially scary, this system takes over, and it takes over *hard*. You've probably heard of "flight, fight, or freeze," and that's part of this system. By limiting the available responses to three simple ones most likely to save our lives, we don't have to rely on the higher executive function parts of the brain that are very good at solving complex problems but not necessarily at doing it quickly.

If there's a potential predator, then we don't want or need higher-order functioning. We need a straightforward, simple brain process that is designed to use the most basic of pattern recognition to decide which of those three actions are necessary.

Our stress cycle is very, very good at giving us the flood of chemicals that make us strong, fast, and responsive enough to handle tigers in bushes but not so good at handling the endless stressful intricacies of office politics. Similarly, our trauma-handling system is good at helping us form patterns—record *stories*—that could keep us out of danger again in the future. Sadly, these stories are often significantly lacking in nuance.

As Robert Burton explains:

> Our brains reward us with dopamine (that "aha" moment) when we recognize and complete patterns. Stories are patterns. The brain recognizes the familiar beginning-middle-end structure of a story and rewards us for clearing up the ambiguity. Unfortunately, the brain rewards us for a good story—one with clear good guys and bad guys—regardless of the accuracy of the story. [...] The brain is not a big fan of ambiguous stories that leave unanswered questions and a big tangle of possibilities. The brain has no interest in *Maybe I have a part* or *Am I blowing this out of proportion?* The part of the brain that goes into protection mode likes binaries: Good guy or bad guy? Dangerous or safe? Ally or enemy?[107]

This is the part of our brain responsible for writing down the stories that make up our personal mental library. This part of our brain is emotional, hypervigilant, and simplistic.

Sometimes the facts of the story are correct, but our brain gets hypervigilant about applying that story to future events, using the smallest triggers as an excuse to rip that book off the shelf like, "Here! I know this one! I can help keep you safe!" What is designed to be a self-protective measure becomes harmful when an over-eager brain rereads that story at the slightest provocation, and in cases of pathological hypervigilance, those rereads go so far as to turn into re-livings. The DSM-V has an entire section on stress and trauma induced disorders, including Post-Traumatic Stress Disorder, which is often characterized by a reliving of the events that created those feelings in the first place. Faith Harper writes in *Unf*ck Your Brain*:

> Our thoughts, feelings, and behaviors come from here. They are rooted deep in our physical bodies, in how our brains perceive the world around us, based on past experiences and current information.[108]

She goes on to say, the way our brains react to stress and trauma is a "*completely normal response*" that's designed to protect us as squishy, edible humans. Quick emotional responses based on past experiences let us get the hell out of dodge when we're in danger. It helps us see orange and black stripes and shout, "Tiger!" and know we need to run away. It throws up red flags when a date is giving off uncomfortable vibes. It has us turning immediately for the trash can when food smells dangerously off.

But, if that's all we were, if all our reactions and decisions were based on what is essentially gut instinct, then we'd miss out on a lot, too. It's our more reasoned side that lets us endure immediate discomfort for future benefit, such as getting a vaccine to prevent future illness or getting off the comfy couch to put on our running shoes to keep up with our exercise routine. Being able to stop, look back, and realize that the orange and black stripes weren't a tiger at all but a stripey plant keeps us from living in a state entirely covered by unpredictable emotional responses.

We need both emotions and reasoned thoughts, but they need to be *in balance*.

What are the stories we tell ourselves about our present and future?

This is one of the sections where we need to get really blunt with y'all. Mostly because these stories we tell ourselves now are so embedded that they don't feel like stories, they feel like facts we can't escape. We promise that they are, in fact, stories, and they are stories that need examining. Just because something is accepted as "true" does not mean that it is factual. And, that difference is all the difference.

Story Title: This Is How It's Always Been, and How It Will Always Be.

False. Whatever "this" is, it's malleable. "This" is something that's been created by people and can be undone by people as well. Your marriage does not have to be this way. Your professional life does not have to be this way. Your mental and/or physical health does not have to be this way. Throughout the book, we'll be talking about ways to change all those things, and our guess is that if we make you uncomfortable at any point, then we're brushing up against a thing you know needs to shift a bit.

In a few paragraphs, we're going to touch briefly on personal and generational trauma, but first, we want to continue with our, probably belabored, soup metaphor because there are some very American things in that broth, which can change with imagination, stubbornness, and a healthy dose of righteous anger. Here's a few of those things.

- Food Deserts: The USDA defines a food desert as a geographical location where citizens do not have quick and easy access to a large variety of foods, and specifically, no access to a large grocery store.[109] Forced to shop at local bodegas, variety is low and prices are high. This can, and routinely does, lead to low academic achievement, eating disorders, and a lot of trauma for people who know hunger this intimately. It doesn't have to be this way.[110] We can pass laws that increase public transportation or create tax incentives for larger chains to operate in food deserts. We *can* ensure that everyone has access to the foods their bodies function best on, we just have to want to.

- Gun Violence: We did a whole podcast series on gun violence in America, and if you want to dive into this any deeper, then we'd recommend searching for "The Culture Cast" on your favorite podcatcher and starting there. This is a subject we're both passionate about, so let us simply and briefly say this: there is no other country not currently in an active armed conflict where children are shot and killed at the rate they are here. The story we tell ourselves is that it has to be this way because the NRA has too much money, and that's a long engrained story. However, it's not the complete truth. Organizations like Moms Demand Action are actively changing policies, which can protect human lives around the country. By shaping the conversation around gun safety, rather than gun control, they've been able to have pragmatic conversations that circumvent the NRA rhetoric.[111] Children do not have to keep dying because of the 2nd Amendment. There is another way.

- State-Sponsored Trauma: This is a *broad* and *large* category, and we're emphasizing those words because they need to be. There are a lot of elements to this category—police violence, the death penalty, the prison industrial complex, disproportionate taxation, low wages, regulations on reproductive autonomy, the entire health insurance network, etc. In the immortal words of Andrew Shepherd from *The American President*, "America is hard work." You'll encounter ways The Man is out to screw you in a myriad of methods throughout your life, and we're frequently told to just get on with it.

We don't have to, though. We can make change. It's hard, and messy, and long, and sometimes terrifying. But, it can change.

However, here's another story title we need to acknowledge:

This is How It's Always Been, And It's Always Been Really Traumatic

Now, that? That's true in all the ways it can be.

Trauma is a big category that we love talking about, and it's honestly too large for this book. Kristen's done two TEDx talks on it, we both looked at it for our PhDs, and we train on trauma-informed leadership. Allow us to summarize some salient points for you.

First, trauma happens to *everyone*. Death, taxes, and situational trauma are all inevitable parts of the human experience. For the purposes of this section, let's define situational trauma as any event which changes the stories you tell yourself about your own life in a way that impacts you negatively. This kind of trauma has the potential to rewire your brain chemistry permanently at any point in your life. This is often combined with generational trauma, in which some of our actual body chemistry is affected by experiences our parents and grandparents went through.[112]

Everything we described above—and so many more cultural realities—can be both situational and generational traumas for people. Let's say that you're an Indigenous person currently living off the reservation. The state-sponsored trauma in your family's life is myriad and stretches back generations.Your DNA will have epigenetic markers telling your body to react in ways shaped by your ancestors trauma.[113] Then, you're in a car accident that does damage to your neck and you become fearful of getting into the driver's seat again. Now, you have situational trauma on top of the generational. Congratulations?

Another situation. You're a college student who has dealt with disordered eating in the past—situational trauma. Then, as part of a class project for your social work degree, you discover that your mother and grandmother both had disordered eating habits. Suddenly, your struggle makes a lot more sense.

One more. You're a parent who is determined not to yell at your children the way you were yelled at. All of your instincts tell you to yell when they misbehave, but you consciously work to overcome them. Eventually, your brain re-writes your epigenetic instincts, and you're able to parent the way you choose to. This is still incredibly stressful, obviously, and a lot of work.

Overcoming trauma—both generational and situational—is completely possible and, we'd argue, necessary. We'd be remiss if we did not mention that there can be a lot of external barriers to doing so depending on the intersections a person occupies, but that doesn't change the necessity. If we don't overcome trauma, then the hormones that our brains release due to traumatic events will control the whole system for far too long. We need to get our rational brain back online as soon as we can post-event, or that traumatic experience becomes a new story that keeps happening instead of something that happened once upon a time.

The more stress and trauma we experience, the more this part of the brain becomes in charge of processing our situations, and the more we're broadly applying these stories to everything that happens to us. And, these experiences aren't just personal, they can be communal, too. When a whole community experiences a trauma, those stories become baked into each individual, the culture of the community as a whole, and even into future generations. We don't have to accept that every story on our shelf is the truth now or ever was the truth. We can archive stories, we can take them out and examine them critically and rationally (especially with the help of a therapist!), and we can move forward, both personally and culturally.

While there are a lot of risks of not doing the above, one of them is that living in a constant state of untreated trauma is a contributing factor to burnout. If you refer back to Section One and our handy sliding scale graphics, this is one of those factors that can mean our stress levels are caught in perpetual cycles which never resolve. For folks who live in perpetual cycles caused by trauma, the established pathways in their brains caused by said trauma means that burnout is even more probable than for others.

So, of course, we need to talk about a communal trauma so massive, so broad, and so recent that we're still living in the fallout: COVID-19.

Chapter 9: The COVID of It All

Let's get something on the table right now: COVID is a big part of this book. It would honestly be silly for us to write a whole book about why burnout is so pervasive and not talk about the global reset button that was the COVID lockdowns and pandemic.

As we write this in the spring of 2023, most countries have declared the pandemic "over." While epidemiologists and immunologists can debate the accuracy of that, as social scientists, we can assure you that it's not. The ramifications of this period of human history are still being figured out, but there are a few things we know for sure:

1. Lockdowns stopped the inertia of work
2. Trauma is real, and we all experienced it, whether you acknowledge it or not
3. We can't go "back to normal" because our "normal" way of doing things is the reason we have a culture of burnout in the first place

When we look back on those first few weeks of the COVID lockdowns in March 2020, it's hard to remember that we had no idea how long it would last, how bad it would get, or how much our lives were going to change. But, looking back now, we can see a lot of patterns that got broken and systems that need changing. The one benefit of a global pandemic was that it forced so many of us to stop. To just stop.

And, when we did, we looked around and saw a world that wasn't working for a lot of folks. People were exhausted, stressed, overwhelmed, unhappy, and unhealthy. We know a lot of people who came out the other side of the worst of COVID and said, "It doesn't have to be this way."

We're two of those people, and it's one of the reasons we were driven to write this book.

What was the state of the pre-COVID American work culture?

Most of the point of Section Two was to present our case about the state of the pre-COVID American work culture. We've added all these ingredients to our burnout soup as we go, making the recipe more and more complex.

Without repeating ourselves too much, let's reiterate some of the most important points we've made so far. Remember, we know that burnout is experienced globally, but we're Americans, we live in America, and we want to talk specifically about American burnout culture.

At this stage, we might sound like we really hate the Puritans, but they gave us a *mess* of a work ethic to grapple with. The pre-COVID American work culture was one that prioritized productivity over rest, profit over people, and constant achievement over balance.

Our highly individualistic culture tells us that we have to have all these priorities, and we have to try and achieve them on our own. We've made almost every part of work and life a moral judgment—from how hard you work and how committed you are to your career, to what food you eat and how you take care of your body.

The state of the pre-COVID work culture was unhealthy and unsustainable. Something had to give, and something did. Amongst all the horrors and the uncertainty, we experienced some real and large-scale societal changes.

How did COVID change American culture?

We've been putting all our burnout soup ingredients into the pot on the stove, gradually turning up the temperature as we add more and more parts to the soup. What the near global COVID lockdowns did was turn off the heat for a lot of folks.

Before we go any further, we have to note that for many, *many* humans, especially low wage earning, hourly folks in service industries, and those essential workers in healthcare, education, and manufacturing, the soup stayed on the hot burner. In fact, for many people, the heat got turned up.

It's no surprise to any of us that the two professions with the highest rates of burnout are teachers and healthcare workers.[114] They lived through extraordinarily high stress periods, and experienced levels of trauma and burnout that the two of us cannot ever come close to grasping. We also cannot ever understand what it felt like to work in a grocery store, or other parts along the supply chain, and to deal with the constant barrage of abuse that was working in a public facing service job during those turbulent years.

As social scientists, it is not surprising in the least that this post-COVID world is seeing a rise in union organizing and workers strikes in response to the treatment of many essential workers throughout the pandemic.[115]

Whether the heat stayed on our burnout soup, whether we got to slow down or had to speed up, wide sections of Americans started to realize that the soup was starting to spoil. We might have taken a taste and realized that this was not the soup we wanted to be making all along. A lot of us realized that some of the ingredients didn't even belong in the recipe anymore.

COVID changed the way Americans valued work because it forced so many of us to stop working. Prevented from maintaining the rigid routine of work life, separated from home life by the dreaded commute, the boundaries between work and home became blurred and even disappeared.

In a culture built to operate at high speeds, to constantly produce to the point of toxicity (more on that later), we had to pump the brakes and slow down. COVID didn't bring us into balance, but it forced rest on a significant subset of a culture that was told from its very founding that rest was for the afterlife. Did COVID change our perception of work and productivity overnight? Not at all. We can all still remember our social media feeds filled with pictures of the hobbies people had picked up during lockdown.

All of a sudden, everyone was learning how to make bread. Or, finally downloading Duolingo. Or, learning a new craft. Or, picking up gardening. We can make the argument that learning a new skill during lockdown was, for many, a way to find control in a world seemingly out of control. A way to create something in a world that seemed on the brink of destruction. A way to keep us from wasting the days away doomscrolling in despair.

But, on the flip side of that coin, was the pressure—the cultural pressure—to be productive. In a 2021 article for HuffPost, Brittany Wong examined the concept of "toxic positivity" specifically through the lens of our experiences in lockdown. She argued that "the pandemic has convinced us that we have to be useful at all times," even when the world is falling apart around us.[116]

Wong used a viral tweet, posted within the first few months of COVID, as evidence of our toxic relationship with productivity:

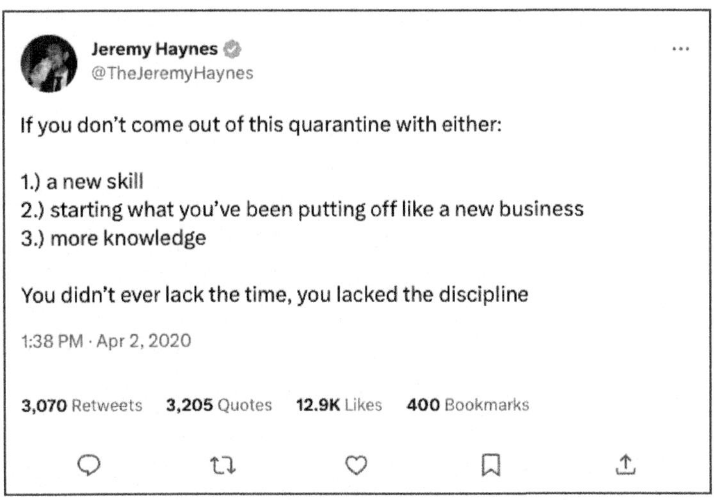
Jeremy Haynes
@TheJeremyHaynes

If you don't come out of this quarantine with either:

1.) a new skill
2.) starting what you've been putting off like a new business
3.) more knowledge

You didn't ever lack the time, you lacked the discipline

1:38 PM · Apr 2, 2020

3,070 Retweets 3,205 Quotes 12.9K Likes 400 Bookmarks

We can all see the influence of Puritanical capitalism dripping off of this tweet, right? All we knew by the start of April, 2020 was that this COVID thing was horrible. It was killing people, we didn't know how to stop it, and we were all living in fear-soaked lockdowns. But, in America, there were a lot of people who thought that if you weren't doing something with all the free time that fear-soaked lockdown gave you, you were wasting it.

But, the longer the soup sat untended on the stove, the more we started to see how many ingredients were making the soup taste funky. We had national conversations, through news media and podcasts, about what it meant to value productivity over well-being. Over rest. Over balance.

It's still a process the world is in the middle of, especially since a lot of these conversations stopped the more we returned to in-person activities and the more the world began to look like it had before the pandemic. It's also a process we strongly believe needs to continue.

The thing that's particularly...persnickety about COVID is that it was both restful for some people and traumatizing to everyone. While Kristen has had some people remark jokingly that they could really use a good lockdown to get caught up on their naps, she can hear the remnants of fear, uncertainty, and overwhelm in their stories. This odd duality is one of the flavorings of the COVID soup ingredients that it's far too early to know exactly what to do with, but we are positive they are present.

How did COVID change the way we work?

The gradual re-emergence out of lockdowns forced us to experiment with different ways to work and to communicate. We all became literate in Zoom or Teams, and we had to learn how to incorporate Slack or Discord into the way we communicate. Many industries that previously proclaimed remote work wasn't possible were forced to make it possible in order to survive.

COVID forced innovations and experimentations—some good and some bad—in so many facets of the American workforce and work culture. The myriad of disruptions to "the way things were" was challenging and stressful, but the forced adaptation created a gap in American culture between what was and what could be.

However, one of the things that didn't change with COVID was our ability as individuals and a broader society to adapt appropriate and healthy stress responses and coping mechanisms. Being forced to live outside the world we knew, and the one we had learned to control, left a lot of Americans with unexpressed emotions and stressors.

The social isolation of COVID took away many coping mechanisms and outlets, forcing people to find other ways to relieve stress or to bury it. As the disruption of COVID continued from one year to two years, we saw dramatic and horrific rises in domestic violence, gun violence, and antisocial public outbursts.[117]

It can be exceptionally difficult to process the trauma of a massive and prolonged communal event. Very few, if any of us, escaped the period of lockdowns unscathed. We've already talked about trauma a bit in the previous section, but we couldn't leave the big T out of a section on COVID.

The pandemic was something that was both deeply personal and uniquely communal. Very rarely in human history has the entire planet experienced an event at the same time. But, though we experienced it together, like all traumas, we did not experience it the same.

What about all the traumas we experienced?

Whenever American culture hears a new and surprising story about a deeply personal trauma, some approximation of the phrase "you never know what someone else is going through" is bandied about on repeat. It's a method of coping, of reminding ourselves that people are more than what we can see, and that, in many instances, we should withhold our judgment of others.

We've already argued that no trauma is comparable, and that goes for our experiences of COVID too. So many individual factors, or ingredients, went into how each American experienced COVID—from their generation, their gender, and their profession, to their mental health, their family, and where they lived in the country.

How do we recognize that COVID was hard for every single person, regardless of their experience?

For so many folks, COVID was a deeply traumatic experience, whether they worked on the front lines as a healthcare professional, or went through a really terrible breakup, or lost their only outlet for stress and couldn't figure out how to cope.

When we added a global pandemic to our culture of burnout, it's no surprise that the rates of burnout skyrocketed.[118] We have a lot of data on the burnout rate among teachers, doctors, and other essential workers, but we didn't look as hard at the rate of burnout across the rest of the country.

Three years on, and we've done a bit more digging. We'll talk more about the relationship between COVID and The Great Resignation a little later on, but there are more stories of burnout and recovery from this period than we realized.

Just like everyone's experiences of COVID are different, everyone's experiences of burnout are different. We humans learn better from stories than from lists of facts and statistics, so we asked a friend of ours to share her personal story of plunging into the depths of burnout and coming out again during her first COVID lockdown.

A Personal Story of Burnout From a Very Good Friend

In 2012, I met and joined forces with another young woman who had been in the process of starting a pet care services company over the last year. Between the two of us, we decided to launch the business as a major endeavor and make it our full-time jobs and careers.

Four years later, the business was thriving. We had rented an office, hired an extensive staff, and were booked solidly 365 days a year from first thing in the morning to last thing at night. We were finally making a comfortable profit and loving the benefits of being our own bosses.

But only a year or so later, I was starting to feel *awful* all of the time. I was tired in a way I could never quite communicate, the kind of deep, bone-set, brain-tired that no good night or spa day could even come close to touching. I kept trying to find ways to dismiss my own feelings. On light days, I'd chastise myself for being so exhausted by what should have been an easy day at work. When small inconveniences sent me into a stress spiral, I wondered if I was cut out for being a business owner. There were nights when my phone rang from a staff member and it took me long enough to summon the energy to make the call back that I had to apologize and make an excuse like being in the shower or cooking. Meanwhile, I'd sat there watching it ring, unable to answer it.

We tried so many things between the two of us: having full weekends off, alternating being on call, hiring more office staff. Nothing seemed to truly work. There was a pervasive, inescapable feeling that I was always responsible, always teetering on the edge of total disaster, that one domino could ruin not just my business but my life. I was constantly waiting for the Next Thing to Go Wrong, even though, on reflection, things rarely did go wrong, or if they did, it was usually minor and easily resolved.

In my "spare" time, I was also volunteering for multiple animal rescues, fostering pets with special needs in my home, offering free tech services to a few local non-profits, and sitting on the board of a charity organization. My husband worked long hours out of the house and made more money than I did, so I also took on the brunt of home-management responsibilities like cooking, cleaning, shopping, doing our taxes, paying bills, and remembering to get the cars' tires swapped twice a year.

Breaks stopped being breaks. I would go on vacation and feel marginally better only to feel worse when I got back home. I started fantasizing near constantly about being rendered unable to do any of these things. Just a *small* accident, like a dog breaking my wrist or twisting my ankle on the ice. Every fiber of my being called for me to just

STOP but I didn't know how; I couldn't. Stopping entirely would mean putting everything on my partner and putting my family's financial well-being at risk. I couldn't figure out how to address this feeling that was eating away at me without losing everything I'd spent ten years now working for.

And then COVID-19 hit.

Overnight, my entire life changed. Our business was closed for all non-essential services, which meant I went from packed-full days of appointments to a few a week at most. All my employees were gone. Everything *stopped*.

I was lucky enough to be in a place to get government support, so financially I was safe, and for the first time in a decade I was able to truly breathe. I spent six weeks confined to my house except for dog walks. I did yoga every morning. I read books. I sat in one place and did nothing, sometimes for hours. You might think this is the point when the healing starts, but it's not. I wish I could say that was all it took to reset, recharge, and restart with a more positive attitude, but it wasn't. No, this was the point that I truly realized something was wrong. Not with me, but with the life I had been living for so long.

This was the first time in all that time that I acknowledged that it wasn't fixable with an on-call schedule or a part-time administrator on the books. I realized that the urge to STOP had been screaming at me for so long and I'd been answering back: *that's impossible, there is no stop*. But now I had stopped. I'd been forced to stop—there was suddenly no going, instead! And it felt like that intense cathartic release at the end of a long crying session.

Over the next two years, I listened to myself better. I gave myself space. I stopped. And then I started again, slowly, carefully. I got a new job

> that I love, that values me, and gives me the time I need to be an object at rest instead of a perpetual motion machine. I started therapy. I learned so much about myself and what stresses me out. I realized that while I still miss a lot of things about my old job, it was never going to get better.
>
> I have an immense amount of privilege to have found lockdown to be more restful than stressful—for so many people it was absolutely the opposite, and it breaks my heart that it took such a massive global tragedy for me to find personal clarity. But if there's anything my experience underlines it's that 1) our cultural expectations make it all too easy for you to blame yourself for your burnout and 2) baby steps are sometimes not enough to tackle levels of stress like this; when it gets that bad, sometimes the only way out is to stop.

COVID didn't just happen to us individually, even though we each have our own story of how it affected us personally. It happened on a collective and communal level in a way that we hadn't experienced as a country in a long time. Certainly, not one that we'd experienced during this age of mass information and technological change.

The Good Doctors are both experts in communal trauma. While we're sure you think that level of expertise is all sunshine and rainbows, let us be honest and say it is some of the most difficult, yet rewarding, work we've ever done. Because of this expertise, when the lockdowns hit, we both started noticing a lot of patterns appearing in American culture that we had seen elsewhere. From the language people used, to the way people responded to communal events and changes, we could see the writing on the wall.

We've been sharing our insights and analysis with anyone who cared to listen, and right now, that's you lovely folks.

Where have we seen communal trauma like this before?

We talk a lot about Northern Ireland in our own lives, and even a little bit in this book. Both of us lived and worked in that place. We earned our PhDs in trauma related topics from Queen's University Belfast. Additionally, Kristen's husband grew up and lived most of his life in Northern Ireland. All of this means that we've had both an insider and an outsider view on what communal trauma looks like.[119]

For approximately 30 years, the small country located at the top of the island of Ireland was subject to an armed ethnonationalist conflict referred to as "The Troubles." While the roots of that conflict go back hundreds of years, the concentrated span from 1968 to 1998 saw the highest rates of death, injury, destruction, and disruption through violent means perpetrated by a number of groups and actors. During that span, nearly 4,000 people died, 50,000 were physically injured, and there were approximately 37 thousand shooting incidents in a geographical location smaller than Connecticut.[120]

For decades, life became a series of adjustments and adaptations. What was once entirely abnormal—army checkpoints, bomb scares, burned out cars, and barricades—gradually became a normal part of everyday life. Governments and politicians came and went, policies changed, but most people in Northern Ireland tried to get on with everyday life. Underlying all of these changes and disruptions was a constant feeling of uncertainty and fear.

Now, if we remove the specific references to violence and Northern Ireland, that paragraph could be written about our experiences during COVID. If we replace checkpoints and bomb scares with mask requirements, travel restrictions, and socially distanced events, then it all sounds quite familiar. Stories we heard of life during the Troubles often came back to both of us as we watched and listened to American's grappling with the height of the pandemic.

So, how did the lovely folks in that Connecticut-sized country cope with the trauma of such a massive societal disruption? If we told you that one of the biggest coping mechanisms we witnessed was traumatic disclosures to strange Americans in pubs, would you believe us? From the moment either of us stepped foot on that soil, we were spotted as Americans. The longer we lived abroad, the more we saw it too. Americans walk differently, dress differently, stand differently, and certainly, speak at different volumes.

We always knew we were different, that we were outsiders, but what we didn't know was that also made us safe to the people living there. In our years living in and visiting that beautiful part of the world, we heard stories about death, pain, grief, and anger. The conversations happened in living rooms, taxi cabs, and pubs, and could range from deeply detailed disclosures about how human ash felt on their skin, to how much they hated going to their grandma's for Christmas because they had to go through army checkpoints. These conversations would not, however, ever happen if Kristen's husband was with us. He is from Northern Ireland himself and, therefore, not a safe person they could say things to.

You see, one of the chief cultural mottos of Northern Ireland is "whatever you say, say nothing".[121] Say nothing about your personal pain, say nothing about the things you overhear in the neighborhood, say nothing about what you know or what you feel. Years of communal trauma—of fearing your neighbor, of worrying about being safe in public, of grieving seemingly unending losses—created a culture of silence. It created a culture where it was normal to drink yourself into oblivion or throw molotov cocktails at the police, but not to talk about your pain. Not with your family, not with your friends, not with your neighbors, and certainly, not with a professional.

The problem with that is, humans can't actually live like that.

Pain demands to be shared because our bodies are not built to carry it alone.

We can choose how to share the pain, or when, and we can do it in ways that move us towards healing or ways that contribute to more pain—but that pain is going to escape. It'll happen in a pub one night after too many pints, or in a taxi to the airport. Or, it will happen in the grocery store checkout when the item you needed is still out of stock. Or, it will happen at the school board meeting when you're told about another period of remote learning. Or, it will happen at a Lunar New Year celebration because you blame Chinese people for the virus in the first place.

The pain will always find a way to be expressed, especially when we don't teach adequate coping strategies or build appropriate support systems. When we aren't honest about the impact of the trauma, people can't be honest about the root of their pain, exhaustion, and burnout.

But, what do we do when that pain, that trauma, that grief is communal? Or, in the case of Northern Ireland and many other places around the globe—what happens when our pain is connected to a cycle of trauma that never really ends even when the event is "over?" And, even more importantly, what do we do when our community has told us to ignore the pain and get over it?

What do we do when we've lived through an incredibly distressing and difficult time and we're told by our government, our industries, and our media that the best way to deal with what happened—the only way to deal with what happened—is to go "back to normal?"

Why is the "back to normal" narrative harmful?

Reminder: "normal" is truly just a setting on a tumble dryer. Head back to our section on intersectionality for a fuller refresher.

We're not saying that the desire to go back to the ways things were before a profound trauma or massive change isn't natural. We would argue it's even a "normal" response to trauma. The problem with that response isn't that it's abnormal. The problem with that response is that it's harmful. Wishing we could go back to before the world changed does a lot of damage. It prevents us from grieving, from healing, and from growing through the traumatic experience. It stops us from seeing the reality of the situation, from seeing what could or should be different. And, sometimes, it stops us from recognizing the ways we can prevent similar things from happening again.

One of the most damaging things we did from the start of the pandemic was try and convince people to participate in public health measures with the promise that if we did—if we could just "flatten the curve" or "stop the spread"—we could return to our normal lives. The longer the pandemic went on, the more severe the trauma and societal disruption, the more harmful that lie became.

The truth was that the pandemic changed so much—the way we saw ourselves, the way we interacted with each other, the way we approached medicine and public health—and we could never return to the "normal" of before, because it no longer existed. Not only was our old way of life gone, but as we said earlier, the pandemic forced a lot of us to examine it more closely and come to the conclusion that going "back to normal" was a bad idea because, as it turns out, "normal" American society and work culture wasn't working for a lot of people.

Remember our friend's story from earlier? She was just one of millions of folks who was only able to see their burnout because the world stopped.

We are not the first, nor the last, place to experience prolonged communal trauma. As social scientists, we always look outside our own culture to see what lessons we can learn about how to deal with the "end" of COVID. With our time working and living in Northern Ireland, we knew there were important lessons to learn from their communal experiences of trauma.

How did Northern Ireland deal with their communal trauma after the Troubles "ended?"

Spoiler alert: they didn't.

After decades of violence, and years of ceasefires and negotiations, in 1998, the major political parties of Northern Ireland signed what is called "The Good Friday Agreement," or "The Belfast Agreement," depending on your persuasion. The people of both Northern Ireland and the Republic of Ireland were asked to ratify it, and they did, overwhelmingly so. It outlined a new form of government, specific access to social services, and more. It's understood as the official end to the armed conflict, and so much good came out of that document and the process of crafting it.

But, a key omission is that the agreement did not propose any mechanisms for people to officially air their grievances and seek restitution. The prevailing cultural attitude was one of relief that the conflict was over, and that life could now get "back to normal." The thing is, there is no going back to it after the world has changed. There is only creating something new, and ignoring what happened doesn't do anyone any favors in that new world.

Over the last twenty odd years since the ratification of the agreement, there were small and large non-profit organizations who stepped into that gap and provided healing, reconciliation, and support for victims and survivors. But, as of the publication of this book, there is no unified governmental response to the Troubles. (In fact, there's no unified or even functioning government at all.)

The process of handing the emotional aftermath over to a cornucopia of nonprofits, religious organizations, and individuals left Northern Ireland grappling with what it meant to be a "victim" of the conflict. Who is allowed to say they suffered? How do we measure that suffering? How do we acknowledge it in a way that is inclusive and healing?

We can, and do, ask these questions about other events of communal trauma—such as who is affected the most by 9/11, or how we remember the fraught legacy of the War on Terror. If we've done our job in drawing these parallels from home and abroad, then you can see how these other examples of communal trauma connect to our experiences with COVID.

Trauma is a living creature, a monster we wrestle, and healing is the path away from it. All of us have an origin story with that monster; most of us have several. How we change as we walk that path is our own personal evolution, and walking the path is the only way to turn a scar into scar tissue. It's the only way we turn trauma into a thing that happened, instead of a thing that is happening.

However, ignoring a problem never makes it go away. Pretending trauma isn't real, or that it never showed up in the first place, or that it didn't change life as we know it only allows that monster to grow unchecked. Instead of being healed from it, we're consumed by it. We can pretend nothing has changed, but everything actually has.

When we experience a trauma, generational, personal or communal, or all of the above, and we do not accept, process, or heal our pain, we stop growing. We become frozen inside our trauma, locked in a position where our pain does not have a healthy outlet, trapped in that story that we relive over and over without a conclusion. But, as we've already said, that pain will find a way out. It always does.

So, what happened when we tried to put COVID in the past tense instead of present tense? What happened to all those folks who didn't see their burnout during lockdown and kept working through that pain and exhaustion?

Everyone remembers The Great Resignation, right?

The Great Resignation was, in part, a reaction to the return of burnout culture when American society emerged from the forced isolation and slower pace of COVID. Helped in part by the "back to normal" narrative, the supply chain disruptions, and the fear of another recession, the American economy broke all the speed limits trying to return to its pre-pandemic status.

COVID forced a slowing down, for a time, but we all know that the pace and the period of reevaluation didn't stick. And, why is that? Because we didn't take that time to explore and understand the deeper cultural context of our exhaustion, of our pain. We assumed we were burned out and exhausted because of the effects of COVID, not in spite of it. We looked to the immediate cause and assumed that the "end" of it was the end of our problems. COVID was "over" and so now we could all go back to our lives the way they were before March 2020.

The two of us watched these conversations, LinkedIn posts, and news stories spread through the country with growing alarm. Humanity has been here before, after all, and we knew it wasn't good.

When America, and the world, began to open up more in 2021, we started to see the different ways the pandemic had changed the way the culture works and the way humans relate to work. To us, it was further proof that we could never go "back to normal." The Great Resignation, first coined in May 2021, represented the first inklings that Americans were beginning to re-evaluate their participation in the labor market.[122]

In August 2021, 4 million Americans voluntarily quit their jobs. The job report and media coverage announcing these numbers spawned thousands of think pieces, op-eds, and analyses on what these job losses meant for the American workforce.

Why did so many people quit their jobs?

As we started to gather data on the reason behind waves of folks quitting their jobs, we could see how the promise of going back to the normal way of working was forcing a lot of people to reconsider their jobs and career paths. One of the big reasons there were high numbers of job loss was that many companies forced their staff to return to the office full-time, and people lost a lot of the workplace flexibility they had grown accustomed to during the pandemic.[123]

The more we paid attention to what people were saying on the job market, the more we heard stories about people being lied to in their job interviews about the possibility of work flexibility. Before COVID, plenty of managers and leaders thought that remote work would kill the economy. During COVID, the data proved that wasn't the case. But, after the pandemic, many of those same leaders and managers expected their employees to go back to the way it was, even if the last few years pointed to how that wasn't necessary to get the job done.

Another major issue with job losses was the lack of accommodation for folks with different healthcare needs. More women than men left the workforce during the pandemic, mostly to take over the caring and sometimes education duties for their children during lockdowns and remote learning periods.[124] Childcare facilities were some of the hardest hit during the pandemic, and many did not reopen after lockdowns. This meant that families with children had fewer options for childcare support. Many women quit jobs when they lost that lack of flexibility with remote work and childcare still remained a challenge.

Similarly, many immunocompromised and disabled people left the workforce during The Great Resignation out of a legitimate fear of returning to work in the office and the continued threat of exposure to COVID-19. The end of remote work policies was especially difficult for immunocompromised workers and put them in "unworkable positions, since company policies may not cover their situations as a result. Going into the office poses a risk to their health—but risking their livelihood by refusing is not an easy choice, either."[125]

But, it's important to note that what started out as The Great Resignation shifted into something larger, a reconceptualization of what the American workforce experience should be. A 2022 article from Harvard Business Review argues that what we all witnessed starting in the second half of 2021 "upended the relationship between workers and the labor market."[126]

The article contends that there were five factors that contributed to this dramatic change in the labor market, and that the situation is far more complex than simple resignations. To keep with the theme of r's, their five factors are: retirement, relocation, reconsideration, reshuffling, and reluctance. They explained these factors as:

> Workers are **retiring** in greater numbers but aren't **relocating** in large numbers; they're **reconsidering** their work-life balance and care roles; they're making localized switches among industries, or **reshuffling**, rather than exiting the labor market entirely; and, because of pandemic-related fears, they're demonstrating a **reluctance** to return to in-person jobs.[127]

Since COVID forced so much change on our society, it will take a long time to navigate our way through these changes and fully understand what our post-pandemic world and workplace will look like. A few months into The Great Resignation, we started to see calls to rename this period of change with some calling it The Great Reshuffle or The Great Upgrade.

Regardless of what you call it, what we witnessed was the start of a reconceptualization of American workers and their participation in the labor market. This is especially true for those folks suffering from burnout. We were all in survival mode for those first few years of COVID, but as we started to live more than survive, we all realized how many things had changed, or how many things still *needed* to change.

How did we go from The Great Resignation to "quiet quitting?"

While historians like nothing more than to put nice, neat brackets around major events, societal change is rarely that tidy. As 2021 transitioned into 2022, we continued to hear more stories of people leaving jobs, fields, and careers for a whole host of reasons. Even though there are a lot of big fancy words for why people kept quitting, from our perspective, it really came down to people realizing they were unhappy continuing in a job that did not see and respect them as a whole person.

In researching for this book, it surprised us to learn that more people actually quit their jobs in 2022 than the previous year. But, as we learned with the first wave of resignations, most people weren't leaving the workforce altogether. They were quitting to take new jobs. Some of the top reasons listed for this continued recontextualization and extended reshuffling was the reality that the post-pandemic labor market meant ample job prospects, higher wages, and flexible work options continued to change the American workforce.[128]

People weren't just quitting their jobs, though. By the Summer of 2022, we had a new concept trending on social media. We should be honest and say that few things pissed off The Good Doctors more than the conversations around "quiet quitting." In fact, our notoriously camera-avoidant team member Eleanor was so upset about it that she joined us on a ranty YouTube Live to talk about it in August 2022.

What we hated about the term "quiet quitting" was how it was used to criticize people for doing something very healthy: setting boundaries. What we didn't hate about the term was that it represented a large-scale cultural shift in how Americans understand our relationship with our culture of burnout. We are in the process of changing the way we talk about and view labor as a culture.

This trend in the great workplace reshuffle first appeared on our radars in March 2022 with a TikTok video from a user called Brian Creely.[129] He captioned his video post "More people are 'quiet quitting' instead of leaving," and the internet proceeded to go wild, yet again. Several things happened with the panic over "quiet quitting," but the biggest difference was around what it actually meant and what people perceived it meant.

From morning news shows to battling TikTok videos, America became enmeshed in an argument where people debated whether "quiet quitting" was "a trendy new term for laziness or a way to push back against capitalism-gone-too-far."[130] Interpretations of "quiet quitting" as laziness or lack of motivation stemmed in part from the term reaching viral status on TikTok, a platform used mostly by young Millennials and Gen Z, and from generational differences on workplace expectations and job requirements.

Can we blame Gen Z for "quiet quitting"?

As generational researchers, we know that every new generation in the workforce is called lazy and entitled. We certainly remember it happening when our generational cohort first entered the labor market. With "quiet quitting," a lot of older leaders and managers (Boomers and Gen X) used the term to criticize Gen Z as being more lazy and entitled than other generations.[131] One of the more toxic responses we saw to the trend was from CNBC contributor Kevin O'Leary who said that "quiet quitting" was "worse than COVID," and "if you're a quiet quitter, you're a loser."[132]

Leaving that horrific hot take aside, we can still ask the question of who is right? Is "quiet quitting" just about lazy kids fresh out of college complaining about hard work? Or, is it more about Gen Z's reconceptualization about how they want to participate in the labor market and workforce? You might guess from our emotional reaction to the term in the first place, where we land on this issue.

With the term rapidly gaining in popular use, its original user, Brian Creely, was called upon to explain the meaning of the term. In an interview with Insider he explained, "It's not being lazy or doing poor work. Quiet quitting is about restoring a healthy balance in your career and work. In other words, you're doing exactly what you're paid to do and establishing firm boundaries."[133]

That might sound entirely reasonable to you, and we agree. But if you are part of a generation who believes that achieving your goals is not possible if you set boundaries, or if you say no to your boss, then you might believe that setting those boundaries is unreasonable and unrealistic. Whether you agree with the definition of the term or not, there's no question that there is a significant drop in engagement across the workforce.

We know that as of late 2022, data gathered by Gallup reported that quiet quitters made up at least 50% of the workforce, and we've seen alarming drops in the rates of engagement starting in the second half of 2021. The study found that it was "especially related to clarity of expectations, opportunities to learn and grow, feeling cared about, and a connection to the organization's mission or purpose." Gallup also discovered a generational element in their survey findings with a specific decline in engagement and employer satisfaction being expressed by those under 35—younger Millennials and Gen Z workers.[134]

In fact, the TikTok responsible for the terms viral status, posted by user known as Zaid Khan in July 2022, speaks to Gen Z's possible discontent with American work culture. Khan described "quiet quitting" as:

> You're still performing your duties, but you're no longer subscribing to the hustle culture mentality that work has to be your life—the reality is, it's not. And your worth as a person is not defined by your labor.[135]

How do we understand these changes in American work culture?

We think you can make the argument that a lot of these changes in the labor market and work culture stem from younger employees, rather than older, as is often the case. In our section on generations, we talked a bit about the demands that Millennials and Gen Z are asking of the workplace and what kinds of changes they are looking for. Because of this, some are arguing that "quiet quitting" is dominated by Gen Z workers—maybe because they can't afford to quit for real or shuffle to another field or career.

In this way, "quiet quitting" is part of Gen Z's natural reconceptualization of their relationship with work. There are more Gen Z workers employed in the US than before COVID, and for those who joined the workforce during the pandemic, they are only now starting to realize what "back to normal" means for their employers and industries. If we consider the impact that being "digital natives" might have on Gen Z's perception of work and themselves, then this period of reconceptualization makes even more sense.

An analysis in *The New Yorker*, from late 2022, lays out the argument for Gen Z's unique merging of their personal self with their work self.[136] The generation of social media and influencer culture has shown them that there are very few hard boundaries between those two identities. Therefore, the remote work of lockdowns hit this generation differently.

What we can learn from this tumultuous period is that "for Gen Z, which had so thoroughly mixed work and self, this suffocating grimness hit at a more personal level. It became clear to many that they needed to separate their personhood from their jobs. It is this transition that generates much of the angst exhibited in quiet-quitting videos."[137] Even though we've moved past talking about "quiet quitting," these cross-generational conversations are still happening online.

Where do we go from here?

Sidney Morss is a popular TikTok creator who has a series of videos on generational gaps in the workplace. In her "Who's bringing napkins? Generation-Gap Pt. 59" video from early May 2023, her stereotypical Gen Z worker replies to the question "Are you quiet quitting?" with "Nobody is quiet quitting. We're working our wage."[138] Whatever you want to call this shift in workplace expectations, it is clear that it's not another short-lived trend.

But, The Youths are not the only workers to declare that their worth as a person is not defined by their labor. We learned from the Gallup survey that 50% of the American workforce is "quiet quitting," but according to the U.S. Census Bureau, Gen Z only makes up 20% of the workforce.[139] Doing some quick math, we can see that there are a lot of workers who are starting to set boundaries with employers who aren't meeting their expectations.

We'll talk more about the concept of toxic productivity later on, but it's worth repeating that the changes we're seeing in American burnout/work culture are nothing new. What is new is that, for the first time in American history, we have an endless supply of platforms to use to talk about our ideas of workplace boundary setting and balance.

This process and discourse is happening in an interactive and collaborative way because of social media and smartphones. It is an interesting social experiment to talk about the importance of setting boundaries on platforms that make money by discouraging boundary setting, and one we'll address later in Section Four.

We've also seen recent examples of high-profile athletes such as Naomi Osaka and Simone Biles setting firm boundaries between their profession and their personhood.[140] Those high-profile, high-performance athletes did something countercultural when they prioritized their mental and physical health over the demands of their jobs. The furor on social media and in traditional sports broadcasting was swift and fierce, but so was the loud support. This is clearly a matter on which people remain divided.

And, with that, our bowls of Burnout Culture Soup are ready to be served, chock-full of individualism, Puritanical beliefs about work, conflict between generations, and rife with stories of trauma, both personal and generational. So, what does swimming in that soup look like for Americans today? In the next section, we're going to explore America's current culture of burnout and the ways it affects us all.

Section Three:

Our Culture of Burnout

"Oh, you're not burned out. That's just a trendy internet word for being lazy."

Craig wasn't surprised, but he was disappointed. He'd thought long and hard about bringing up his current state of overwhelming anxiety during his performance review and this was demonstrating his greatest fears. "Sir, with all due respect—"

"I guess you can take a few days," his boss said with a heavy sigh, as though Craig was asking for a corner office and a seven figure pay raise instead of a four-day work week for the next six months. "There's nothing mission critical on your calendar. Just don't make a habit of this, Craig. You're a rising star in the company and taking time off when you're not sick might stand in the way of a promotion."

"Thank you," Craig said, biting his tongue so he wouldn't snap back that he *felt* sick. It would be better if he settled for whatever his boss was willing to give him than fight for something that may not happen.

So Craig took a few days and came back to work. His already existing symptoms of persistent anxiety and difficulty focusing continued. He would call in sick on the days he couldn't get out of bed, and over time, he noticed that his boss' prophecy had proven correct. He was routinely passed over for plum assignments and promotions. But his mental health wasn't exactly heading towards regulation either, and he only felt worse since his performance review. But he felt lost and unsure how to change anything, so he just kept showing up and hoping something would change.

If Craig's story sounds familiar, we're sorry. We know versions of it happen every day, all over the country, to employees at every level of an organization. Americans live in a culture of burnout, and now that you know a little bit more about how we got here, the values that have built this narrative as our reality, we can look at what living in a culture of burnout is like and what that means.

To add even more metaphors to the mix, if the last section examined the bricks of American culture, now we're going to look at the house we built and what it's like to live in it. First, we'll review how the values the Puritans gave us evolved into the present-day, including our cultural perspective on success and productivity. Next, we'll examine how gender roles play a massive part in the prevalence, experience, and type of burnout we experience (and the research being done on it!). And, finally, we'll dive into the deep, dark well that is the Wellness Industrial Complex.[141]

Chapter 10: **Puritans Remix: America's Version**

Let's revisit our good friends, the Puritans, to talk about the ramifications of their past beliefs on America today, and which elements are particularly American.

While other cultures experience burnout—and we'd never claim they don't—the version Americans experience is particularly our own. Just like you can only get a proper Philly cheesesteak in Philadelphia (do not get Kristen started), you can only get *American* burnout by being in America.

We've been talking through this idea in presentations, keynotes, and Zoom calls for years now, and the reactions are generally the same. As soon as we break down Puritan theology, people's eyes light up, and you can actually see their brains working to rewrite their understanding of themselves.

So, here are three elements that the Puritans left us as our ideological inheritance and how they *specifically* relate to America today.

You're Only a Good Person if You Work Really Hard

It would be hard to find a concept that is more embedded in what it means to be an American than this. Because we have attached a moral value to hard work, we have created a culture of burnout that valorizes exhaustion and criticizes rest.

Though this concept was around for a good few hundred years, it sank its nails into the American imagination when we connected moral judgments around the need and use of government assistance programs. In Ronald Reagan's 1976 Presidential campaign, he started telling the story of the "Welfare Queen."

Linda Taylor was a real person who was convicted of welfare fraud in 1974, but the true story of her life, and her abuse of the welfare system, got lost in the Reagan administration's demonization of anyone using welfare.[142] The idea that anyone on welfare was lazy and morally corrupt took hold during the 1980s, and America forever solidified the notion that you can *only* be a good person if you work hard.

In more recent years, we can see this attitude in our cultural worship of Silicon Valley tech start-ups—the Steve Jobs, Bill Gates, and Elon Musks of the world. This attitude is why we have "hustle culture" and people quipping, "We all have the same number of hours in a day as Beyoncé."[143]

We've all been a part of those conversations where people brag about how busy they are, how little sleep they are getting, and how successful it has made them. Kristen's mental off-switch is nonexistent, and ignoring the thoughts that tell her resting is being lazy is usually chemically impossible. Even when it is possible, she feels defeated by the whole notion and often just keeps working.

Recently, when we were talking to a dear friend about how hard Kristen works, how many hours a day she works, and how little sleep she gets, we weren't surprised to get this response: "Oh you must be exhausted, that sounds so hard…but I'm not going to lie, I'm a little jealous. I wish I could get that much done." Kristen was explaining how toxic and harmful her work patterns were, and our friend, very much a product of this Puritanical capitalism, was jealous of her productivity.

Working Hard Means Doing It All Alone

Our second concept from the Puritans finds a lot of purchase in our culture of burnout because of two deeply held and pervasive myths of American life: the myth of bootstraps and the myth of the lone cowboy—and each evolved into the myth of the lone genius.

When we talk about achieving success or being a productive

member of society, we often use the phrase to "pull yourself up by your bootstraps" to refer to a person's ability to overcome the circumstances of their birth, or life, and succeed on their own. We're both fascinated by the origins of words and phrases, and so, naturally, for this segment of the book, we did some research on the origins of this phrase. We were actually shocked, but not surprised, to learn that the phrase originally meant "to try to do something completely absurd."[144] To pull yourself up by your bootstraps is actually physically impossible. John Swansburg wrote this about the toxicity of the bootstraps myth:

> The very language we use to describe the self-made ideal has these fault lines embedded within it: To "pull yourself up by your bootstraps" is to succeed by dint of your own efforts. But that's a modern corruption of the phrase's original meaning. It used to describe a quixotic attempt to achieve an impossibility, not a feat of self-reliance. You **can't** pull yourself up by your bootstraps, anymore than you can by your shoelaces. (Try it.)[145]

The origins of the phrase date back to 1834 when it appeared as a snarky newspaper response to the discovery of perpetual motion. From those curious beginnings, how did it come to reference a "self-made" person? The meaning of the phrase started to change in the early 20th century. It now represents America's irrepressible spirit and our ability to rise "purely through rugged individualism."[146] This myth often negates the reality of the situation and how many Americans have only found generational wealth through the aid of government assistance.

Take our enterprising pioneers as an example. Why did they leave the comfort of the East Coast for the expanse of the West? In part, because of the Homestead Acts, a government benefits program that granted them land. Though it doesn't fit with the national narrative of the self-made man, close to one quarter of (mostly White) Americans owe part of their generational family wealth to the Homestead Acts.[147]

The myth of the lone cowboy comes from a similar misrepresentation of life in the American West. This myth was also founded on the idea that working hard means doing it alone. It is the most potent symbol of our individualism, even though most cattle ranchers worked in groups, and most western towns outlawed guns.[148] We romanticized the notion of man taming the "uncivilized" west, and then, we perpetuated that myth through print media, Wild West shows, and eventually western movies.

So much of American culture is built on the fetishization of cowboys as the ultimate Americans—inaccurately portrayed as loners who took the law into their own hands. The stranglehold of this Puritan ideal has constantly taught Americans that oneself is all anyone *should* need to succeed. As mentioned above, this became the more recent worship of the lone genius. Jobs, Bezos, Zuckerberg—America tells the story that these men did all the work by themselves to be billionaires. Just like the cowboys didn't do anything truly alone (they did not raise their horses, or build the towns they visited, or own the land they settled on), these men did not arrive at innovative technology on their own.

We can also see this reflected in the changing style of American homes over the centuries, which we touched on earlier in Section Two. What better way to show that you don't need community, that you can look after yourself and your own family, than to move your social life from the front yard to the backyard? Jungle gyms and swimming pools, and other backyard accouterments, became the hallmark of a successful American lifestyle, while also reinforcing the primacy of the nuclear family over the community.

Rest Is For When You Are Dead

This one is probably the most straightforward. How many times have you heard this in your life? How many times have you *said* this? How many times have you driven yourself into exhaustion thinking, "If I just get one more thing done" or "If I work through dinner, I'll finally be caught up" or "I can't afford to take a vacation right now, work is too important"?

Americans are obsessed with working hard and are convinced that doing so is the only way to have success. It's been baked into our American identity since the Puritans first stepped foot on Indigenous land.

But, all this talk of being successful and being productive and being good members of society brings up its own set of questions. What even is "success?" Why do we value productivity? And, is too much productivity a bad thing?

Chapter 11: America's Obsession with Success and (Toxic) Productivity

This section is full of statistics because some of these topics are the easiest to quantify into research. This may be overwhelming (we're not numbers people either), but we ask you to stick with us because the numbers are compelling. They paint a pretty stark picture of the consequences of living in this soup.

What is "success," really?

Our broth formed the base for a soup that tastes a lot like "American work culture is obsessed with productivity and success." But, is success something we can even define? Are success and productivity related? What do Americans think success really looks like, anyway?

Your gut instinct answer probably has something to do with money.

Several researchers explored the connection between money and happiness and tried to figure out if there is one, and the answers have varied a little bit.

You might have even heard of the $75,000 threshold. The idea came from a 2010 Princeton study where Daniel Kahneman and Angus Deaton determined that day-to-day emotional well-being "kind of leveled off" once a person made $75,000 or more, whereas, before that, an increase in salary correlated to an increase in happiness.[149]

In 2018, a larger study by Purdue University declared the happiest income point to be $95,000, where they saw a bump not just in day-to-day emotional well-being but also in overall, grander life satisfaction. They even noted a drop in happiness levels when someone made more than $105,000 per year.[150]

We don't need to define a specific "happiness salary," which would change year-to-year and area-to-area anyway, to understand why this is the case. It's not just about what makes you happy but about what makes you unhappy, what stresses you out.

At the lower end, not being able to maintain a basic standard of living where you can afford a safe, comfortable place to live, enough food, healthcare, and at least the basics of entertainment and social activity is going to have very obvious and negative impacts on your day-to-day happiness and comfort. The stress of having to choose between rent and food, the constant threat that a sinus infection or a broken ankle will bankrupt you, or the fear of not being able to afford the childcare you need in order to go to work and support your family are stressors that weigh heavily on Americans all across the country.

But, as salary increases, so often does responsibility, obligation, and liability, which can create stress. Those noting a drop in happiness after a certain point are likely working longer hours, are dealing with heavier workloads, and are more likely to be managing others.

The APA's "Stress in America" study in 2022 found that 83% of Americans cite inflation as a source of stress, with 69% saying the economy was a source of stress and 66% saying money. Those who are stressed by money are most stressed by not having enough to pay for basic needs, and of those stressed out by money, 55% reported that it causes fights or tension in their family. Those who are feeling stressed by a lack of money to pay for things in the present are also much more likely to be making under $50,000 a year, the study found.[151]

Not having enough money is stressful, and we know prolonged stress can lead to burnout. But, is having money the same as being successful?

Americans seem to think so, ranking "more wealth" as the most common factor they'd need to feel their social status had increased.[152] It was followed by freedom/autonomy, respect/recognition, and less responsibility. Only 2% said what they needed was fame.

When asked, "If you haven't 'made it' yet, what's missing," 67% of Americans said a higher income. 22% said their dream job. Worth noting—the top three things that defined making enough money to consider yourself successful were: never having to worry about medical bills, being able to loan money to family and friends, and being able to donate a significant amount to charity.[153]

Other signs of success included reaching a higher level of education, working from home or with a shorter commute, and living with a drastically larger amount of time off. The difference between the American average at the time of the study in 2018 and where the participants drew the line for "making it" wasn't hugely disparate in a lot of categories, but for time off, the current average was 2.8 weeks and the success threshold was 5.3 weeks. You're going to see this as a recurring theme in this book. What Americans seem to want most is relief from that which is most stressful. Success, to us, is enough money not to worry about it and enough time to spend it enjoying ourselves.

Those seem like worthwhile pursuits, especially when we consider how these factors relate to happiness. Americans want to feel secure and happy. Safe, comfortable, and able to provide the same for their families. So...how did that seemingly wholesome desire become so toxic?

What is toxic productivity?

As with many things, this attitude becomes dangerous when it becomes extreme. A desire to grow and improve oneself, move up the ranks at a job, and make enough money to feel comfortable and safe is not inherently bad, but it is oh-so exploitable because it's very difficult to draw a line between a healthy amount of ambition and a sinking into toxic productivity.

This is a term you've probably heard loads, but you know by

now that we love a good definition, so let's see what we found.

Erika Ferszt, founder of Moodally, calls toxic productivity "the evil love child" of workaholism and overachieving, explaining, "The culture we live in loves employees who are toxically productive. You know you can call them at any hour of any day, and they will respond."[154]

HuffPost defines toxic productivity as "an unhealthy desire to be productive at all times, at all costs. It's the need to go the 'extra mile' at work or at home, even when it's not expected of you."[155]

"Even time that's not spent on work or family is supposed to be somehow 'productive'—the precarity of American jobs and the rise of hustle culture have led to a 'feeling that you need to get something out of all of your time,'" says Jenny Odell, author of *How to Do Nothing*.[156]

Basically, what we're saying is, toxic productivity is The *Real* American Dream. The Puritans would be so proud!

If we have the Puritans to thank for the foundations of toxic productivity, then we have popular culture and media to thank for making it an aspiration or an achievement worth overworking for. "Success," and all that it means in a uniquely American context, is a story that we tell ourselves as a country.

From the first publications selling financial independence and land through Manifest Destiny, all the way up to Instagram influencers peddling free vacations for product promotion, we have been told the story that "success" means financial wealth.

Since the emergence of TV shows into the American cultural imagination, we've told countless stories of people achieving "The American Dream" through hard work, grit, and determination. Each generation gets a seminal example of what this dream should look like. Boomers got *Leave it to Beaver* and *The Mary Tyler Moore Show*, while Gen Xers got "greed is good" from *Wall Street* and Robin Leach touring extravagant homes on *Lifestyles of the Rich and Famous*.

What about us younger folks? Millennials grew up in an America where MTV was almost known more for reality TV than music videos. We were shown the model of monetary "success" through hit shows like *Cribs* and *Pimp My Ride*. Gen Z is perhaps the unluckiest generation of all, since the advent of social media platforms gave us the rise of "influencer culture" and the belief that anyone could become rich and famous by making a viral video, promoting a product, or finding a click-worthy gimmick.

In most of these stories, the victor "wins" through hard work and without much time spent on their privileges and support systems. These stories do not grapple with intersectionality and wage inequality. In this version of America, "monetary success is the *only* success."[157]

We both grew up being told that all we needed to do to reach our own piece of The American Dream was to work hard. In this way, The American Dream "promotes a notion of individual upward mobility without government help, but if this dream were viable for *all* Americans, these gaps would be balancing themselves over time."[158]

For too long we have used the "bootstrap" theory we outlined earlier to hide the systems of inequality and oppression that make it impossible for most Americans to emerge from underneath the weight of toxic productivity and our definition of "success." If we want to find our way out, then we have to start telling different stories, and that's yet another reason why we are writing this book.

Toxic productivity sends the message that sitting still is pointless laziness. Rest isn't just neutral, it's actively wasteful of the time we could be spending achieving, producing, creating, earning. And, everything we do, regardless of why we do it, can be making us money and, therefore, pushing us up the ladder of success. Every hobby, interest, skill, and activity are opportunities for "side hustles" and turning down extra hours or added responsibilities at work are not just occupational failings, but personal ones, too.

Toxic productivity is a huge reason that so many people cannot stop producing, even during a COVID-19 lockdown. Remember the tweet we shared in our COVID chapter, berating us for lacking discipline and willpower if we didn't come out of lockdown with a new skill or accomplishment?

We are also surrounded by apps, games, and other forms of entertainment that boost engagement through accomplishing tasks.[159] The "gamification" of our lives has led many of us to believe that we need to achieve or accomplish something in order to get any form of validation or celebration. Even mindfulness or wellness apps push you to create a streak of engagement and reward you when you do.[160]

In addition to a need to find self-value in overwork, Derek Thompson at *The Atlantic* identifies something else that makes hustle culture so easy to fall prey to: a need to belong. Hard work and godliness are closely tied together in American culture, even for those who don't subscribe to any specifical spiritual beliefs, and so, "workism" becomes a new religion for those in need of something greater than themselves to subscribe to. He contends:

> Many highly educated workers in the white-collar economy feel that their job cannot be "just a job" and that their career cannot be "just a career": Their job must be their calling. [...] What's the problem with people calling their jobs a calling? Some people simply love their job, and it would be ridiculous for me to tell them that actually, they are quietly suffering from some disease they cannot perceive. But many of them are also adherents to a cult of productivity and achievement, wherein anything short of finding one's vocational soulmate amounts to a wasted life. They have found a new kind of religion—one that valorizes work, career, and achievement above all else.[161]

Work isn't just a means to put food on the table and maintain a stable society, it needs to provide fulfillment and a deep meaning to your life. How can we even begin to explore the concept of work-life balance when work is supposed to be your whole life?

Throughout this book we've been setting up the premise that:

> We are a product of a fast-paced culture where people desire purpose and belonging. It's no shock we get sucked into corporations, schools, and workplaces that promote hustle culture. Bottom line: It's not our fault, but we can still take back some control.[162]

If the American ideal of "success" comes from our Puritan background and the unrealistic American Dream, then toxic productivity is what happens when we marry those ideas with capitalism and our 24/7 culture.

We've already shared with you the impact of the 24-Hour news cycle. But, in reality, our whole lives now operate 24/7, making it that much harder to shut off, to stop working, or to set boundaries.

Anat Lechner, a Clinical Associate Professor of Management at NYU argues that the old distinction of working 9 to 5 is for the 20th century. They state, "We live in a culture that is 24/7. Social media is 24/7, communication is 24/7, Amazon Prime is 24/7, everything is 24/7," and we don't have those fixed boundaries that we used to: where you went to work, left work, maybe went for drinks, went home and went to bed.[163]

The culture of burnout does not want us to have set boundaries between work and non-work. Toxic productivity, or what some call "the cult of overwork," means that "the need to perform and over-perform has made it incredibly challenging to keep up with the continuously cycling hamster wheel that is the demands of work."[164]

How much are we actually overworking?

Americans work more and get less time off than almost any other industrialized country.

There are three ways in which Americans are overworked: number of jobs, number of working hours, and lack of time off.

Number of Jobs:

- Deloitte found that 46% of Gen Z and 37% of Millennials work a side hustle, with another study finding that across generations, 39% of working Americans work a second job.[165]
- Compare this to the 1980s when rates of moonlighting among employed Americans went from 4.9% in 1980 to 6.2% in 1989, and this was seen as a "rapid increase."[166]

Working Hours:

- Americans work an average of 1,791 hours per year, 428 hours more than workers in Denmark.[167]
- Of the 38 OECD countries, the only countries working more hours per year than the US are Chile, Mexico,

Greece, Korea, and Costa Rica.[168]

- The U.S. is one of only four of these countries which has no statutory maximum length of the work week.[169]

Time Off:

- The U.S. has no federal mandate for paid sick leave and no legally mandated annual leave, up against countries such as France and the U.K., which offer over a month's worth of paid working days off, each year.[170]
- The U.S. has no federal policy for paid parental leave, and the average length of leave taken (paid or unpaid) is 10 weeks. The OECD average is 18 weeks paid. Just over the border, in Canada, the average length of maternity leave is around 40 weeks, all paid.[171]
- Parental leave also isn't available to everyone. Only 23% of Americans in private and civilian industries have access to paid leave and only 26% of government workers do.[172]
- On working days, employed Americans spend almost as much time working as they do on all forms of personal care combined, including sleep, over 30% of each day.[173]

So that means Americans are more successful, right?

If money means success, then all those working hours should result in the richest, most prosperous generation in hundreds of years, shouldn't it? But working Americans are feeling the pinch of the post-COVID economy, rising inflation, stagnant wages, and potential stock market instability.

Here are a couple quick stats to give you sense of Americans' economic concerns:

- 50% of Americans say they are worse off in 2023 than they were in 2022, the highest the number has been since 2009.[174]
- Wages in the U.S. have stagnated since the early 1970s. Between 1979 and 2020, workers' wages grew by 17.5% while productivity grew over three times as fast

at 61.8%.[175]

- Wage inequality continues to climb, with the gender and race gaps widening in recent years.[176]
- Inflation peaked at 9% in the summer of 2022, the highest recorded rate since 1981.[177]
- The average consumer good cost 6.4% more in January 2023 than in January 2022. "Consumer goods" are anything you buy and use yourself, versus something manufacturers create and then use to make something else. [178]

The side of the equation where working more gives us more of what we want (financial security, freedom, time to indulge in things we love) has fallen to the wayside—heavily impacted by the data we listed above, not to mention other issues like student loan debt and rising housing and healthcare costs.

With these economic trends and lingering issues of instability and inequality, work on its own has become a marker of success. We take pride in our exhaustion because if we don't, what else is it all for? Also—the good old Puritans taught us that we should take pride in our exhaustion because working hard, even to the point of exhaustion and burnout, means we're good people.

Psychologist Jacinta Jiménez explained to *Fortune* that there's "this belief that constant hustle and stress are fundamentally intertwined with success, and so we see busyness as a source of pride. It gets us trapped in this shared delusion that relentless productivity and constant hustle only come with rewards, only an upside—not at a costly price."[179]

So, what is that price, anyway?

What damage is overwork doing?

Not to be dramatic, but overwork can literally kill us.

Globally, the WHO found in a 2021 study that overwork killed 745,000 people in a single year. Anyone who works 55 hours or more per week bumps their risk of stroke up by 35% and their risk of dying from heart disease up by 17%.[180]

While only 5% of Americans work hours this extensive, under

the global rate of 9%, there's no legal protection to limit working hours in a week, and our average hours are creeping up. From 2010 to 2021, the average hours worked per year shifted from 1,772 to 1,791.[181]

The health damage also isn't an on-off switch that flips at 55 hours. Overwork is the single largest factor for occupational disease, and Americans are trending up on all fronts.

Part of the impact of overwork is the direct damage that chronic stress does, especially to our hearts. The other part is the way it eats away at the rest of our lives, making it harder to sleep enough, eat healthily, get exercise, seek preventative healthcare, and tend to our personal needs and relationships. It also makes it more likely that we'll reach for unhealthy coping skills like smoking, alcohol, and unhealthy eating habits.[182]

The damage is disproportionately gendered, too.

We're going to spend much more time in the next chapter breaking down the impact of gender on burnout, but it has to be measured here. The cult of overwork is hurting guys, gals, and nonbinary pals alike—but in different ways.

2014 research into overwork and its relationship to the gender wage gap drew some pretty strong connections. Researchers found that between 1979 and 2007, the prevalence of overwork exacerbated the gender wage gap by about 10 percent of the total wage gap.[183] Why would it do this? Because of our gendered expectations of who performs paid work and unpaid work.

The researchers drew the connection by stating, "Employees who work long hours can only do so with the support of other household members, usually women, who shoulder the lion's share of unpaid-work obligations."[184]

And, this isn't even taking into account *unpaid* labor and the toll that takes. In 2021, new studies showed that workers around the world were working 9.2 hours of unpaid overtime per week—up from 7.3 hours in 2020.[185] And, the reality of the situation is that our culture of burnout is encouraging that upward trend. The state of the 21st century work culture means:

> Co-working spaces are filled with posters urging us to "rise and grind" or "hustle harder." Billionaire tech

> entrepreneurs advocate sacrificing sleep so that people can "change the world." And since the pandemic hit, our work weeks have gotten longer; we send emails and Slack messages at midnight as boundaries between our personal and professional lives dissolve.[186]

We keep harping on the impact that stress and burnout have on our bodies and minds for a reason. Productivity is at its worst when it causes actual harm. It reaches toxic levels when our relationship with work (and our self-worth) is unbalanced. It also has a negative impact on our sense of self, our ability to relax, and our ability to build self-esteem, or feel accomplished or satisfied.[187]

Overwork doesn't just damage health, it damages relationships too. Think about all of the living that fits into the "life" part of the work/life balance equation.

What do you need in order to do all those things? Time.

What does the American burnout culture reliant on toxic productivity *not* want you to have? Time.

A 2021 *Vox* piece argued that the "cult of overwork" made Americans bad neighbors and essentially bad fellow humans. It argues that "prior to the pandemic, work was a huge obstacle to community involvement" because "American capitalism in the 21st century has all but destroyed the concept of free time."[188]

Lack of free time means lack of engagement with others. It means lack of relationships and lack of community. This is how the culture of burnout not only survives, but thrives. It is built to capitalize, literally and figuratively, on our beliefs that we have to keep working and we have to do it all alone.

We do not have the time in this book—nor are we labor experts—to dive into the various intersections of American capitalism and its impact on different categories of workers. However, what we do know is that for many people, "The pressure to maintain our precarious lives makes it all too hard to look out for anyone but ourselves."[189] When we add to that a culture that tells us the only way we will truly be successful is by doing it ourselves, it becomes clearer to see why it's so darn hard to get off this "continuing cycling hamster wheel" of toxic productivity.

And, despite all this, employees who work too hard and too much aren't even necessarily value-added to the companies they work for. During our COVID chapter we already discussed the concept of "quiet quitting," and we certainly believe that toxic productivity contributes to the high rates of that as well. But, how can we tell the impact of toxic productivity before we get to the quiet quitting, or not so quiet quitting, stage?

Just because an employee is attending work for a certain number of hours doesn't mean they're providing their company with their best work or a measure of efficiency at completing their assigned tasks. Deloitte's recent research into mental health and the British workplace found two other consequences of a work culture that overvalues productivity and undervalues boundaries while not providing adequate support. They describe high instances of both "presenteeism"—where employees work when they are not their most productive—and "leaveism"—where employees struggle to disconnect from work, especially in our "always on" culture.[190]

If we don't address the root causes of presenteeism or leaveism, then they can lead to other bigger problems of engagement. When people can no longer stay on the hamster wheel of overwork, we see increased rates of absenteeism, quiet quitting, and burnout.

When our culture ties productivity to worth, it's easy to see how we can slide deep down into the well of needing to squeeze every ounce of productivity out of the day. This urge is driven from within and without—a deep-seated urge to be hustling 24/7 matched with employers who reward those who go that extra mile in their eyes. An employee who's working too hard is seen as value-added, regardless of whether those extra hours really are valuable or not.

What does this mean for the way we view success and productivity?

A 2021 BBC article on the cult of overwork concludes that we are at a crossroads when it comes to the relationship between toxic productivity and burnout. From their perspective, and ours:

> We can prioritise [sic] our wellbeing, or prioritise sending an email at 0300 [AM] because it'll impress the boss. Letting people work from home can only go so far in easing

> the burden it has to be up to the workers to stop making burnout somehow desirable, and up to the companies to stop making the workers feel like they should.[191]

Believe it or not, the power (and choice) to dismantle the culture of burnout—for ourselves and for our society—is in our hands. But, there are a lot of barriers preventing us from starting, and choosing health over productivity is counter-cultural.

Perhaps this is all best summed up by the search results on Etsy for "your worth is not measured by your productivity." Nearly a thousand products come up, from cute stickers of coffee pots to knitted vegetables holding signs to adorable sloths, perhaps intended to embody the idea of slowing down and taking a break.

But, for how many of these talented creators is their online store a "side gig?" Who among them feels their art must be profitable and not merely a hobby? How many are up until two in the morning printing shipping labels to eke every cent of productivity out of the day while Etsy racks up billions in profits merely by providing a platform for selling?

Not all of them, of course, but it's certainly something American culture asks of all of us. Stick a smiling sloth to your monitor reminding you that your worth is not measured by your productivity, grab another cup of coffee...

...and then get back to work.

Chapter 12: Gender Roles and Burnout

> Mark was fine.
>
> He was balancing a business, a family, and a new startup that was expanding rapidly to multiple states and even other countries, but Mark was fine.
>
> He'd had this cough for a few years, and he wasn't feeling his best, but Mark was fine.
>
> Until Mark wasn't.

We're sure a lot of you resonate with Mark at this point—you, too, are fine. We hope your story doesn't take the next step that Mark's did, which is that he ended up in the hospital for a few weeks. He was eventually diagnosed with multiple comorbidities, all of which could have been treated faster had he realized he wasn't actually fine.

But, what we really want to highlight about Mark's story is that throughout this entire ordeal, he *never* put up an out-of-office notification on his email because he was *still* fine. He was in a hospital bed, but he was still trying to handle it all. He was hooked up to breathing machines, but he was still unable to delegate key tasks because he was fine, dammit.

But, Mark wasn't fine.

He was, however, raised in the American culture of burnout, with a giant heaping dose of masculinity. Gender roles are no small piece of how both society and individuals handle burnout.

So, here's another root vegetable to add to our cultural stew: what gender you identify as matters a whole heck of a lot.

We may be dating ourselves here, but remember that SUPER popular book from the 90s, *Men are from Mars, Women are from Venus*?[192] Whether or not you read the book when it took America by storm, that phrase quickly became a cultural shorthand for the biggest differences between men and women.

Though men and women are not, in fact, from different planets, the way they experience the world, and their own emotions, can make it seem as though they are at times. Since the early 1990s, we've expanded the larger cultural understanding of gender to include trans, gender fluid, and non-binary folks. But, by and large, we still rely on a lot of the gendered stereotypes that informed that bestselling book and our cultural understandings of what it means to be an American man and an American woman.

For the majority of this section, we will be talking about two gender expressions, man and woman. We firmly believe that gender is a socially constructed identity that has a whole range or spectrum of different expressions (which we'll explain in a moment); however, when it comes to understanding gender roles and burnout, society still operates largely on the gender binary. Likewise, while there exists a good deal of research on how men and women experience burnout differently, there is not yet significant research conducted on how gender diverse people experience burnout.

Before we get into the nitty gritty of whether or not burned out men are from Mars and burned out women are from Venus, we need to set the ground rules for how we, *The Good Doctors*, talk about gender and gender roles.

It's time, once again, for everybody's favorite part of books... definitions!

What is gender?

Let's start with the (complicated) basics. There is a difference between biological sex and gender identity. Though gender and sex are often used interchangeably, they, in fact, have very different meanings. As American society continues to grapple with the expanding alphabet of human experiences and identities, and we add words such as transgender, intersex, non-binary, and gender fluid to our vocabularies, it becomes even more important to establish the clear differences between the two categories.

There are loads of places we could go for definitions of these terms, but we really like the way that our friends at the Canadian Institutes of Health Research (CIHR) lay them out. They define sex as:

> Sex refers to a set of biological attributes in humans and animals. It is primarily associated with physical and physiological features including chromosomes, gene expression, hormone levels and function, and reproductive/sexual anatomy. Sex is usually categorized as female or male but there is variation in the biological attributes that comprise sex and how those attributes are expressed.[193]

From their helpful explanation, we'll pull a couple key parts. It is important to remember that sex is a "biological" designation that is usually broken down with "physical and physiological features," and that it is "usually categorized as female or male." In short, your sex is determined by biological attributes that you are born with, usually classifying you as having female sex or male sex.

As terms, female and male are often confused with boy and girl, and man and woman, so let's move on to the CIHR's definition of gender.

They define gender as:

> Gender refers to the socially constructed roles, behaviours [sic], expressions and identities of girls, women, boys, men, and gender diverse people. It influences how people perceive themselves and each other, how they act and interact, and the distribution of power and resources in society.
>
> Gender identity is not confined to a binary (girl/woman, boy/man) nor is it static; it exists along a continuum and

> can change over time. There is considerable diversity in how individuals and groups understand, experience, and express gender through the roles they take on, the expectations placed on them, relations with others and the complex ways that gender is institutionalized in society.[194]

Oof, that is quite a lengthy description! But, the detail here is one of the reasons we really like it. There's a lot to unpack, but for our purposes, we want to highlight a few important points.

First, gender is a "socially constructed role." This means that gender is not something we are born with, like biological sex, but it is, instead, something that society creates, or constructs. Gender is taught through societal ideas of what it means to be a "man" or a "woman." Though diverse gender expressions have existed since time immemorial (hello, Ancient Rome), as a society we created and enforced a gender binary—meaning only men and women—are the "normal" and "acceptable" forms of gender expression.

Therefore, the second part of the CIHR's definition is doing a lot of work to dispel the misconceptions that gender is a binary, that gender is fixed, and that our understandings of gender have not changed over time. We know those are misconceptions because we have the history and the statistics and the personal testimonies to prove that they are.[195]

Even if we only believed that all people were either men or women, there's a lot of evidence to show that those identities and expressions changed over time. Whether through the Suffrage movement of the late 19th and early 20th centuries, or through the Third Wave Feminist movement of the 1970s, women (and men) have been changing our ideas of what it means to be an "American" woman (and man) for quite some time.

These movements changed the roles that men and women were expected to perform in both a personal and cultural context. Gender roles play a significant part in how men and women typically experience burnout, so let's make one more stop on the definition train and unpack the concept of gender roles.

What are gender roles?

As we were talking about writing this section of the book, Kristen reminded Erin of the time she saw a sticker on display at the University of Leeds that claimed, "Cinnamon Rolls, Not Gender Roles."

Through various feminist movements (or waves) of the 20th century, women continued to push back against the gender roles assigned to them by their family, friends, husbands, and wider society. When we delve into it a little more, it should be no surprise that cinnamon rolls are more popular (gender roles rarely come with cream cheese icing).

We don't want to leave you hanging without our promised definition, though, so let's start there. The one we landed on comes from the work of the European Institute for Gender Equality and the UN Women's Training Centre Gender Equality Glossary. They describe gender roles as:

> Collectively, gender roles often determine the traditional responsibilities and tasks assigned to women, men, girls and boys. Gender-specific roles are often conditioned by household structure, access to resources, specific impacts of the global economy, occurrence of conflict or disaster, and other locally relevant factors such as ecological conditions. Lik.e gender itself, gender roles can evolve over time, in particular through the empowerment of women and transformation of masculinities.[196]

Several things jumped out at us from this definition that were important for us to include. First, gender roles are both *personal* and *cultural*. This means that you will have a certain understanding of your gender from your personal experiences, beliefs, relationships, but also from what society tells you it expects from your gender. Second, gender roles vary across different cultures, but certain factors like "household structure," "access to resources," and participation in the local and global economy almost always play a significant part.

Third, gender roles "determine the traditional responsibilities and tasks" assigned to the genders. In societies that are organized along the gender binary, gender roles determine the tasks and responsibilities assigned to boys and girls, and men and women. We hope, at this stage, you're starting to see how gender roles have a serious impact on every part of society—including the division of labor inside and outside the home.

The final point we'd like to draw out of this definition is that, like gender, gender roles evolve and change through time. As we mentioned before, the Third Wave Feminist movement of the 1970s pushed back against a lot of the restrictive gender roles in place in American society, which had previously limited the sphere of women's influence to their home and family life.[197] Activists such as Gloria Steinham, Shirley Chisholm, and Betty Friedan began to talk about and to demand not only more rights for women, but more expansive and inclusive gender roles for everyone.[198]

Similarly, as all gender roles continue to expand and to change, we've seen the rise in stay-at-home Dads. We've seen musicians and actors like Sam Smith and Bella Ramsey come out as non-binary, and we've seen fictional soccer coaches like the character Ted Lasso show us that empathy and compassion are masculine traits as well.

Though we've come a long way, there is still a long way to go, and traditional gender roles still heavily impact how men and women (and all the folks in-between) live and work in American society.

How do gender roles inform work roles for men and women?

We've expanded our definition of workplace to include: *any organization or group of humans that you have a commitment to providing your time, energy, and expertise to*. This new definition of workplace allows us to consider all the myriad ways and places a person can burn out—from the traditional 9-5 job to volunteer positions and caregiving responsibilities. For this reason, we want to talk about the categories of paid and unpaid work as a way to separate the work of compensated employment and all the other parts of life that still take work and that aren't often included in conversations on burnout.

At the core of the relationship between American gender roles and work lies the traits and values our culture places on men and women. A 2017 Pew Research Center report stated that when men and women are asked about gender differences, "Women who perceive differences generally attribute them to societal expectations, men tend to point to biological differences."[199] This means that women are more likely than men to recognize that gender roles are socially constructed and, therefore, have the potential to change. Men are also more likely to believe that traits associated with their gender are a part of their biology and, therefore, are fundamental to how they see themselves and are unchangeable.

In 2018, Pew expanded their research into gender to ask which traits society values, and which it doesn't, for both men and women. Their results produced some valuable insights on how men and women relate to and identify with their work. In this survey, 75% of respondents identified the word "provider" with men, and it was a trait exclusively classified as male.[200] The study also found that "leadership" and "ambition" were more associated with men than women. This helps us understand not only how men and women view themselves, but how these views can influence how they work and how they burnout.

Another 2017 Pew study found that even if women are earning more at their jobs—a clear sign of societal progress toward gender equity—"most Americans place a higher value on a man's role as a financial provider."[201] 71% of their respondents said, it is "very important for a man to be able to support a family financially to be a good husband or partner," while only 32% said the same for women.[202]

Basically, this research shows that, for many men, their ability to gain and keep paid work in order to fulfill these societal expectations is a huge part of how they see themselves as men.

In comparison, this same survey found the words most positively associated with women were "beautiful," "caring," and "compassionate."[203] While "leadership" and "ambition" were considered positive attributes for men, they were usually considered negative attributes for women. Whereas the results showed that men need to be financial providers in order to be considered good partners, they also found that for women to be considered good partners they needed to be caring and compassionate (90%) and contribute to the household chores (63%).[204]

What stories do these statistics tell us about gender roles and work roles? *The End of Burnout* author, Jonathan Malesic, argues studies like these tell us that "even as gender roles seem increasingly flexible and open to revision, we are still a society where men attempt to prove their manhood through their performance at work."[205] Malesic goes on to argue that to address men's burnout specifically, "We have to acknowledge that consciously or not, our society still largely equates masculinity with being a stoical wage earner" and that the "signature patterns in male burnout each reflect an enduring breadwinner ethos that does not serve men well."[206]

We'll get into male-specific symptoms of burnout later on, but we wanted to hammer home the point that American masculinity is deeply tied to this "breadwinner ethos," which means they have to be the primary wage earner in order to be a good, successful, and supportive provider.

How do gender roles impact paid and unpaid work?

While we are still a society that tells men they are "good men" because of their ability to perform paid work, we are also still a society that tells women they are "good women" through their ability to perform unpaid work. You may have heard the phrases "unpaid work" or "unpaid labor" talked about more recently, especially when we had a lot of conversations about what life looked like for people during COVID-19 restrictions, lockdowns, and societal shifts.

Evaluations of what constitutes unpaid work have revealed a shocking gap in the labor performed by men and women. In *Invisible Women*, Caroline Criado Perez dedicated an entire chapter to exploring the impact of unpaid work on women. Through her research, she found that, globally, "75% of unpaid work is done by women, who spend between three and six hours per day on it compared to men's average of thirty minutes to two hours."[207] That is a glaring difference between not only the amount of unpaid labor that women undertake, but also between the amount of time spent on that labor.

If you're still unsure what exactly unpaid work might entail, let's break it down to give you a better idea. Veerle Miranda's study of unpaid work around the world defined it as:

> The production of goods and services by household members that are not sold on the market. Some unpaid work is for the consumption within the family, such as cooking, gardening and house cleaning. The products of unpaid work may also be consumed by people not living in the household, e.g. cooking a meal for visiting friends, helping in a soup kitchen for homeless people, mowing the lawn of an elderly relative, or coaching the local football team.[208]

This definition fits with our understanding that a workplace is any group of humans you dedicate time and energy to. Unpaid work includes all household labor, childcare, caring for an elderly relative or community member, shopping, and any volunteer positions. And, just like American society expects men to perform the role of the breadwinner, American society expects women to perform the role of the homemaker and caregiver.

These gender roles and expectations go back a long way, and as we've seen, even over the pandemic, it's quite difficult to unlearn and to change these expectations. Nearly 2 million women left the American workforce during the first few months of the COVID-19 pandemic, accounting for 63% of all job loss.[209] Most, if not all, of those women, left their paid work to devote all their time to unpaid work, especially when their children were in remote learning environments and required not only childcare but also educational support.

So, what does all this lovely information mean about how men and women experience burnout? Basically, because we have these different societal expectations for the roles that men and women perform, men and women generally have different stressors, burn out over different tasks and responsibilities, and process burnout differently.

When we live within these limited gender roles, we also limit our ability to understand the real root causes of burnout. Just as these gender roles are deeply embedded in our culture, so, too is burnout. It is not an individual problem faced by workaholics. It is a cultural problem potentially faced by every American, and gender plays a big part in what it looks like and how it feels for men and women.

While this chapter is going to continue to be chock full of statistics and recent research, we also firmly believe in the power of stories to educate. Before we dive into a further understanding of gender roles and burnout, we've got another personal story to share.

A Personal Story of Caregiver Burnout

Hey, y'all, it's Erin here, and I wanted to take this opportunity to share my own experiences with caregiver burnout.

Just like our friend's story of burnout, my story also begins with that old nugget COVID-19. For context, when I moved home from Northern Ireland in 2016 at the end of my PhD, I moved back in with my mother in order to save money. Flash forward four years later, and by the start of the pandemic, my mother's physical health had deteriorated significantly, and I had gradually begun to take up more of the caring and household responsibilities. Just for fun, she added into the mix a serious arm injury, ever increasing and debilitating chronic pain, and significant mobility issues.

Don't get me wrong. It was all "fine" during the first year of lockdowns. I was at home anyway, what did it matter if I did most of the cleaning? My mother is considered high risk for infection, so of course I was going to do all the shopping. After her arm injury, she couldn't really do any more gardening, but I gained a newfound love for it while taking over its management.

Slowly but surely, all this extra unpaid work began to add up. Once I began to travel again for work, and the outside world crept its way back in, I often found myself short of temper, frustrated, and even resentful toward my mother. She had been a caregiver—a nurse and mother by calling—her whole life and I had a hard time understanding and empathizing with how she was feeling and what she was unable to do. I kept waiting for it to change, for her to get better, for me to feel less stressed by the neverending list of tasks it took to run the household.

I was having a particularly hard weekend a few years ago when a close friend said to me, "Oh, so this means you are her primary carer now." And honestly, until that moment, I hadn't really allowed myself to consider using the word "carer," and I know that was part of what was contributing to the feelings of anger and frustration. In my mind, we were two "equals" living in the house, and I was tired of her not being able to pull her weight. But in that moment, I realized that line of thinking was deeply unfair, to both my mother and me.

Changing my perception of the situation, and realizing that she likely would never be physically able to return to her former level of productivity, was a massive perspective shift. I would love to tell you that after that realization I skipped into the future, free from any continued stress because of my new role as caregiver... but that would make me a liar.

This is the part of the story where gender comes into play. I have one sibling, an older brother who is also single, child-free, and lives nearby. Yet, for several years, I struggled to ask him to take on more responsibilities, to ask for help. And while my brother and I have super progressive understandings of gender roles, I still think we struggled under the invisible yoke those gender roles placed on us both.

Let me be clear, no one has *ever* told me that I have to do it all, that I can't ask for help, or that it's not okay to say I'm struggling. And yet, those are the core feelings at the base of my stress. The tape in my head plays a loop of, "Well, I live here too, so I should just take care of it," and, "I don't really need help, I can find a better way to manage my time," and, "if I just get these last few tasks done, maybe I'll have time to rest."

During rough patches, I find it extremely hard to take a break, to actually stop on the weekends, and to keep a calm and positive attitude. Simultaneously, there are many days where getting out of bed is the hardest thing I can ask of myself. My brother and I have had several honest conversations throughout the last 18 months, and we are working on clearer communication. I have been able to ask for more help, but it's still a work in progress. I have to work hard to remind myself that I am allowed to be more than a caregiver, and that even if I don't "need" help, it's totally okay to ask for it.

As I evaluate all the unpaid work I do, I've become increasingly interested in understanding why these are tasks I feel like I should be doing, why it feels more "natural" for me to assume the cooking and cleaning duties, and how I have to be intentional about overcoming these deeply rooted gender norms. The more I study burnout for this book, the more I recognize my symptoms and see how American burnout culture has perpetuated them.

In personal and professional settings, I also face a lot of stigma from other folks, mainly women, who think that I don't have enough stressors to be burned out. Just because we believe that trauma is not comparable doesn't mean that lots of humans aren't trying to medal in the Suffering Olympics. Sometimes I am told I can never be as tired as other women because "at least I don't have a husband" or "I'm lucky I don't have kids" as though those are the necessary requirements for women to burn out.

I wanted to share my story because I wanted to say that stress is stress, exhaustion is exhaustion, caregiving is caregiving—whether it's for your 5-year-old daughter or your 75-year-old mother.

We live in a culture that tells people, especially women, that balance means being able to "have it all." This often means that we have to work professionally *and* adhere to traditional gender norms, all the while feeling lucky that we live in a developed nation where we are privileged enough to have so many opportunities to be a productive member of society.

As with our friend's personal story of burnout from our chapter on COVID, I want to acknowledge the privilege that comes from being a middle class, highly educated, White woman in America. This means I have more access to resources and support, and fewer barriers and stigmas attached to my gender and race.

But—we all have an uphill battle when it comes to addressing the gender imbalance in unpaid work and caregiving. Both of those factors are big contributors to rates of burnout, and help explain some of the biggest differences between how men and women burnout.

Lest you think this is how I will leave my story, worry not. I have found a lot of practices that help me work towards balance and away from burnout. I'll be back in Section Four to share what works (and what doesn't work) for me. *waves*

Wait. Back up. How did we get gendered forms of work in the first place?

As we've been gradually adding the gender ingredient to our burnout soup, it's time for the final few measurements—the real meat of the issue—how men and women process burnout. Given what we've shared with you about gender roles for men and women in American society, you might conclude that men burn out during paid work and women burn out during unpaid work. Since those are the areas most commonly associated with their gender, and since it is the type of work where they undertake the most labor, it would seem to make sense.

However, what burnout researchers have discovered is that even though paid and unpaid work still cause high levels of stress for both men and women, their symptoms of burnout tend to show up in situations counter to their gender roles. The reasons for this difference come straight out of the expectations placed on traditional gender roles in American society and out of the way we've coded both paid and unpaid work based on these gender roles.

These gendered expectations are long time ingredients in the recipe and are so integral to the soup that we start to train boys and girls for these roles when they are children. This starts from the toys they play with—both of us remember practicing childcare with our Cabbage Patch Kids in the 1980s—to the way parents raise their children through the household chores they have them learn—boys usually helping fathers with yardwork and girls usually helping mothers with cooking and cleaning.[210]

From a very early age, we place boys and girls into these narrow definitions for *when* they are allowed to work and *how* they are allowed to work, so that by the time they are seeking professional paid work as an adult, these gendered expectations are so deeply ingrained that they can't envision any other way. What this means is that we have defined paid work by how a man does paid work and, simultaneously, defined unpaid work by how a woman does unpaid work.

Returning to some of the surveys we cited above, the narrow and specific gender roles placed on men and women make more sense when we look at the language we have to talk about them. In the Pew's survey on gender-associated traits, the traits most strongly associated with women, like "kind," "caring," and "compassionate" are traits we associate more with caregivers.

As mentioned, "provider" was *exclusively* used for men alongside associations with "strong," "ambitious," and "leadership." In both instances, when the association with one gender was viewed as positive, it was viewed as more negative with the opposite gender. The two biggest differences occurred with "ambitious" and "compassionate" where "ambitious" was viewed as an overly positive trait for men and as an overly negative trait for women, and "compassionate" was viewed as an overly positive trait for women and as an overly negative trait for men.[211]

What does this teach us about how society perceives gender and different types of work? We've learned that, as a society, we've forced people into very narrow roles that do not leave room for gender diverse interpretations and expressions. And, it certainly doesn't leave a whole lot of room for people who attempt to change those gendered roles and expectations.

What's the difference between burnout in men and women?

Because we start teaching children their gender roles and work roles almost from birth, we can understand how children develop stronger coping mechanisms around the work most associated with their gender. Girls learn that they are always supposed to be performing unpaid caregiving work, and so, they learn how to cope with those demands and stressors. Boys learn that they are always supposed to be performing paid work, outside the house, and so, they learn how to cope with those demands and stressors.

So, where does that leave us?

First, men and women are more able to deal with the stress of paid/unpaid work because their coping mechanisms are deeply rooted in their gender roles. Second, because these types of work are highly gendered, men and women are more likely to experience burnout in the type of work where they haven't developed coping mechanisms.

Very often, people cannot express or see burnout symptoms within their gendered form of work. It can be incredibly difficult for men to talk about or express burnout at paid work, and it can be equally difficult for women to talk about or express burnout at unpaid work. For many humans, burning out in these types of work is associated with a failure of either masculinity or femininity.

If a man does not want to be a worker, then he is a failure of masculine norms. If a woman does not want to be a caregiver, then she is a failure of feminine norms. On the other hand, if women decide they do not want to do paid work, then that is acceptable because they are expected to be a caregiver, and if men decide they do not want to be caregivers, then that is acceptable because they are expected to be the breadwinner and provider. People express burnout in the safest workplace to express it because it is the opposite of their assigned gender realm of work.

When you combine these gendered expectations with the Puritanical influence on American capitalism, we get a deep identification with work—both paid and unpaid—that tells us that in order to be a good person, we have to be a good worker. Burnout scholar Dr. Jonathan Malesic argues that in Britain and America, especially, "We have developed a quasi-religious faith in work as a source of not only security, stability and material comfort, but of identity, fulfillment, prestige, happiness, purpose, meaning."[212]

Because we have this intense personal identification with our work and attach it to our identity, when we burn out, we don't see the cultural barriers that helped encourage our burnout but, instead, see it as a personal failure. In other words, "When we give it 110% and it fails to yield the desired results, many of us take that as a deep personal failing."[213]

If work is a part of who we are, and we "fail" at it, then, more often than not, we bury that failure in a toxic cycle of shame and guilt. When we personalize failure and burnout, we make it much more difficult to talk about and much more difficult to treat. When people are ashamed of their actions, or lack of actions, they are less likely to speak about it or seek help.

So, what does the weight of all these gender expectations look like in terms of burnout symptoms? Keep reading to find out (unless you need to take a break first, because that was *a lot*).

How does burnout feel for men and women?

Let's revisit the three main characteristics, or symptoms, of burnout identified in the WHO's definition. They found that burnout looks like: "1) feelings of energy depletion or exhaustion; 2) increased mental distance from one's job, or feelings of negativism or cynicism related to one's job; and 3) a sense of ineffectiveness and lack of accomplishment."[214]

What burnout researchers are discovering is that not only do men and women experience burnout in different forms of work, but they also experience different symptoms. These symptoms are also closely tied to gender roles. It's all part of the same soup, after all. A quick Google search will show you that most analysts believe women are suffering from burnout more than men. But, gender burnout scholars are also quick to point out that several gender traits might help to hide male symptoms of burnout.

Let's tackle burnout in women. Studies conducted within the last year found that 42% of women experience burnout and that burnout is the number one reason women are considering leaving their jobs.[215] According to another study, the impact of the COVID-19 pandemic is partly to blame. This study found:

> Women are shouldering a much heavier burden of household labor and caregiving during Covid-19, and it's taking a toll—they're experiencing physical symptoms of stress and burnout at up to twice the rate of men.[216]

From burnout research, we see that the most common symptom women experience is exhaustion, both emotional and physical. When we factor in the added stress of the changes wrought by the pandemic, we start to see the context for these higher rates of burnout in women. One of the most significant reasons for burnout in women, and their removal from the workforce, is the fact that they are significantly more likely to have unpaid work responsibilities.

A 2017 study that examined how women balance paid and unpaid work found that many women spoke of their exhaustion as a primary reason for their struggles with this balance. They argued, "One of the most significant effects of women's struggle to balance their responsibilities was that of tiredness and the constancy of doing something at any given time, without time to rest or recuperate."[217]

When women have so many responsibilities that they feel they do not have time to stop or rest, they push themselves until their exhaustion forces them to stop. What we have learned is that when women decide to limit the stress from work, they often choose to eliminate part or all of their *paid work* responsibilities before they ever think of eliminating any *unpaid work* responsibilities.

Why don't we know more about burnout in men?

From our perspective, it is no surprise that keeping women in the workforce post-COVID continues to be an uphill battle. In contrast, as a society, we've never had a problem keeping men in the workforce because "we are still a society where men attempt to prove their manhood through their performance at [paid] work."[218] This is, again, in part due to traits we associate with their gender roles and in part due to how and where their symptoms of burnout manifest.

Most researchers find that men tend to exhibit burnout in terms of "feelings of negativism or cynicism." Malesic argues further that cynicism in men "is commonly taken as a sign of competence. As a result, the stern manager, the hard-boiled detective and the brusque physician are all male-coded cultural archetypes."[219]

This means that our perceptions of masculinity and associated traits make it more difficult to identify burnout in men, especially since they tend more toward cynicism (depersonalization) than exhaustion. Since we tend already to have "emotional distancing" as a masculine gender norm, it's harder to see burnout in men. What we have created in America are very narrow gender norms and roles that do not allow for emotional exposure or growth, especially when it relates to talking about burnout.

If men are always supposed to be working—the "breadwinner ethos"—and we expect them to be withdrawn and cynical, then how are we ever supposed to know when they are reaching burnout on the Stress-o-Meter? We have created situations in which their symptoms are invisible. Similarly to women, men have more developed coping mechanisms for high stress situations in paid work, and we often see their burnout symptoms manifest in relation to unpaid work—usually in relation to childcare and parenting.[220]

The lack of capacity that men typically have to talk about and express their own emotions is another important impact of gender roles on burnout. When talking about the pervasiveness of the "male-coded cultural archetypes," Malesic noted that "emotionally open male figures have not yet fully supplanted them."[221]

Basically, the current definition of masculinity within American's minds is more likely to be John Wayne than Ted Lasso.

Because we have made it culturally "abnormal" for men to talk about their feelings, Malesic argues, "When men encounter problems at work or elsewhere in their lives, they are much less likely than women to talk about it, in either public or private," and "are about 40 percent less likely than women to seek counseling for any reason."[222] All this adds up to mean that accounts of burnout in men are very hard to find.

So, it's possible that we talk so much more about women and burnout, in part, because we have the data to back it up. When we're trying to understand how we got stuck in this burnout soup, it's important to consider all these different contexts. Concerns around men's mental health are not new, but we don't usually combine those conversations with ones about burnout.

With significant cultural barriers in place, it's no surprise that men don't talk about their mental health. A recent survey found that for those men who haven't sought mental health treatment, 29% didn't because they were "too embarrassed," while "20% say there is a "negative stigma" associated with talking about their mental health."[223] This survey also found that the two biggest factors in the men's mental health were work pressure (32%) and financial issues (31%), further supporting the belief that the "breadwinner ethos" is prevalent among most men.

If men are not capable of experiencing burnout in paid work, then the only sphere left is unpaid work. Most burnout research found that men exhibit a level of emotional detachment and a lack of involvement with aspects of unpaid work—usually childcare duties and household chores such as food shopping, cooking, and cleaning.

Where does that leave us?

We've ended up in a place where women burn out at work and men burn out at home because that's where they're "allowed" to.

On the flipside, women do not burn out at home and men don't burn out at work because they're *not* allowed to. Living with these restrictive gender roles, we've accepted the premise that burnout within your gendered form of work isn't burnout, it's failure.

Yikes.

This means that in American society no one is having productive and holistic conversations about why we have a *culture* of burnout. When we don't challenge the narrow and restrictive stereotypes of our traditional gender roles, we don't allow people to be fully human and we continue to perpetuate our culture of burnout.

We have to get to a place where honest conversations and systemic change can help us gain more control over our emotional state and move toward a culture of balance.

Before we get to the solutions bit, we have one more ingredient to add to our soup—and it's a whopper. We cannot talk about burnout culture in America without discussing its relationship with capitalism. Because Americans believe that being a good person means working hard, we've created a perspective on wellness that is deeply tied to our ability to make a profit. It's a concept that we (and others) are calling the Wellness Industrial Complex, and it's time to start unpacking what it means, how it works, and why it needs to change.

Chapter 13:
Wellness Industrial Complex

Hannah just started a new job in the financial administration department of a large construction contracting company. Her first few weeks involve all the usual corporate onboarding: filling out forms, doing safety training, and learning about her benefits as an employee.

Halfway through her second week, Hannah is invited to a meeting to introduce the company's employees to their brand new workplace wellness program. A chipper and fast-talking representative from a corporate wellness app company is introduced and walks the team through how to use the app.

"In just five minutes a day, you can improve your scores in areas like mindfulness, resiliency, and focus!" the helpful representative informs them. "View your workplace leaderboard to motivate you to open the app every day."

Hannah notes down her login code, downloads the app on her work phone, thanks the representative, and goes back to her emails.

Six weeks later, after a conversation with her fiance about starting a family soon, Hannah asks HR at her company what her parental leave benefits would look like.

There aren't any.

We wanted to start this section with a small vignette that we feel quickly encapsulates our modern problem with wellness, Workplace Wellness Programs, and the Wellness Industrial Complex. Hannah's story exemplifies how many corporations are relying on Wellness Programs—usually outsourced to a third party—instead of practicing wellness as an organization. As social scientists, and more generally, as humans, we're convinced that paid parental leave is an integral part of wellness, and yet, America is one of only six countries in the world that doesn't have it.[224]

Before we get into what wellness means to us in Section Four, we have to spend some time understanding how we got to the place where Hannah's story is far too common. You might have started this section and thought, "How did we get to this Wellness Industrial Complex?" Or, "What actually *is* the Wellness Industrial Complex?" And, so, we'll be breaking these parts of the burnout soup into nice digestible chunks. After all, when you look at our burnout recipe, there has to be a reason the Wellness Industrial Complex is such a massive ingredient.

The Good Doctors' American Burnout Soup

TIME TO COOK: *403 years*
SERVES: *Entire US population*

INGREDIENTS

- The stock of Puritanical beliefs (broth)
- 1 spoonful of dried US history and culture
- 2 tbsps intersections spice mix
- 1/4 cup each of generations (finely chopped)
- Season to taste with the stories we tell (collective & individual)
- 2 cans of chunky gender roles
- 3 lbs. of ground Wellness Industrial Complex

DIRECTIONS

1. Simmer the stock of Puritanical beliefs for 400 + years
2. Slowly stir in the US history and culture, intersections, gender roles, and finely chopped generations.
3. Season to taste with the stories we tell
4. Brown the Wellness Industrial Complex in a skillet, then add, stirring regularly
5. Serve with fresh capitalism and don't enjoy!

Someone who is *well* is someone who can't be suffering from burnout, right? Our goal should be wellness for everyone in our workplaces, in our organizations, and in our families. But, what does wellness really mean? Or, rather...what has it come to mean?

Oxford Languages gives us this when asked to define wellness:

> The state of being in good health, especially as an actively pursued goal.[225]

"An actively pursued goal." And, there's nothing American capitalism likes more than using an actively pursued goal to sell you something.

Our concept of wellness has been twisted and tainted into something you can buy. McKinsey & Company estimated the global wellness market to be $1.5 trillion dollars. Yes, that's "trillion" with a T. They also found that in the U.S. in 2021, 48.2% of respondents gave wellness higher prioritization in their life over the last 2-3 years.[226]

Clearly, Americans care about wellness, and they're willing to pay for it. But, is paying for it working?

In other words, is paying for wellness making us well?

Despite the increasing interest in wellness, American workers are struggling with their mental health more than ever. More than half (59%) of all American workers report experiencing at least moderate levels of burnout, which is 9% higher than in 2021 and 2% higher than in August 2020.[227] And, we all remember what was going on in the summer of 2020.

The data tells us that Americans are *even more* stressed out now than we were during the height of the COVID-19 pandemic. Of those employees reporting higher levels of burnout, 86% also reported experiencing other mental health challenges such as anxiety, depression, and trouble sleeping. And, about half of both employees and employers report that their burnout and mental health struggles have a negative impact on their job performance.

And, what did these burnt out employees want more than anything? Time.

When asked which options would be most helpful in dealing with burnout, ranked first a majority of the time were: paid time off, flexible scheduling, and permanent work from home options.

What was less popular? Participants ranked virtual mental health coaching and workplace wellness programs in first place only 3% and 2% of the time.[228] After reading the data and talking to our friends who work for places with such programs, we can't say that we're surprised.

Addressing the wellness and mental health of each member of an organization is a critical part of reducing burnout, increasing productivity, raising job satisfaction, lowering employee turnover and being part of an organization you can be proud of. However, Corporate Wellness as an industry tells us this is a problem we can solve by signing a check—download an app, host a one-day wellness seminar, send out an email reminding everyone that it's National Mental Health Awareness Day. Problem solved.[229]

We have to stop thinking of a lack of employee wellness on a corporate level as a tick-box problem that needs to be solved. Wellness isn't something you can offer or provide to your employees. It's an individual experience that is going to be different for everyone. Look back at that definition of wellness we mentioned earlier: *the state of being in good health*. By what metric are we defining good health?

As an example, we used to think of BMI as a metric by which we could define health, and businesses jumped right onto that. The show *The Biggest Loser* became corporate as companies sponsored and supported employee group weight loss competitions, with benefits for those who participated and even punishments—while not explicit, often social, like promoting peer-pressure or enabling team rewards—for those that didn't.

Season Five of *The Office* captures this perfectly in their two-episode season opener "Weight Loss." Corporate runs a company-wide weight loss competition, and the branch with the most cumulative weight loss will win—you guessed it—extra time off.

It does not escape our notice that the prize for participating in a competition about "wellness" is the thing people report would help them *actually be well*. If only they didn't have to earn it by making themselves more unwell. In the episodes, the teams go to extreme lengths to diet, overexercise, and attack and pressure their coworkers to have lost more weight by the final weigh-in.

We know now that BMI is an inaccurate and downright discriminatory measure of health, which was even recently confirmed by the AMA.[230] We know that abrupt, rapid weight loss does not lead to a long-term lower maintained weight[231], and we know that being thin does not mean a person is healthy.[232] And, yet, a quick Google search for "workplace weight loss challenge ideas" returns 165 million results, many of which were published in the last couple of years. One link recommends a modern take on *The Biggest Loser* challenge—"maintain don't gain!"—where the goal is simply not to gain those extra pounds over the holidays.

Even ignoring the fact that weight loss of this nature is neither healthy nor maintainable, and that weight is not an indicator of health, a competition like this makes no space for humans who have a desire or a medical need to *gain* weight. Or, even worse, it requires them to disclose personal information they may not wish to disclose in order to be excused without social pressure from the event. What about pregnant employees who need to gain to grow their child? What about those who are recovering from illness or surgery?

What an employee weighs is absolutely none of their employer's business. If a doctor has made a different distinction, then so be it, but overall? No. Encouraging weight loss for financial gain has proven detrimental for contestants on the show *The Biggest Loser*,[233] and the whole thing can lead to increasing feelings of internalized shame. For people who are already feeling some sort of way about their bodies, having focus on it can lead to increased isolation from the team—going against the very thing these initiatives are usually attempting to do.

Furthermore, 19% of participants in the AFLAC study on workplace mental health who reported experiencing moderate to high levels of burnout cited an additional struggle with disordered eating or a diagnosed eating disorder.[234]

Yeah. A fifth of burnout sufferers are also fighting a personal battle with food, and yet, companies feel that workplace wellness should involve dictating what a healthy relationship with your weight should look like—whether that's losing or maintaining or even just tracking—dangling rest as a reward for conforming.

We'll be honest, this kind of practice makes us a little grumpy. Actually, a lot grumpy. Bodies and weight are two things we discuss a lot in our work. Our YouTube comment section is full of folks who are harmed by this kind of practice, so we're particularly prickly about this feature of Workplace Wellness Programs.

All of these elements—who should lose weight, what does Workplace Wellness mean, how can we take care of ourselves and each other—are acts performing under the giant circus tent of the Wellness Industrial Complex (WIC). Examining what American culture thinks about being well, how we married wellness and capitalism, and how our employers and employees approach wellness, can all be understood by examining the potent ingredient in our burnout soup: the WIC.

In order to understand where we are, we have to look first at how we got here. First stop, let's unpack some of the key ideas around "wellness," from the origins of the term to how it got big enough to have its own industrial complex.

What does "wellness" even mean?

We started this section of the book by including the Oxford Languages definition for wellness: "The state of being in good health, especially as an actively pursued goal." For a rather simple definition, there's actually a lot going on there. While we agree that true holistic well-being is an active, not a passive, state, let's throw in a couple more definitions to see if we can come to a clearer picture of what wellness really is.

The Global Wellness Institute (GWI) is a nonprofit organization deeply embedded in and dependent on the continued functioning of the WIC. As soon as Erin uncovered that thread, we knew this would be an interesting ride.

They define wellness as "the active pursuit of activities, choices and lifestyles that lead to a state of holistic health."[235] Again, this definition seems fairly straightforward, and perhaps a bit more specific in using the word "holistic," which means "whole" (so holistic health is health of one's whole self instead of merely one part). Further on in their descriptions, they also stipulate that wellness has to be "driven by self-responsibility."

This emphasis on "self-responsibility" is key to analyzing the development of wellness, especially with our understanding of the

Puritanical origins in this country. Remember: in order to be a good person, part of the Puritans' belief was that we had to do it on our own. Now, we're not saying that your own well-being is not your responsibility, but we are saying that the current culture of burnout we find ourselves in is due in large part to the hyper-individualized nature of how wellness is sold to the masses.

One of the great ironies of the WIC is that it depends on both a hyper-individualized approach to wellness—it is your job to fix your health and well-being—while also relying on the mass produced and marketed nature of the universal quick fix.

Buy X product to fix your problems, but do it on your own because your burnout is your responsibility/fault.

One of the earlier critiques of "wellness"—from way back in 1988—comes from Arthur Barsky's book *Worried Sick: Our Troubled Quest for Wellness*. Highly critical of this "new" movement, Barsky claims that wellness is "health through self-control and will power."[236] He also argues:

> Although sensible preventative measures relating to nutrition and lifestyle are highly desirable, this new concept goes further, to say that good health is not a gift, not mere good luck, not the product of heredity or regular everyday activities, but, rather, the result of willpower, resolve, and dedication to the goal of wellness.[237]

It's starting to sound more and more like a Puritanical approach to "wellness," isn't it? We are "good" at wellness if we have the willpower. If we work hard. And, we are a good person if we are well or good at wellness. If we define wellness within the realm of willpower and hard work, then it is a short jump to be able to say that people society deems unhealthy—people who are fat, people who are addicts, people who don't do physical exercise, people in chronic pain—are lazy, unmotivated, and unworthy of help.

Basically, framing wellness as a matter of willpower allows us to believe it is a moral position—you are either a good person or a bad person—depending on the state of your own wellness. This understanding takes wellness out of the realms where we can analyze features such as socio-cultural factors, comorbidities, and genetic differences. It makes it an *individual* problem, not a *cultural* problem.

Barsky also argues that one of the larger problems with wellness is its overemphasis on physical health. We'll talk more about this in Section Four, but it's important to unpack here first. Barsky makes the distinction that:

> Physical health is not the same thing as happiness, optimism, satisfaction with life or self-fulfillment. We need to be clear about just what we can and cannot expect to result from the pursuit of health. It is an illusion that controlling our health means controlling our lives.[238]

How many of us have had the thought at some point in our lives, "If I can just lose 10 more pounds..." or "I just need to stop eating all this candy..." or "If I could just manage to commit to my gym membership, things would fall into place..." In a world that increasingly feels out of control to us mere mortals, finding ways to control our physical bodies is quite a natural coping mechanism.

But, why have we historically focused on our physical bodies and health? Since its earliest days, wellness has often been about emphasizing how good physical health can and should lead to good overall wellness. But, when were its early days? Where did this word and concept come from? You've got questions, and we've got answers. It's time to delve into the fascinating history of wellness.

How did we get here?

As we live through yet another revival of wellness in American culture, there is a corresponding renewed interest in the origins of the idea of wellness and how the industry has developed. While most people believe that our current obsession with wellness dates to the 1970s, the term was first popularized in the 1950s by Dr. Halbert L. Dunn.[239] When he published an article in the *Canadian Journal of Public Health* in 1959, he coined and defined the term "high-level wellness" as "a condition of change in which the individual moves forward, climbing toward a higher potential of functioning."[240]

To us, that sounds a little too much like word salad, but Dunn refined his points. In his work, he differentiated between good health—*the absence of illness*—and wellness—*an active and ongoing pursuit.* As the so-called father of the wellness movement, Dunn was one of the first to argue that good health is a passive state, and wellness is an active state. This concept of wellness emphasizes an individual's health and their responsibility to pursue their own wellness. It does not account for any cultural, economic, environmental, racial or gender factors that might contribute to, or detract from, their general health and well-being.

Though the term "wellness" first found regular use after Dr. Dunn's advocacy in the 1950s, researchers into the history of wellness have found much earlier iterations of the movement. Lest you think that the time of the Puritans was as far back as we would go in the culture of burnout time machine, have we got news for you.

Our first stop is actually all the way back to 3000 BCE in the land that became India and the dictates of Ayurveda.[241] These stories started as an oral tradition and were later recorded in the Vedas, the four sacred Hindu texts. The Vedas represented "a holistic system that strives to create harmony between body, mind and spirit."[242] We can also trace a lot of our understanding of holistic health and well-being to principles of Traditional Chinese Medicine, dating from 3000 to 2000 BCE.

Next up in our history of wellness tour is a stop at the height of the Industrial Revolution. In her article, "The False Promises of Wellness," Daniela Blei traces ideas of wellness back to the late 19th century when "newly prosperous Europeans created a wellness culture that went by another name: 'life reform.'"[243] For the first time in the history of humans, the mass production of goods and the revolution of a range of industries created an emerging middle class. With this new class of workers came both wealth and leisure time, which allowed for the time and space for people to pursue avenues of wellness.

Life Reformers experimented with an array of wellness activities including vegetarianism, raw food diets, open-air exercise, nudism, spas, and sunbathing. Blei contends that although the "aesthetic ideal of the lean, muscular body may derive from Greek antiquity," it was the "life reformers who turned the well-cared-for physique into a virtue."[244] We can trace the idea that wellness was a moral judgment back to the time of the Life Reformers.

Doctors jumped on this new wellness bandwagon, and the late 19th century saw the establishment of sanatoriums all over Europe. Depending on their geographical location, these sanatoriums offered natural spring baths, mud treatments, various athletic pursuits, and other holistic treatments. Alongside the Life Reformer movement we saw the proliferation of "new intellectual movements, spiritual philosophies and medical practices" across the United States and Europe.[245]

The Global Wellness Institute notes that a "number of alternative healthcare methods that focus on self-healing, holistic approaches, and preventative care—including homeopathy, osteopathy, chiropractic, and naturopathy—were founded during this era and gained widespread popularity in both Europe and the United States."[246] Through the Life Reformer and other movements, wellness quickly became associated with capitalism. Those with the resources to pursue these new forms of health and leisure were able to expand on the concept of wellness through their consumption of goods and services.

Blei notes a troubling trend that "through consumption, nineteenth-century wellness culture promised health and, by extension, success and personal fulfillment."[247] Her analysis also notes a striking number of similarities between the end of the 19th and the beginning of the 21st centuries, namely a technology revolution, capitalist expansion, wealth concentration, labor insecurity, and with it, status-related anxiety. When looked at through this lens, it is possible to see how and why we are living through another surge in the WIC and its various consumable goods and services.

Perhaps the most troubling correlation is not with the emergence of wellness movements in general, but the specific connection between health, wellness, and physical beauty. Blei concludes her critique of wellness by arguing that the far more consequential lesson from the Life Reformers is that in their "pursuit of a more natural, disciplined lifestyle, [they] blended health with beauty. It didn't take long before a person's outward appearance was taken as an indication of their physical, spiritual, and mental health, a development that would have dangerous, even deadly, consequences."[248]

Queen Victoria, Street Urchins, and the WIC

Queen Victoria reigned over England for a really, *really* long time. Sixty-three years, seven months, and two days to be exact, and she had an enormous amount of cultural influence during that time. Coronated in 1838, and married in 1840, she was a trend setter from the beginning. Instead of wearing royal robes at her wedding as her predecessors did, she wore a simple white dress and rode in an open carriage—traditions that are still held today.

The Britain of her time was... a lot. Jack the Ripper happened on her watch, as did high rates of poverty, violence, putting people in prison for having debts, and nationalist uprisings in Wales, Scotland, and Ireland. By all accounts, Victoria was not concerned with any of those things as she saw her role as setting the tone for the people. If they weren't following her tone, that was not her fault.

Victoria herself was very vocal about her beliefs regarding gender, even remarking once that giving women the vote would be a "mad and wicked folly."[249] She was deeply socially conservative and believed that people should stay in the social classes to which they were born. She also modeled for her subjects that one's social class was tied to one's morality.

Okay, so what does any of this have to do with the WIC?

Because Victorian England was *obsessed* with bodies. Covering them, punishing them, healing them through country air. Victoria was only 5'1" and generally petite. When she was crowned, she looked like the teenager she was, and small waists became even more of a trend than they already were. The conditions in London were abysmal for human life, but instead of fixing it, Victoria encouraged her subjects to remove themselves to the countryside for fresh air and light physical activity. Not actual physical activity, though, because then you may begin to look like a laborer and that simply would not do. Because if you were a laborer, that meant you were possibly poor, which meant you were most likely immoral.

For a more colorful description, see any adaptation of (or the original) *Oliver Twist* by Dickens.

We've read speculation that nearly all the blue blooded women in this era suffered from disordered eating, and we can absolutely believe it. Have you ever worn a Victorian corset? It's not something either of us recommend if you enjoy eating and/or breathing.

Sex, in particular, was something only enjoyed by the "lower classes." It was had by the upper crust, but not to be enjoyed. At least, that was the public narrative, which is what we're most concerned about here. Between the Puritans and wealthy Americans of the 19th century emulating English customs—think wealthy American turned landed gentry Cora Crawley from *Downton Abbey*—America has adopted this really wacked-out view of bodies. If you enjoy your body—either by eating food you enjoy, having sex you enjoy, doing physical activity you enjoy, basically doing anything you enjoy that doesn't involve politely sipping tea—then you must be an immoral person.

Sounds a little like Instagram influencers saying that if you don't try their cleanse, you don't value your health, doesn't it?

What are some more recent takes on "wellness?"

We already know there was a significant surge in interest in wellness in the 1970s. The massive societal shifts of the 1960s—the Civil Rights movement and political assassinations, the failure of the Vietnam War and the Watergate scandal—led to an increasing distrust with governments and institutions.

This distrust spilled into the health and medical field, and the wellness movement of the 1970s was categorized by three traits:

1. robust individualism,
2. distrust of western medicine
3. and a commitment to self-optimisation.[250]

As we start to break down the key ingredients that make up the Wellness Industrial Complex, we can see that each iteration of the larger movement puts an emphasis on individualism.

The 1970s also signified a major period of growth in Workplace Wellness Programs, which we will address soon. But, this decade also marked the time in which the word "wellness" moved out of the realm of medicine and into the general public's lexicon. In fact, during this period, an "informal network of physicians and psychologists began to create comprehensive, multi-dimensional models of wellness, wellness assessment tools, and to actively write and speak about their concept of wellness."[251]

What happened from the 1980s to the 2000s was the further mainstreaming of wellness ideas and practices. During this time period, wellness became enmeshed within medical science and recognized by government organizations and institutions.[252] As we add to this part of our soup, the particular realities of the start of the 21st century—major media expansion and technological growth, economic instability and a global pandemic, stagnant wages and large scale wealth accumulation—we can see that our recipe for the culture of burnout has to include our historical and contemporary perspectives on wellness. All of these realities also contributed to the creation and sustainment of the Wellness Industrial Complex.

Maybe now you're starting to see why our recipe calls for 3lbs of the WIC.

However, we're still missing one more major ingredient in the history of wellness, and that is the foundation of Workplace Wellness Programs (WWPs). Their creation and progress can be easily tied to the various wellness movements, and for good or ill, wellness programs are now a staple of almost every workplace culture.

When did Workplace Wellness Programs become a thing?

You'll be shocked when we tell you that we can trace the origins of workplace wellness to the late 19th century. We know, knock you with a feather. Though these practices were far from established programs, they did start to change the conversation about how employee health and wellness should be treated, both on- and off-site.

The Industrial Revolution not only revolutionized the global economy and workforce, it also brought into focus questions about workers rights, health and safety, and eventually physical health. To be clear, these conversations were good things! For a stark example of why, google "Triangle Shirtwaist Factory Fire."

We get the first inklings of workplace wellness with the John Pullman company in Chicago in the 1870s, when they created an athletic association for their workers. Though it may seem the most basic of offerings, it was considered countercultural when, in 1894, John H. Patterson began offering morning and afternoon breaks for his employees at the National Cash Register Company in Dayton, Ohio.[253]

A lot of the changes in the American workplace and workforce demands were highly influenced by popular publications that addressed the larger health issues facing workers. For example, Charles Turner Thackrah's book *The Effects of the Principal Arts, Trades and Professions and of Civic States and Habits of Longevity* (that's some title), published in 1831, argued for the importance of reducing standing hours, improving ventilation, and limiting work hours as measures that would help preserve the health and lives of employees.[254]

As employers continued to argue about employee health and well-being, workplace wellness became more commonplace. Considering that there were *zero* protection laws for workers at the time, and "cotton lung" was a common diagnosis, this was not the worst decision.

In his article on the forgotten history of worksite wellness programs, William McPeck categorizes the evolution of American Workplace Wellness programs into four phases.[255] Let's journey through them:

- Phase 1: The Social and Recreational Phase (1870s—1940s)
  - Started with the introduction of the athletic association at the Pullman Company in the 1870s and culminated with the creation of the National Employee Services and Recreation Association in 1941. The goal of this association was to spearhead efforts to create employee recreation programs across the country.
- Phase 2: The Fitness Phase (1950s—1970s)
  - Began in the 1950s with a shift in focus from social and recreational health to physical fitness. This is also when we see the specific development of employee fitness programs. One of the early features of these programs is that they would specifically target employees with the highest risk for health conditions.[256]
  - PepsiCo began their employee fitness program in the late 1950s, and in the 1960s, Sentry Insurance, Rockwell International, Xerox Corporation, and NASA all joined the fitness party.
  - The 1970s saw a continued focus on employee fitness programs. Workplace Wellness Programs were also significantly impacted by the passage of the Occupational Safety and Health Act (OSHA) in 1970 and the expansion of Employee Assistance Programs (EAPs) beyond their original focus on alcoholism.
  - In 1979, Johnson & Johnson launched their Life for Life program, which was one of the first programs to provide a physical health assessment and targeted wellness support to those with high BMI, poor

nutrition habits, and minimal stress management techniques.

- Phase 3: The Medical Phase (1980s—1990s)
  - Came about with the advancement of diagnostic testing revealing a rising concern with chronic diseases and cardiovascular health.
  - When the increased attention on chronic diseases was combined with the escalating employer healthcare costs in the 1980s, we saw workplace wellness programs becoming more focused on aligning with medical models of treatment.
  - The dynamic duo of rising costs and the reliance on the medical model meant the Medical Phase saw the creation of health education programs, Health Risk Assessments (HRAs), biometric screenings, and initiatives targeted at helping individuals change specific behaviors deemed to be unhealthy.
- Phase 4: The Fusion Phase (2000s—present)
  - Represents the final marriage between the traditional medical model and all the alternative forms of wellness developed through the middle part of the century.
  - At this point, the Workplace Wellness market is saturated with drives to "help" individuals achieve wellness—as defined by their employer.

Throughout all these phases of wellness, a near constant factor is the need for programs to be highly individualistic. Even though these programs were developed to be implemented on a corporate and cultural level, the focus still resorted back to the familiar discourses around an individual's responsibility and willpower to overcome their own poor health. The Wellness Industrial Complex thrives in a state where our individual differences, considerations, and health concerns drive a capitalist economy where there is an endless supply of support—for a cost—for all those lovely individuals.

What makes a 21st century Workplace Wellness Program?

Workplace Wellness Programs, in their current state, are a major ingredient in the Wellness Industrial Complex, and we knew that going into this book. But, we had a lot of unanswered questions about them: what are their stated benefits and goals? Are they working and how do we know? And, what are some of the big changes that have led us to where we are now—a culture of burnout? We also cannot talk about the current state of WWPs without addressing the impact of the COVID-19 pandemic on the focus of these programs, what they offer employees, and whether or not they are actually helping to make and keep people well.

We hit our first roadblock in trying to understand the reality of WWPs when attempting to find a definition for what they are and what they cover, and we aren't alone in that confusion. Mujtaba and Cuvico contend that "one initial problem with any examination of wellness programs in the workplace is that there is no statutory, regulatory, or uniform definition of the term 'wellness program.'"[257]

Right, okay. We just kept digging to see if anyone did have a concise definition.

We found a 2013 evaluation of Workplace Wellness Programs that provides a much more comprehensive definition of what workplace wellness programs entail:

> Employee wellness programs are an organized, employer-sponsored program that is designed to support employees as they adopt sustainable behaviors that reduce health risks, improve quality of life, enhance personal effectiveness, and benefit the organization's financial position.[258]

They've given us quite a laundry list of benefits and goals that, unsurprisingly, shift toward how employee wellness can eventually benefit the corporate bottom line. When any wellness practice is deeply embedded in a corporate setting, there will always be financial considerations to contend with. We are not saying that is inherently a bad thing, but if we further examine the stated goals of current WWPs, then we might uncover why they can be viewed as problematic, and not necessarily cost effective.

What are the goals of WWPs?

We found several sources that agree upon the three main benefits of an employee wellness program. These benefits are:

1. Lowering the direct health care costs to the organization,
2. Increasing productivity, and
3. Reducing absenteeism.[259]

A 2013 Rand Health survey found that "employers overwhelmingly expressed confidence that workplace wellness programs reduce medical cost, absenteeism, and health-related productivity losses."[260] Zula et al's evaluation of WWPs also listed possible benefits such as improved morale, increased ability to recruit and retain quality employees, and increased worker loyalty and commitment to the job and company.[261]

Now, we can all begin to see how the Puritanical idea that hyperproductivity is a moral trait shows up in workplace wellness. Even though we've been studying this topic for years, it was actually striking that we did not find anywhere in the top 3 listed benefits (or 3 supplementary ones) of the WWPs a prioritization of the improved health and well-being of the employees.

Mujtaba and Cuvico are even more explicit that employers believe, "If the people are healthy, educated, and happy they will be better able to increase productivity."[262] Employers are coming straight out and admitting that the primary goal of Workplace Wellness Programs is to *increase productivity*, not—that we can find stated in any accessible research—to improve the health and well-being of the individual employees and thus the overall health of the corporation or organization.

Let's pause on that, shall we? Improved health and well-being is not listed as a top priority of WWPs.

So how do WWPs measure success?

If the primary goal of the WWPs is to increase productivity, then we need to look at the methods they are using to reach these goals. In the 21st century WWPs system, there are two main issues impacting the effectiveness of the programs: 1) the "carrot and stick" approach of incentivizing and penalizing and 2) the collection of employee health data by insurers and employers.

Mujtaba and Cuvico's research shows that many programs employ the "carrot and stick" approach, in which the "carrot" is incentives to participate in the WWP and the "stick" is some form of penalty for not participating. Other research found that more than two-third of employers who had at least 50 employees and some form of formalized corporate wellness use financial incentives to encourage program enrollment and participation, while ten percent within that category use incentives that are tied to health-related standards.[263]

Needless to say, there are a lot of critics of the "stick" approach. There are arguments that the "stick" approach increases "the potential for discrimination and harassment at the workplace" for the failure to participate in the program or to meet specific corporate goals and mandates.[264] Others argue that using penalties to encourage or enforce participation "will erode the informed consent of the employee-patient in medical decision-making."[265]

Does this sound great? No? Let's add more fuel to the fire.

In her extensively researched article on the negative effects of workplace wellness, Elizabeth Brown says that "employers have an ever-widening range of tools to gauge their employees' health, fitness, and likelihood of developing diseases—all of which affect corporate spending on health insurance."[266] Were employers concerned merely about limiting costs and determining the appropriate budget, we would be less alarmed. However, Brown further argues that many of these programs, applications, and the data they collect are not considered under major health and discrimination laws, such as the ADA and HIPAA.[267]

In a rather frightening scenario, she also notes that "evaluating an employee for a promotion based on the likelihood that the employee will develop an expensive health condition later in life, based on her wellness program data, would not invoke disability law because no specific disability is invoked or perceived."[268]

Are you worried yet? We are, too.

What we have learned so far is that, like all the other elements in the WIC, WWPs adopted the belief that an individual person's health is a moral assessment and valuation on their ability to contribute and be productive.

Do WWPs actually work?

Basically? Not really.

We've all heard the colloquial stories from friends and family about the latest health initiative at work: the weightloss challenge, the meditation app, the online mental health assessment.

We've already argued that their primary goal is not to help people achieve and maintain their wellness because, in order to participate in the culture of burnout, we have to be measured on our productivity and contribution (especially to the economy). If they aren't meant to keep people well, then we can't easily measure if they are working to do that. We can ask if they are helping companies save money, decrease absenteeism, and increase productivity, since those are their real goals anyway.

According to the Kaiser Family Foundation's 2020 Employer Health Benefit Survey, 81% of large companies offered their employees access to corporate wellness programs in 2020.[269] With such a high level of implementation, one would assume that these corporations have a decent amount of data to suggest that these programs work.

In our attempts to find the hard facts on whether WWPs are effective at all, there was...not a lot to find. A 2012 review of the impact of worksite wellness programs for the RAND Corporation found that there was some data on reducing healthcare costs, but not a lot of accessible studies and not a high number of monetary savings were available.[270]

Similarly, writing in 2017, Brown found that most employers don't know if they are saving money through WWPs. She found data that more than half of employers surveyed in 2010 reported that they did not know their programs' ROI (return on investment).[271] We also found some puzzling results from the 2012 Rand Health survey. The authors state that in the survey:

> Employers overwhelmingly expressed confidence that workplace wellness programs reduce medical cost, absenteeism, and health-related productivity losses. But at that same time, only about half stated that they have evaluated program impacts formally and only 2% reported actual savings estimates.[272]

With the belief, albeit unfounded, that WWPs help reduce employer costs for healthcare, it's not surprising to see a rapid rise in their use. If WWPs are supposed to help reduce employer healthcare costs, then we would expect to see them throw their weight behind measures that would minimize those costs.

But, we don't. They're not even lowering insurance premiums! The cost of premiums for family coverage rose 27% from 2010 to 2015, and they had the same rate of growth from 2005 to 2010.[273] Rising premiums means rising costs for healthcare coverage altogether, and these rising prices are then passed on to the employer.[274]

When we, as a society, view human beings as productivity machines whose real value is in their ability to stay healthy so that they can work more and harder, then we develop a perspective on wellness that is more concerned with cost savings than happy and healthy employees. And, it seems, those cost savings don't even need to be backed up with real data. The mere *feeling* that a program is saving money is good enough to press on with it.

What about the ACA? Wasn't it supposed to fix all this?

Um…yes and no.

We don't really have the time or the space to dig into all the arguments for and against the passage and implementation of the ACA, but we cannot talk about workplace wellness programs without talking about how that particular piece of legislation changed the workplace wellness game.

A lot of the research we collated on WWPs mentions the requirements placed on corporations with regards to employee healthcare and benefits. We learned that Workplace Wellness Programs are a primary component of the ACA and that the "ACA allows employers to reward workers who participate in wellness programs, and penalize those who refuse, with discounts or increases of as much as 30 percent of their insurance costs."[275] In fact, we found that the primary purpose of most WWP programs to date is to comply with the ACA and to reduce employer-sponsored health insurance premiums.

The ACA significantly impacts the way we think about and implement workplace wellness programs.[276] The main problem comes down to this: these "voluntary" WWPs are not really voluntary if employers are forcing employees to decide between divulging personal health information that could be used in a discriminatory practice or buying unaffordable and limited private health insurance coverage.[277]

Are you really going to talk about the COVID of it all (again)?

Yes. Sorry/not sorry.

Well before the mere thought of a global pandemic and health emergency was anywhere near our radars, the U.S. healthcare system was already heavily burdened by chronic diseases. Research from the early 2010s estimated that treating chronic diseases accounted for over 75% of national health expenditures.[278] One of the biggest questions currently facing the U.S. healthcare system is how COVID-19 and lasting impacts of the virus will be classified. Since we are still so close to the height of the pandemic, there's a lot of data we won't have, simply because medical science takes time, and we won't know how recovery from COVID-related illness will evolve over time and with new medical treatments.

At this stage, we all likely know someone who is still recovering from a COVID infection, whether it is Long COVID or the ramifications to other bodily systems. We personally know people who haven't been able to return to work and who are permanently disabled or severely limited in what they can do, specifically because of their illness. We all know that COVID changed so much about how we think about work; it's one of the chief reasons burnout is such a popular topic these days.

Some of the critical questions facing WWPs are: how will CO-

VID change how employers understand the goals and outcomes for the programs? Will COVID be considered a pre-existing condition for new hires? How will companies plan for and support the high numbers of people with long-term and evolving health needs? There's only so much we can know about it right now, but we wouldn't be our curious selves if we didn't start asking these questions now.[279]

Briefly, Kristen is going to put on her business owner hat and explain her view on this messy topic.

Our Parent Company's Perspective on WWPs

I cannot tell you the number of times that someone has pitched me a workplace wellness program. It comes from insurance companies, workman's compensation lawyers, and other sellers of business-to-business services. My brother (who owns the company with me) and I will listen dutifully and then ask a few questions they never have answers for. What if our employees don't use smartphones? What if we feel uncomfortable with anyone else tracking their mental health? Does this account for ESL speakers or different cultures? What about people who are not used to thinking critically about themselves—do you have onboarding for their mental health?

From what I can tell, everything I've ever been pitched is entirely designed for white, middle-income, white collar workers who spend most of their days at desks. Sure, this may be a decent sized portion of the population, but it doesn't even really serve them. It doesn't account for *any* differences between people and reduces the entire concept of wellness down to participation in an app—which we've already gone over in this section.

> And that last bit is what really gets my goat. My brother and I are *extremely* concerned about our employee's well-being. It's right there in our mission statement: "to impact lives and create holistic wealth." That last bit is what matters — how are we creating physical wealth, economic wealth, spiritual wealth, emotional wealth for our employees and stakeholders? By my account, it's by paying people a living wage, offering flexibility for childcare needs, and other sundry activities that hopefully remind our folks that they're humans to us and not just an employee identification number. It's messier, sure. It involves a lot more conversations, but our employees also know that we give a damn about them beyond what they do or do not click on an app.

Now, after all this, you might still be thinking, "Why are they being so critical of Workplace Wellness Programs? Surely, it can't be a bad thing to offer folks different options to improve their health." And, from the outside, we can understand that question. However, our contention throughout this entire book is that when we rely on broken systems to support societal wellness, we're not actually practicing holistic and inclusive well-being.

Workplace Wellness Programs—and the WIC by extension—are all about the bottom line. WWPs are specifically designed to use all available methods to determine if the workforce is working hard enough, efficiently enough, if they are healthy enough to do the job and keep the investors happy. From our perspective, they treat wellness as a slogan, not as an authentic method to improve the health and well-being of their folks.

When these ideas are developed within a culture of burnout, they will be designed to perpetuate ideas of health and wellness in a way that keeps Puritanical productivity at the forefront of the employers' goals. That, in and of itself, is pretty solid evidence that the workplace wellness system is broken, but we'd like to spend a few more words giving you some more of the nuts and bolts of why that is the case.

Why is the Workplace Wellness system so broken?

In short? Because slap-tape-on-it or throw-money-at-it solutions are easy, and promoting and supporting true, holistic wellness and well-being in an organization is hard. We're not going to lie and pretend it's not. In fact, this whole book is about how we have to choose the harder, scarier path instead of the easy, familiar path if we want to see true change. And, we *do* want change.

Also, if we're completely honest, business is often entirely about metrics—key performance indicators, revenue goals, cost of customer acquisition—and wellness isn't truly measurable in this way. So, as the industry grew, it became more and more clear that money could be made in the world of corporate wellness. Companies who sold products and services designed to improve wellness had to come up with ways to show their products worked, regardless of whether those results were an accurate reflection of any real improvement in wellness.

Not only is measuring things about people's bodies not...great, but it prioritizes a concept of physical health as the be-all and end-all of well-being, and it's simply not. In Section Four, we're going to introduce a different perspective on wellness that can serve us all better, because being and feeling well is *good* and valuable and improves quality of life for everyone.

Before we get there, we need to make sure our approach to well-being takes two very important things into consideration: 1) you can't buy wellness and 2) everyone's perspective on what constitutes their own wellness is going to look different. This perspective, at first glance, doesn't look like it makes anyone any money; in fact, it might look costly instead.

Basically, what we're saying is that because we have created disordered workplace cultures and expectations, anything that is a byproduct of those disordered cultures carries that disorder. In short, workplace wellness as a concept is simply not fit for purpose because it comes from our toxic and disordered workplace cultures.

So, really, why is the workplace wellness system so broken?

Because of the Wellness Industrial Complex.

What is the Wellness Industrial Complex?

In the book *American Detox*, Kerri Kelly defines the Wellness Industrial Complex (WIC) as "extreme materialism masquerading as spiritual practice."[280] We agree.

What does that look like? It's the Instagram ads telling you to buy this tea, or the yoga teacher who says you can be free of your trauma if you take this course for $219.95. It's an app that promises that in just five minutes a day, your employees' mental health will improve so you no longer need to worry about burnout.

We've already hinted at some of the key ingredients that make up the Wellness Industrial Complex. Now, it's time to take a magnifying glass to the recipe and see what we're really cooking with.

Basically, the Wellness Industrial Complex is what happens when you take all the major ingredients of our current wellness culture and mix them together with unencumbered capitalism and the increasing power and control of social media and technology. As a refresher, when we broke down the key ingredients of "wellness," two of the biggest characteristics were an overemphasis on the importance of physical health and a sense of pretty intense hyper-individualism.

In 2021, *The Guardian*'s Sirin Kale argued that the "polluting tributary in wellness's fresh, clear stream has always been its unwavering insistence that health is a choice rather than something genetically predetermined or socially ordained."[281] A major part of understanding how "wellness" fits so well into the Puritan work ethic is that it views being well as an individual choice. If we view wellness as a choice, then it is something we have control over.

Going back to Arthur Barsky's contention, we can see how the modern iteration of wellness still operates under the illusion that: 1) Physical health is the same as physical well-being and 2) If we can control our physical health, we can control our lives.[282] Therefore, the purpose of the Wellness Industrial Complex is to help folks understand that they *can* control their lives through controlling their health but *only* if they accept that they are going to have to buy or consume or invest in some wellness product to do so.

Thanks?

We're now going to combine all the ingredients of the WIC together by using some rather astute analysis by Lizzie Braicks-Rinker from her 2022 TEDx at the University of Washington "Your body is talking to you, are you listening?"[283] Braicks-Rinker claims that the three largest problems facing wellness culture today are hustle culture, diet culture, and the illusory truth effect. She argues that at the core of "hustle culture" is the idea that "resting or quitting something is a failure."[284]

A wave to the Puritans, who even though they are long dead and gone are still wreaking havoc.

Braicks-Rinker uses Nadia Craddock's (a UK-based body image researcher) definition of "diet culture," which is "a belief and social expectation that we're a more worthy person if our bodies are a certain way."[285] Her 3rd factor is the "illusory truth effect." The illusory truth effect can be understood as "the more we see something, even if we *know* it's not real, the more we believe it could be true."[286] In short, this effect describes what happens to a culture like ours when everyone carries around smartphones—what Kristen calls "fear machines"—and relies upon technology we don't fully understand to provide us with all the information we could possibly want (and then some).

Since Braicks-Rinker uses a lot of terms we know not everyone will remember, we've distilled our recipe for the WIC into 4 essential ingredients:

1. An obsession with physical health and beauty
2. A hyper-individualistic perspective with a focus on individual solutions
3. A use of social media marketing, advertising, and algorithms
4. A permanent and co-dependent relationship with capitalism

To us, any aspect of wellness culture that includes these 4 ingredients is a part of the Wellness Industrial Complex. That means every private gym, exercise or wellness expert, Multi-Level Marketing (MLM) wellness scheme, self-help book, Instagram and TikTok influencer, Workplace Wellness Program and corporate wellness initiative, tea brand, juice cleanse, diet, clothing and fashion trend (hello, athleisure), and every tea, oil, scrub, incense, and salt lamp you can sell. Every single part of our larger wellness culture operates within the broad tent of the Wellness Industrial Complex.

Now, just because we are critical of the *system* of the Wellness Industrial Complex, does not mean we don't engage with it. We both use products and services that fall under the big tent of the WIC. Kristen loves pilates, massages, acupuncture, and aromatherapy. Erin has already talked about her dedicated yoga practice, which she pairs with a love of herbal tea, holistic chiropractic care, and aromatherapy.

Through lots of trial and error, we have found parts of the WIC that actually help us work toward holistic well-being. We're not saying these individual elements are bad. What we're saying is that when they are combined with our four essential ingredients of the WIC, they can tip over into manipulative, toxic, or abusive. When we make well-being about making money or making a moral judgment, that's where we have to take a step back and ask some hard questions.

What do we need to know about the role of gender in the WIC?

We're going to kick this off with a little exercise partly adapted from how *Invisible Women* talks about the gender gap and partly from the closing argument courtroom scene in the 1996 classic film *A Time to Kill*.

Let's take another look at that long list of all the parts of wellness culture that make up the WIC. In our rather lengthy sentence, we listed:

- Private gyms
- Exercises or wellness experts
- Multi-Level Marketing (MLM) wellness schemes
- Self help books and wellness retreats
- Social media influencers
- Workplace Wellness Programs

- Tea brands, juice cleanses, and every diet imaginable
- Clothing and fashion trends
- Teas, oils, scrubs, incense, and salt lamps galore

Read over that list, close your eyes for a minute, and then reflect on these questions:

When thinking about the items on that list, who do you imagine most of those products and services are geared towards? How are they marketed and advertised? What arguments are made for why anyone needs these products? When you think about it, who is selling these products? Who are the brand ambassadors or models used by the companies? What do they look like?

Now...we want you to be honest.

How many of those items on the list do you think are for women? How many are marketed to them—for the purpose of losing weight, starting that new relationship, reevaluating your life path? How many of those items are sold by women? Marketed by super thin, gorgeous models selling the next juice cleanse craze? How do you think this affects women of all ages, but specifically those in menopause?

We're not saying that big parts of the WIC aren't geared towards men. Of course, gym memberships and protein powders and Under Armour workout clothes have significant gender elements to how they are marketed. However, we know that the WIC is a trillion dollar industry, and we couldn't write about burnout without talking about why so much of the money made off the idea of "wellness" is made off women and by women.

How do women engage with the WIC?

Statistically, we know that women experience higher rates of burnout than men. When women are faced with symptoms of burnout, where do they turn? In trying to understand all the various ways the gender gap impacts women, *Invisible Women* talks about how the medical and scientific fields have failed to understand and research key differences in gender.

The book's thesis is that because most of modern society is founded on and operates off of a default male bias, women are often left behind or left out.[287] This is true throughout the history of medical science. From what we know about the female anatomy—ovaries were called female testicles until the 17th century—to how medicines are developed—the COVID-19 vaccines were not tested on people who were menstruating, so they had no idea the impact the drugs would have on menstrual cycles—women have been "chronically misunderstood, mistreated and misdiagnosed" by the medical profession for centuries.[288]

Sit with the phrase "female testicles" for a minute. Wooooooow.

As more and more people study the high levels of women's participation in wellness culture, the more relevant their contentious relationship to Western medicine becomes. We know that Western medicine has a history of not taking women seriously, especially when those women are non-White, non-heterosexual humans. Women's relationship to medicine breaks down on the lines of intersections and:

> Women's symptoms have been seen as psychological rather than physiological, and they have been told that their ailments are "all in their head". Poor women, women of color, fat women, and gender non-binary people all face a magnified version of this, and their symptoms can go for years without accurate diagnosis. To combat this, women are now told to "trust your body" or to "listen to your symptoms" but such advice can be difficult to follow in the face of a system that distrusts women as reliable sources of bodily knowledge.[289]

If we add to these ingredients the socialization of women by American society—where there still exists a high level of stigma against menstruation, sex, and sexuality, as well as the weight of traditional gender roles—then women's relationships with their medical providers become complicated at best and toxic at worst.[290] Therefore, it should not be surprising that "women are increasingly attracted to a wellness industry that hears women and believes them when they say something is wrong. The wellness industry not only appears to take their symptoms seriously, but it does so in a way that feels respectful and empowering."[291]

When we see the insidious aspects of the Wellness Industrial Complex in full force, we realize that many of the more toxic elements are built to exploit women's lack of trust in traditional medicine. In a society where bodily autonomy and agency are at risk everyday, and in a culture where the medical community has a history of not believing women about their bodies, many times resulting in injury or death, where else are women supposed to turn? Not only does the WIC hear and believe women, but its various proponents also promise that their product or service will cure all that ails them.

Quoted in a 2023 Elle article about the rise of the wellness industry, Dr. Pooja Lakshmin (author of the book *Real Self-Care*) labeled the wellness industry the "tyranny of self-care" where women "are being sold breezy fixes in pastel-coloured packages, then made to feel at fault when they don't work."[292] Using the framework of this "tyranny of self-care," we can understand both why the products and services in the WIC are so popular and also so potentially damaging. This matters to burnout because women are now likely to self-medicate with solutions marketed to them by potentially predatory sources, rather than have trustworthy access to medical solutions for the root causes of their complaints.

What about all the women who sell "wellness?"

Of course, women are not just consumers in the WIC. Sirin Kale provides an excellent summary for the state of wellness and how it relates to burnout, especially for women:

> We have had more than a decade of the modern iteration of wellness. A decade of vagina candles, chia bowls, coffee enemas and spirulina shots. A decade of burnt-out, anxious, unhappy women seeking to detoxify their bodies, rebalance their chakras and recentre their divine femininity, ideally while losing weight. The global wellness industry is worth about $1.5tn—and for every saintly Yoga With Adriene there are thousands of grifters pushing untested therapies on impressionable people.[293]

The American culture of burnout is the worst it has ever been. We have never been more stressed, anxious, depressed, and generally unhappy as a society than we are now. Since we aren't addressing the cultural reasons for our burnout, we continue to jump from quick fix to quick fix, hoping that the right combination of candles, enemas, pills, and shots will solve the problem we've never been able to crack.

This leaves a lot of people vulnerable not only to the "grifters" of the WIC, but to a whole host of folks who buy into the idea that selling doTerra essential oils or LuLaRoe leggings can not only help people who need those products, but can also "empower" women to work their own "side hustle" and to become their own "lady boss."[294] Yep, we're talking about Multi-Level Marketing (MLM) operations.

We can't really talk about the role of gender within the WIC without unpacking MLMs. They have long been a research obsession of Kristen's, and she's got capital T thoughts and capital F feelings about how they target specific subsets of women and how they fit into the grand scheme of the Wellness Industrial Complex.

What do we do with the candles that promise to heal us?[295]

"Hey hun, been a while! Hope you're great. I've got this new side hustle and I thought of you immediately."

"I see you've given birth recently, congratulations! Did you know Rodan + Fields has a great cream for getting rid of your stretch marks?"

Have you ever been a victim of one of these kinds of messages? They're so ubiquitous that they're almost a joke now. But, they're also a significant part of the WIC.

Multi-level marketing (MLM) is a simple system, really. Using LuLaRoe—the besmirched clothing MLM—as an example, they work like this. Becky is looking for a night out away from her kids and to meet other moms, so she goes to a party at Simone's house for LuLaRoe. Becky hears that this is a great way to make friends, gain a community, and make some extra cash, so she buys the $499 starter pack. This gets her a box of clothes delivered to her home that she can now sell on at a profit.

But Simone is now in Becky's "upline," as the person who recruited her, and will make money off of everything Becky sells and then every other person Becky recruits, as well. The real trick here is that, in fact, both Simone and Becky will make more money off recruiting than they will off the clothing.

Becky realizes that her starter kit doesn't have a lot of the clothes that people are buying, so she tells Simone that she's worried. Simone tells her that's no problem—just order more inventory. Oh, and she should also recruit more people to join her team! At this point, statistics tell us that Becky is probably taking in less than $10/mo in revenue and spending at least $500 a month to keep her "side hustle" afloat.

If this sounds like a pyramid scheme, you are not wrong. MLMs are careful to say that they're not pyramid schemes, which are illegal under the FTC, but if we're honest, the lines are *really* blurry. For our money and for the purposes of cultural and psychological effects, an MLM is any company where you can make more money by recruiting others to sell under you (a downline) than you can off selling the products themselves.

Another piece of the WIC is that they are largely targeted at women—not only in the products themselves, but in the sales structure. We'll get into this a bit more in a little while, but the largest proportion of MLM sellers are Mormon and evangelical housewives.[296] It allows them to provide money to pay for incidentals without threatening their husbands' role as breadwinner. It can also be done from home, and it's advertised as something you can do around your kids' schedules.

Especially about wellness, the FTC took action against doTerra (a peddler of essential oils) for claiming their oils could prevent COVID-19.[297] They also targeted several other companies when their "consultants" were proven to be claiming their products could do the same.[298]

Please note, you'll find a lot of anti-MLM advocates use "cult" language for MLMs. Many do exhibit behaviors that behave a lot like cults. Some—like NXIVM—use MLMs as the hook into the larger cult. However, not every MLM is a cult, and to paint broad brush strokes defeats the purpose of our conversation. Instead of investigating if the woman in your DMs is a cult member, ask yourself if buying their product will put actual money in their pocket or if most of that income will go to their uplines and the CEOs at the very top. If so, then you're better off finding another company for your leggings, nail wraps, or essential oils.[299]

Additionally, not every single woman in an MLM is evil or manipulative or stupid or any of the other words we've heard used for these ladies. Everyone has their own reasons for joining, and for leaving, and we are simply pointing out the disparities in the *system*, not any specific women and their choices/behaviors.

Why is the WIC so darn toxic?

Right, so we've given you a lot of information about the Wellness Industrial Complex, one of the most complex ingredients in our burnout soup. Before we move on to solutions to this whole soupy mess, we wanted to spend a few moments discussing the four key elements of the WIC and what makes them so toxic and harmful.

Perfectionism

As more and more people become vocally critical of wellness culture and all the various parts of it, we are starting to find more analysis about how our wellness goals keep veering into dangerous territory. A 2023 article for online outlet Refinery 29 argues that if your motivation to self-improvement through some form of wellness is not realistic, then you run the risk of slipping toward perfectionism.[300] This is a common problem within the WIC because the industry depends on being able to sell you the idea that "through your actions alone you can achieve your 'best self.'"[301]

Perfectionism can thrive in an environment with a strong foundation of moral judgment, which is another reason why it's a big element in the WIC. In her article for *Refinery 29*, Sadhbh O'Sullivan contends, "The reason why many people pursue perfection is because they believe themselves to be fundamentally not good enough in the first place—a belief that is a core motivator for people getting into wellness."[302]

At the start of this section, we shared with you the deep and lasting influence of the Puritanical worldview, which is based on working hard, strong moral judgments, and a fierce belief in individualism. Following these principles to their logical conclusion and incorporating key aspects of 21st century capitalism—e-commerce, social media, and mass produced, cheap products—it seems pretty clear how we got the wellness culture we have.

The notion of perfectionism has a long and lasting negative effect on our engagement in wellness culture and our own self-perception. With this much pressure on ourselves to achieve "wellness," what happens to us when something doesn't work? What are our coping mechanisms? And, more importantly, does the WIC want us to have coping mechanisms? Writing from her own experiences, O'Sullivan noted, "When yoga or smoothies or expensive spin classes are meant to help you reach clarity about yourself, it can be mentally jarring when your daily anxieties or dissatisfaction about your body does not go away."[303]

Oooooof. We've felt this so many times, and we're betting you may have as well. Remember, this stuff is baked in, and you're not a failure for believing it.

The Wellness Industrial Complex leaves a lot of room for you to try every method under the sun, but the framework of this form of experimentation is all wrong. The WIC has created a vicious and inescapable cycle of "wellness" products to try to reach your end goal of "being well." But, wellness is not a finish line we cross, declaring ourselves well and never having to address any aspect of our holistic well-being again. However, the WIC thrives on its ability to sell you the "perfect" solution to your problems—in fact, it depends on it to survive. Modern day wellness exists in a constant state of movement, always encouraging consumers to buy, subscribe, invest, and repeat until you are "well."

The biggest problem with perfectionism is that humans aren't perfect. It's an unachievable goal, and that's the point. If wellness is a place we should all strive for but never get, then the Wellness Industrial Complex will continue to chug along, making money off of our individual insecurities and our collective belief that we can control our lives if we control our health.

One part of the WIC that has prayed on our insecurities for decades is diet culture, and perfectionism is a powerful tool within it. Since our culture places a social and moral value on a largely unachievable beauty standard, there exists a plethora of products aimed at helping you reach that version of "perfection." In her heartbreaking opinion piece for the *New York Times*, the novelist Jessica Knoll reflected on her relationship with her body, with diet culture, and with what she perceived to be wellness. Knoll admits, "I called this poisonous relationship between a body I was indoctrinated to hate and food I had been taught to fear 'wellness.'"[304]

Honestly admitting how she bought into the pressure to be perfectly well, she realized that "when you have to deprive, punish and isolate yourself to look 'good,' it is impossible to *feel* good. I was my sickest and loneliest when I appeared my healthiest."[305] The more we explore the various methods that the WIC uses to convince people to engage, to consume, the more we understand that an industry built on the false promise of perfection cannot also be concerned with achieving holistic well-being.

Life As A Fat Lady

Hello, Kristen here, your resident fat friend for this book. I hope I'm not your only fat friend, for the sheer fact that there are a lot of us, and many are quite lovely, and you should know us! But for now, I'd like to tell you a little of my journey with my body and the WIC.

I was first put on a diet when I was nine. My incredibly well-intentioned mother—who I adore and will hear nothing spoken against her as she's also a human in this soup—was worried about my weight and took me to Jenny Craig. I would now like to ask how in the living hell did someone not tell her I was too young for this? But the answer is that they could make money off of us, so off I went. Since that fateful first failure, I've been on the grapefruit diet, the cottage cheese diet, Atkins, South Beach, Weight Watchers—between 1992 and 2011, I was on every trendy diet you can imagine.

None of them helped me change my body

permanently.

All of them impacted my relationship with my body and with food.

I look back now on photos of me as a kiddo. I thought I was a whale (which several kids in my life called me, so thanks!). I was a kid who might have been more active, but wasn't anywhere near my self-perception. I *loathed* myself. I was completely convinced I'd never get married because who could love someone who looked like me? I even remember wishing I was anorexic a few times because those girls were skinny and wasn't that the most important thing?

If I am completely honest, I work toward body acceptance most days. Body positivity feels far too out of reach. 40 years of being told that my body is other people's business (yes, I have been moo'd at from cars), that it isn't "right", that it doesn't fit (don't get me started on airplane seats or roller coasters)—those 40 years take a toll. The first time I saw someone remotely my size on a movie screen who wasn't a joke was in 2007's *Hairspray* musical directed by Adam Shankman, and I was in my 20s.

I'm much more comfortable talking about my body now than I was in my teens or 20s. I want to thank folks like Aubrey Gordon and Ashley Graham for giving me language to understand that the WIC is the enemy, not my body. My body has kept me alive, is doing her best, and while she probably does need to move more, she's not a moral failure because she prefers reading over running.

I also need to briefly recognize my privilege as a fat person who still physically fits into most of the world. While I cannot buy clothes everywhere off the rack, I can at many places. Though they are often uncomfortable, I do fit in airplane seats and on rides at Disney World and in the driver's seat of a car. My social media is filled with people who cannot do any of those things, and their stigma and oppression is much, much greater than mine.

As I wrestle with body acceptance, I see it as my responsibility to get people used to the idea that "fat" doesn't mean bad. When I call myself fat, folks often correct me and say, "you're not fat, you're beautiful." Pals, listen to what you are saying. Or, "I don't see your size, you are just you." Cool, but if you were describing my body to a stranger, you'd probably use my size at some point. "Fat" should be value neutral—it's a reality, merely a descriptor. The WIC is the one who gives it the negative connotations it has.

But just like every other part of culture, we can change that and reclaim bodies from the tyranny of the WIC.

Individualism

The second key element of the WIC is our cultural understanding that burnout, or more broadly being unwell, is an individual problem with an individual solution. The WIC continues to dominate our understanding of holistic well-being because it is able to tap into how our culture views health through a "hyper-individualistic moral frame."[306] One of the reasons why this frame is so successful in America is because of how it relates to the cultural values we imagine exist at the heart of what it means to be American.

If a new company or influencer can sell the idea that their product will get you to achieve perfection as an individual, without any cultural context or support, then they have found a recipe in their cookbook that is very financially lucrative and sustainable. By employing these two elements as their model for "wellness," the Wellness Industrial Complex ensures those who participate are always focusing on the parts of themselves that need to be "fixed" in order to be a good person, to have value, to be attractive, to be successful.

Cultural Appropriation

The third element is the legitimate concerns about how wellness appropriates concepts, practices, and beliefs from other cultural traditions and faith systems. Poorna Bell states, "Wellness—particularly white wellness—has a bad reputation for taking on other cultures, repackaging them with whiteness alongside pretty pictures and hashtags, and booting the original culture out of the process."[307] We can see this alarming trend of appropriation emerge with the explosion of online influencers selling spiritual crystals, weight loss yoga practices, or fasting as a form of meditation. One of the clearest examples of the damage caused by cultural appropriation is the very popular burning of white sage.

Bell outlines the history of the significance of this practice to Indigenous peoples, the original inhabitants of this continent, and how the wellness industry perpetuates lasting cultural damage. Few of you may know that the burning of white sage was banned by the U.S. government until 1978 because it was illegal for Indigenous peoples to practice their own religion. Flash forward to now, and white sage is co-opted by largely White wellness culture to the detriment of Indigenous peoples and their spiritual practice. The increasingly high demand for the plant led to a rise in illegal poaching practices and over-harvesting. The overuse of this plant for wellness purposes means that Indigenous peoples do not have adequate access to it for their sacred rituals.[308]

Climate Change

The fourth element we want to mention is the ethics of WIC labor practices and their impact on the climate/environment. We found a number of in-depth explorations into whether or not claims of sustainability within wellness culture are accurate. In short, it appears that a lot of consumers in the WIC are sacrificing ethical work environments for the convenience of their access to products and treatments.[309] From the overharvesting of frankincense in Somalia to the questionable and dangerous labor practices of quartz mines in Madagascar, there appears to be ample evidence that the capitalistic drive of the WIC is spreading its toxicity throughout the global economy.

What does the WIC want from us?

The Wellness Industrial Complex does not want you to evaluate and analyze what you need, what your body needs, what your relationships need, or what you can afford. It does not want you to take your time, or to do research into new treatments or products. In order to keep chugging along, the WIC needs you to keep spending, because that is what happens when "late-stage capitalism merges with hyper-individualism."[310] One of the best explorations of this answer that we read was *The Gospel of Wellness* by Rina Raphael, and we'd encourage all of you interested in this topic to read it for yourselves.

Actual holistic health and well-being takes an investment of energy and time. People who are in burnout on our Stress-o-Meter have no energy and time to give to that process. This is part of the reason that the "take a pill and you're all better" solutions are so appealing to folks. How many of us have all thought at some point: "I wish I could just fix this," "I wish I could just feel better," "I wish I wasn't in pain." Those are all valid thoughts and feelings. Our culture of burnout wants you to think that there are easy solutions to your health and well-being problems.

But, we've all tried things that haven't worked. We've all tried the diet that made us sick, got the workout equipment that didn't give us a "beach ready body," or bought the crystal that didn't cure our eczema. Those are all solutions that the culture of burnout wanted us to buy into. It is a culture that is built on the fallacy that "the human mind is a drill sergeant and the organs of our body obediently fall in line."[311]

It is a culture that says if we just work hard enough, if we are a good enough person, if we do the "right" things, then we will be a person of value. It says that we will be worthy of good health and that well-being can be earned.

That culture is telling you that you need to participate in the Wellness Industrial Complex to get better. It is telling you that your burnout is your fault and, therefore, your problem to fix. It is a culture that relies on the contradictory belief that there are quick fix solutions to what ails you, but there is also no quick fix solution that will ever really work. It means that the wellness industry is one that "needs to continue to grow on the back of people's discontent."[312] This is the culture of burnout and wellness we have built. But, that culture is lying. Therefore, what we are saying is that real well-being—authentic, holistic well-being—is countercultural.

So what does all this mean?

You are exhausted *not* because you need to be, but because your culture decided your worth was tied to your output. However, just like all other things culturally constructed, it can be deconstructed. That's also going to be very, very hard. That which is culturally embedded is also *personally* embedded. You may be reading this and nodding along but still feel stressed when you need to take a day off work, or you expect an employee to work from home while they recover from COVID. Maybe you say yes to volunteering every weekend because if you don't do it, who will?[313]

It's extremely difficult to shake the deep-seated beliefs that all us Americans were raised on: our hard work equals our worth and our lack of productivity is a personal failing. Thankfully, or maybe disappointingly, cultural shifts are also slow. We don't expect this to change overnight. As we've seen, even massive global events like COVID-19 don't always force rapid change, even if it helps underscore that a change is needed.

So, we teach our children better than we learned. We find different stories to tell ourselves. We explore other people's lived experiences. We read stories, ask questions, and embrace differences. We reject Workplace Wellness Programs and the Wellness Industrial Complex and other exploitations of a desire for personal well-being. And, the shift begins.

Now that we've gone through every part of our recipe for burnout culture, from the past through where we sit now, it's time to talk about what we do with it and how we change it. We wouldn't be writing this book if we didn't believe that systems and cultures can change. It's going to be hard work, but all lasting change is, to quote Thomas Jefferson in *Hamilton* the musical..."let's go."

Section Four:

Solutions

We've just spent the last three sections of this book explaining that Americans (and much of the rest of the Western world) are living in a culture of burnout. Productivity is hailed as the ultimate measure of worth. Ill-health, trauma, and suffering are worthy punishments for the lazy or weak, and differences of all intersections are threatening, othering, and uncomfortable.

So, what do we do? This is the part of the book where we need to get countercultural: burnout is the culture we live in now, so to change that, we need to explore countercultural options. We need to talk about things that might make you feel uneasy at first, options that push boundaries and ask us to reframe our thinking about things that feel so fundamental to our humanity that it's totally out-there to ask for new perspectives.

This is hard to do. Never once in this book (we hope) have we ever suggested that this isn't really hard work, because it is. Changing your patterns of thinking and ways of seeing the world is not as simple as flipping a switch. It's contant work. It's work that will never be finished. It's a habit, a practice, a daily challenge for the individual, and as it builds, it becomes a movement that can truly shift the culture we live in.

We *can* move from a culture of burnout to a culture of balance.

We see these sorts of culture shifts all the time—it's not a wild proposal to make! Remember our discussion about wellness culture? Drinking herbal tea and doing yoga and practicing mindfulness used to be seen as countercultural, the purview of hippies and health nuts. Now, it's a multi-trillion dollar industry, and even your grandma is tracking her steps on her smartwatch. The good news is that cultures are not fixed. They change, they grow, they evolve all the time, and we have a history of making countercultural ideas part of the cultural norm.

What is a culture of balance?

Simply put, a culture of balance is one where societal supports, structures, and expectations all promote each individual's right to cultivate balance within their lives.

How do we get there?

We believe that while it's difficult, it's not complicated. There are four areas we can all shift perspectives and decisions towards to achieve a culture of balance instead of a culture of burnout. It's not an overnight change, but it can be a gradual shift. The more dedicated we are, however, the faster the change can happen. You can make changes in your individual life, in your relationships, and in the organizations you are a part of, and you can push for bigger, more systemic change, too. It can be better for us, even better for our kids, and significantly better for their kids.

First, we believe empathy is the core of all of this. Empathy is the skillset that allows us to ask more questions and make fewer assumptions. And, it's also, probably, not quite what you think it is (we'll get to that very soon).

Next up, we need to talk about interpersonal relationships and boundaries. What they are, why they're important—not just for the boundary-setter, but the boundary receivers as well—and how we create balanced environments where individuals' boundaries are respected.

After we clarify what boundaries are (and are not!), we want to give you some clear tools to use to understand what ones you may need. We call this rubric "The 4 Rs" and it's how we now think about the concept of "rest" beyond the conventional use of the word. It's more than sleeping, it's more than a bubble bath, it's more than a vacation. We're talking about deep, personalized, mental and physical shifts. Yes, rest *includes* sleep, but it's so much more than that.

We see Chapters 14-16 as the tools you will need to cultivate your own holistic well-being, which we will cover in Chapter 17. Your own well-being comes from your work through understanding empathy, setting and keeping boundaries, and finding your 4

R's. In contrast to the Wellness Industrial Complex, this section will also discuss how we can declaw the capitalist grip on our health and comfort.

With tools that support these four areas in our toolkits, we can promote thriving over coping and promote balance over burnout.

What is the difference between coping and thriving?

It's important to explore the difference between developing coping skills and restructuring a broken system. It's also deeply important to stress that *both of these things are part of the solution.* Our main purpose in writing this book is to take a step further out and look at burnout from a cultural perspective instead of focusing on the individual, but of course, it's individuals who make up our society and individuals who have the power to shape the path that cultural shifts take.

Most publicly accessible material on burnout focuses on the individual. It begins with what is burnout and what causes it and, then, how to fix it. But, the how to fix it sections tend towards what we would classify as coping skills and not as structural re-building.

Coping skills are techniques, practices, and activities that help us deal with a stressful situation or a stressor.

This can mean so many different things for different people and for different stressors they're facing. You've probably seen a hundred different things posted on social media under tags like #self-care, and it's true that a glass of wine, a good book, and a bubble bath are popular coping skills. But, there's a lot more tools in the toolbox for people to access.

For some people, coping skills look like counting to ten, squeezing a stress ball, taking a vacation, laughing with their best friend, writing fiction, going to the gym, painting landscapes, or growing flowers. They can also look like deep breathing techniques, supportive mantras, mindfulness practices, and self-talk that challenges irrational thinking cycles. Some coping skills are hobbies we love, some are practices that focus on physical well-being, and some are therapeutic strategies that are best learned with the help of a mental health care provider.

Coping skills assume that stress is part of life, which it is. You won't see us here arguing that a culture of balance means no one ever gets stressed at any point. We *all* need coping skills for stress because there will always be stressful things about being a human. But, the more intense and more constant and more *pointless* that stress becomes, the more difficult it becomes to maintain those healthy coping skills and the less they work.

Remember way back at the beginning when we talked about how burnout is the result of becoming stuck in a heightened stress state for so long that there's no fully coming back down? You pass that point on the Stress-O-Meter, and then, you live there. Coping skills can help you do two things. They can help you live in the world, and they can help you make the levels of stress something you can manage and survive. Oftentimes, you can't control the stressors, but you can cope with the impact they have on your life. They can also reduce those stress feelings, either in a moment of peak stress, or as an overall management technique. Will coping skills alone bring you back down past the threshold of burnout? It may be a wishy-washy answer but: it depends.

There's going to be a lot of wishy-washy answers in this section, actually, but for good reason. It simply varies too much from person-to-person, and the experiences of burnout cover a wide enough spectrum that it's hard to pin down exact answers. So, we'll say it like this: coping skills *can* reduce your stress enough that you're able to come back down out of a burnt out state, but it's certainly not a guarantee that they will on their own. And, if you're not able to address or reduce any of the actual stressors themselves, then there's a good chance the effectiveness of the coping skills will wane over time. Just like you're not supposed to be in a perpetual state of stress, it's also difficult to maintain a perpetual state of coping without hitting a wall.

With that in mind, we want to separate out thriving skills, *and* we want to highlight how a culture of balance both mitigates the need for coping skills as a way to deal with burnout and makes thriving skills something that's baked into our expectations of life in this country instead of something countercultural.

What are thriving skills, then?

Thriving skills are the things that we feel contribute to a life with less stress in it in the first place. It's like eating leafy greens to prevent feeling tired, or doing pilates to prevent getting sore from sitting all day. Or, getting vaccines to prevent serious infection.

Our working definition is thus: Thriving skills are preventative measures that frame the expectations we have for ourselves and that others have for us so we maintain lower baseline stress and drastically reduce the risk of burning out.

While a coping skill might be painting with watercolors, a thriving skill is the boundary setting required to make sure you have two hours every week, unbothered, to spend time painting.

We often entangle the things which help us deal with stress we experience and the things that help us prevent stress in the first place, but it's important to consider them separately and together. General stress is unavoidable, but particular stressors often are avoidable. While a car breakdown, or a scary storm blowing in, or a loved one getting sick are stressors we need to cope with, an uncomfortable work environment, lack of support from a partner at home, or a full-time job that doesn't pay a living wage are stressors we (we as a culture, though not always we as an individual) can reduce or even do away with entirely.

A culture of balance means everyone has access to a toolkit of both coping skills and thriving skills that work for them. It also means giving grace to others, both in understanding of their own personal needs when it comes to coping and thriving, and also prioritizing their humanity over their productivity.

Chapter 14: Empathy

When Kristen was in 10th grade, she read the most *incredible* book. To this day, when people ask her about books that she'd press into the hands of anyone, this one is always in the top five. She's read it dozens of times, seen the modern stage adaptation twice, and still gets goosebumps when she thinks about Gregory Peck in the movie.

The book is *To Kill a Mockingbird.*

The story is thus: 10-year-old Scout Finch is having a normal summer in her small Alabama town when her father, Atticus, changes that by taking on a Black man as a client. The Finches are White, and all of the powerful people in town are, as well. What follows is a meditation on otherness, community, and grace that makes the book a classic. At one point, Scout asks Atticus why he's okay being ostracized by the rest of the town for representing his client. He informs her that no one really knows anyone until they've walked around inside their skin for a little while.

This idea that you can't judge anyone until you walk around in their skin became foundational to how Kristen saw the world.

The adage is often misquoted, however, and people change Atticus' word "skin" to "shoes." Needing to walk around in someone else's shoes as a definition of empathy is plastered on motivational posters and bumper stickers alike.

But, somewhere in the last few years, she realized something was missing from both definitions. You can't really walk in anyone else's shoes—your feet aren't the same, your journey isn't the same, you won't see that path the same way they do. You *absolutely* cannot walk around in someone else's skin—you cannot inhabit their experiences with how their own body moves through the world. What we can do, instead, is seek to understand what the world looks like from their perspective and experiences.

That small change in perspective, that subtle twist, is all the difference. It's the shift between believing we can read someone's mind and know them fully and realizing that the best thing we can do is to ask more questions, make fewer assumptions, and try to understand their context and story.

So, Atticus was right...kind of. We offer this amendment to his dictum:

You can't truly know a person until you do everything you can to truly know a person—ask more questions, make fewer assumptions, and build empathy.

What is empathy, anyway?

When you hear the word empathy, you might think about your friend Carol who cries every time one of those Sarah McLachlan SPCA commercials comes on or, perhaps, about a therapist saying "I know how you feel." Maybe the first thing that comes to mind is Deanna Troi from *Star Trek:The Next Generation.* These are all reasonable associations, but we're going to spend some time breaking apart what our general understanding of empathy is and building back up into a new definition that, to us, suits our culture quite a bit better.

But, wait, isn't empathy about feeling other people's feelings?

No, actually.

A lot of definitions of empathy you'll find sound a lot like the one Roman Krznaric provides in his book, *Empathy*: "Empathy is the art of stepping imaginatively into the shoes of another person, understanding their feelings and perspectives, and using that understanding to guide your actions."[314] Sounds really good on the surface—imagination is a key to curiosity, which we know is a key to empathy and understanding is at the core of everything, but that pesky word "feelings" is the hangup here. Can we truly understand what anyone feels?

Most popular understandings of empathy make the core assumption that it is possible for one human being to know, beyond a shadow of a doubt, what another human is feeling.

We actually can't.

We're really, really good at guessing. There's a lot of research that investigates whether a human feels something they *perceive* another person to be feeling, which finds that, yes, we do! Christian Keysers, of the Netherlands Institute for Neuroscience in Amsterdam, studies our ability to mirror what we see—how watching others' experiences fires our own neurons:

> When we witness what happens to others, we don't just activate the visual cortex like we thought some decades ago. We also activate our own actions as if we'd be acting in similar ways. We activate our own emotions and sensations as if we felt the same.[315]

But, there's a critical part, here, that we always seem to leap right over when this science gets translated to our pop concept of empathy: "*as if we felt the same.*" We "activate our own actions as if *we'd* be acting in similar ways." This is absolutely key because we don't mirror the experiences we *know* to be happening to others, we mirror the experiences we *perceive* as happening to others.

And, there are so many things that affect the way two different people may experience the same thing. For example, when participants in a study were given placebo painkillers, they reported lower levels of pain when they received a shock than those who weren't given the placebo. Makes sense; placebos work!

But, then, those same participants watched someone else get shocked and were asked to rate the other person's pain. The participants who were given the placebo also rated the *other* person's pain as lower than those who hadn't. They perceived the pain they observed as less, because their own experience of pain was also less.[316]

Everything we experience as we grow and change and interact with the world also grows and changes the way we experience things to come. If even a placebo can alter someone's experience of pain, then think of the way chronic illness might change that, or a naturally high pain-tolerance. What about those who are caregivers to loved ones who they see in pain every day? It's our lived experiences, our culture, our families, our joys, and our sufferings, which give each person their own reactions to their experiences, our own feelings cocktail.

And, because of that, we fundamentally cannot *know* what another person is feeling.

What about empaths, then?

Empaths certainly are a thing in science fiction shows, but in real life…not so much. At least, not the way we tend to think about them.

As we've already covered, there is a vast difference between our perception of how someone else feels versus knowing how someone else feels. The studies we just discussed do make it clear that some people have more attentive "mirror neurons" (the parts of the brain that see the experience of another and reflect that same experience in ourselves), but that simply means they are more likely to have their own, personal response to someone else's experience rather than that they are actually able to read another person's feelings the way that Professor Xavier from *X-Men* reads minds.

What is possible, however, is that some people are much, much better at using pattern recognition to predict the behavior of people they spend a lot of time with. Some people are more observant, better at seeing repeating patterns, and better at de-centering their own experience to evaluate more accurately what someone else *might* be feeling.

In fact, there's research to prove that this happens frequently to survivors of elongated trauma, such as living with an abuser. In order to survive, that person becomes very attuned to the moods of others and tries to anticipate what's about to happen. It's still about perception and learned behavior, however.

This has a lot to do with the stories we tell ourselves. Join us on an imagination journey for a minute.

Let's say Amy's husband, Jake, frequently comes home drunk. When this happens, he often hits Amy. The story that she tells herself—based on a lot of credible evidence!—is that when Jake comes home drunk, she will get hit. Her body and brain will make decisions based on that story.

While Amy's brain does not know how Jake is *feeling*, it can make some educated guesses based on past experiences and the fact that those past experiences happened with enough frequency that Amy is highly sensitive to Jake's behavior. Amy picks up on more subtleties in Jake's expressions, movement, and speech patterns, and then, she uses those cues to survive.

We already discussed how trauma rewires the brain, and this is a perfect example, because the flipside to this hyper-attention to Jake's terrifying behavior is that it colors Amy's perception of others' feelings just as much as those who haven't lived through abuse and struggle to de-center themselves.

Amy starts to see threats in non-threatening behavior. She makes her own assumptions: that people she is vulnerable with will hurt her, or maybe that those who are inebriated are inherently dangerous. Her lived experience makes her very, very good at reading certain specific circumstances as a survival method.

In *Leaving Isn't the Hardest Thing*, Lauren Hough's searing memoir about living a life shaped by trauma, she explains how that played out for her:

> I grew into a person you see as empathetic. But it's not empathy. It's survival...I don't just memorize how you like your coffee. I memorize everything. I know how you like to be woken up in the morning. I know you're having a bad day before you do, and I've got a list of ways to fix it.[317]

So, while being an "empath" isn't truly possible, being a highly sensitive person *absolutely is*. And, not everyone gets here from a traumatic experience! Erin is naturally more sensitive to the vibes and energies of others than Kristen, who has trained herself to be aware of those things in order to be an effective communicator.

It's always important to remember, however, that even the most sensitive, in-tune person is still making nothing more than an educated guess about how another person feels. It's not something we can ever know for sure. Treating empathy as if it's something you're born with or not, a mystical skill that allows you to all but read others' minds, also pays a disservice to those highly sensitive people. Not only does it perpetuate the myth that empathy is about emotions, it expects them to *know* what other people are feeling all the time. That pressure can be exhausting, too.

I guess that means empathy doesn't really exist, then?

We said first we'd tear down the current cultural view of empathy, but then, we'd build it back up again. So, let the building commence. Here's our definition:

> Empathy is the consistent and intentional decision to choose understanding over assumptions towards yourself and other people.

In some ways, it's not that different to the meanings we just discussed. Empathy is about understanding, and it's about other people. It's about our interpersonal relationships. But, in other ways, this definition is the antithesis to previous notions of empathy. It is *not* about assumptions, which flies in the face of a lot of what has been said about empathy since it started being studied.

As soon as empathy becomes rooted in an assumption ("I see someone cry so they must be feeling sad, so I feel sad too"), it is, inherently, no longer about the other person. When we give weight to the idea that we can know what someone else's experience is, we erase their actual experience and color it over with assumptions.

How can we argue that being an empathetic person means relating to others better, forming stronger bonds, and being more sensitive to others' feelings, when the core concept is based around a confidence that everyone else's experiences and expressions of feeling would be a perfect reflection of your own?

Here, we can introduce the related, but not identical, concepts of sympathy and compassion. Again, there's no solid, understood, and accepted definition of either of these things, and honestly, it's not that important to have them. Instead, we'd like to divide up these concepts into three categories: feelings, understanding, and actions.

Feelings

Feelings can be activated by a lot of things. Sometimes, they can be activated by our own experiences and, sometimes, they can be activated by observing, imagining, or hearing about the experiences of others, whether real or fictional. We read stories and feel the joy of a first kiss or the fear of a haunting presence. We listen to our bestie gripe about their failing marriage and feel frustration on their behalf. This is the purview of the old definition of empathy that we've discarded. We're not saying these feelings are bad—they're an integral part of the human experience and an important way to connect with others—but there's a clear border they can't cross and that's within ourselves.

Our mirror neurons can only tell us what we might feel in a certain circumstance; we can only create feelings in ourselves that we have some basis for connecting to. Sympathy is a feeling. It's a feeling of sadness, pity, or reflective pain at the suffering or misfortune of others—we could say it is the opposite of Schadenfreude, really! But, remember, sympathy can lie to us about what others are experiencing, so we have to engage with it with caution, especially when it spurs us to action.

Understanding

Understanding is what we've been exploring in this chapter and the new way we want you to view empathy. It's a conscious effort to de-center your own experience and recenter someone else's. It's an acceptance that different people are different, that everyone is diverse, and that we cannot *know* what someone else is feeling. Understanding requires that we set our emotional responses aside and get curious about the emotional responses of other people. It requires engagement.

Action

Action is where compassion enters the chat. It's sometimes considered "empathy put into action," but that doesn't really work. It requires feelings to create action, and by now you can imagine how we're itchy at the idea of tying feelings to anything external. So we have to be careful to clarify *exactly* what we mean by empathy so that we can get to an actionable understanding of compassion.

We find that there are four major downsides to basing action on feelings alone:

1. It becomes too easy to overwhelm our capacity for emotional processing when compassion relies on first having an emotional response to a situation,
2. It excuses a lack of action from those who do not or cannot summon an emotional response to a situation,
3. It ties the emotional response itself to the act of compassion and erodes the need for actual action, and
4. As we've just established, our feelings can lie to us about the best actions to take because they can lie to us about what the other person is feeling or needs.

When empathy is a matter of understanding and not of feelings, compassion *can* be empathy put into action in a way that does make sense. We simply have to center understanding as a key part of the definition.

Sympathy becomes optional—it's an emotional response that's out of your control and one that you may or may not experience in a given circumstance. We don't need to put moral weight on sympathy.

Empathy is the active practice of cultivating understanding. And, compassion is taking developed empathy and turning it into action designed to help others and make your workplace, neighborhood, community, country, or planet a better place to live.

When Our Grandmothers Died

To illustrate the failings of empathy as an "I know how you feel" situation, let us share our two very different experiences of the loss of our grandmothers:

Kristen: My paternal grandmother passed in August of 2016 after a lengthy time living with dementia. We called her Bedste, a derivative of the Danish word for grandmother, and she was a central figure in my life until her death. She was the first person to take me to Broadway, igniting my love of theater and my deep belief that Andrew Lloyd Webber's musicals were not for me. I stayed at her house in North Jersey for weeks in the summer—playing in her backyard pool, taking trips to the library for reading material, eating frikadelle (basically, Danish meatballs which are *life changing*), learning old hymns that she taught me as we drove around in her boat of a car.

She was a complicated person, as we all are, so my memories are not entirely rosy. She was a person with her own baggage and inflicted harm, as we all do, but I know in my soul that she loved me. Her death was a slow process—we knew it was coming for the simple fact that she was less and less herself as years went on. The last time I felt like I had her with me entirely was my wedding in February 2014. That didn't mean that when she breathed her last breath it wasn't painful.

While the grief was not all consuming as it might have been without so much warning, it still left a hole in our family. When my brother got married in 2018, and his first child was born in 2020, I remember thinking how much Bedste would have delighted over those events.

My maternal grandmother, who we called Nanny, died in March 2018, and her death was just as devastating as Bedste's. I was *incredibly* lucky to have two grandmothers who I know loved me and who were present in my life and who pepper all of my childhood, adolescent, and early adulthood memories. That's not the case for Erin.

Erin: My father's mother died in January 2014, a year and a half before Kristen's Bedste. I had a very different connection with her as a grandmother. I did not have a relationship with her at all as an adult and had a complicated and fractious one with her as a child. Part of that is because of her relationship with my Dad, which was also complicated and fractious, and her relationship with my Mom, especially after my parent's divorce when I was six. Because of these relationships, stories, and memories, I did not have a particularly emotional reaction to my grandmother's death.

I was living in Belfast at the time and that distance made her passing even more remote. I didn't tell a lot of people that she had died, but I did tell Kristen. She knew a lot about our relationship already, and so she knew to let me process it in my own way, without any of the pressures of what "appropriate" grief was supposed to look like. When her Bedste died 18 months later, I knew that even though we had both recently lost our paternal grandmothers, we did not have comparable experiences or emotions. So, I did not try to placate Kristen by expressing how I understood her feelings, or telling her about my own experiences with the hopes that it would help her grief. I don't remember what I said to her specifically, but I can guarantee you I didn't say, "I know how you feel."

We've often talked and taught how this phrase is one of the most damaging when it comes to attempting to practice empathy. If I said that to Kristen, or her to me, it would have been a lie. Though we had the same thing happen to us — the death of a grandmother — our relationships with that person, with our family, with any form of faith or belief system, our lived experiences and worldviews all meant that we had radically different experiences with their deaths.

We know the phrase comes from a place of genuine concern and desire to connect with others, but we know from our experience that it was the last thing either of us wanted to hear. Empathy is

> not about knowing what another person is feeling, or sharing the same emotional response as them. We argue all the time that that's not really possible. If we hardly know what we're feeling most of the time, how is someone else supposed to? Instead, empathy is about asking questions and listening. Empathy is about understanding. When we get to that place of understanding, when we see that person for their whole self and see what they need in that moment from us, then we can be truly present and supportive.

Once you have this new view of empathy, you start to see the way it applies everywhere you look. If we show you footage of two people on a couch watching a scary movie, both tense, a hand over their mouth, eyes wide, can you tell which one loves scary movies and which one doesn't? Both may be experiencing manufactured terror, but only one is enjoying it! If you're someone who loves watching scary movies, then those mirror neurons we talked about will light up all the parts of your brain that have a good time while being spooked right out of your seat, and you might assume that both people are also having a good time.

But, what if that footage, instead, made you curious? To us, empathy means instead of thinking, "watching that scary movie looks fun," we ask, "I wonder if those people are enjoying watching that scary movie as much as I would?"

The hard part, here, is that assumptions are easy. They are internal, immediate, and instinctual. It is built innately in us to make rapid-fire assumptions. Curiosity is harder.[318] Seeking understanding is even harder. It involves truly connecting with others, not just imagining a connection. It means pushing your own boundaries by seeking to understand experiences and emotional reactions that are vastly different from your own. It means de-centering yourself, which takes constant work to do.

Does that mean I can learn how to have empathy?

Yes. In fact, we argue that empathy is a mandatory requirement for being human, and it's critical to developing more compassionate workplaces and organizations. Deanna Troi's powers as a being that could sense others' emotions were because she was a half-Betazoid alien, but actual empathy is a skill we can learn, develop, and grow just like any other skill. It's a skill that will improve relationships in all areas of your life.

Roman Krznaric proposed six habits of highly empathetic people,[319] and while we like some of his perspective, it's not without issue. So, here, instead, is what we've discovered through years of training and research on empathy to be the five habits of highly empathetic people:

1. *Get Curious*
Instead of making assumptions, ask questions. When a question pops into your brain and you don't know the answer, see if you can find the answer or find someone who knows the answer. If someone does or says something you don't understand, instead of assuming you know why, ask questions. Try asking open-ended questions that give other people a chance to expand and explain, and really, actively listen instead of waiting for your turn to talk.

2. *Consume More Stories*
Studies show that we all learn more and are more likely to have our perspectives shifted by stories rather than by stats or lists of facts.[320] Read memoirs, watch documentaries, listen to podcasts about people or groups of people you don't normally consume media from. If you find your fiction reading is in a rut, then try an author from another country. Even stories that aren't explicitly about others' lives (like memoirs) still expose you to different lived experiences. Don't be afraid of subtitles!

3. *Push Your Social Media Out of Your Comfort Zone*
Another way to consume more lived experiences is to have a look at your social media feed with a critical lens. Think about our section on intersectionality and diversity. How

many different types of people in how many different ways do you follow? And, we're not saying you have to seek out Twitter activists and sign up for newsletters about protest groups (though, if you want to, by all means). This is more about getting a peek at lived experiences that are different from yours. So, maybe, if you're into BookTok, then find an Indigenous author to follow. Or, if recipes on Instagram are your thing, then try a few from a country you struggle to point to on a map. Expand the way you think about social media and find some people in your areas of interest who have different lives.

4. *Seek Understanding Instead of Condoning*

There's often a gut instinct response to behavior or words we find personally reprehensible; we can't condone the behavior so we disconnect entirely from the person as a person. We back out of empathy and even demonize or other the person in question because it feels safer to exclude people who horrify us from being human. But, engaging in empathy with people we disagree with—even deeply, deeply disagree with: 1) is good empathy practice and 2) does not mean we have to condone their behavior. We can explore understanding someone else's position, lived experience, and perspective without needing to agree with their opinions or support their choices. Empathy means taking the time to acknowledge that different people are different and all people are *people*. It means making space in your mind to explore other ways of seeing the world.

5. *Look Inside As Well As Outside*

Having empathy for others isn't the only important thing—so is having empathy for yourself! You are a person with needs and experiences, maybe traumas, maybe fears. Your lived experiences change you and will continue to change you, and you are diverse in your own ways. Taking time to reflect on the stories you tell yourself about yourself is just as important as taking time to examine your gut instinct responses to others. Look not only at the depth of your empathy practice but at the scope. Are you getting curious about yourself? Your neighbors? Your co-workers? Other countries, cultures, and people groups? What about history?

Considering these five things as you navigate the world and your relationships can help you start shifting your perspective to one of default empathy. No one is perfect. Empathy will always be something to strive for more of, not something to finish or check-off. Making it an active choice to engage with is the most important step, and the more you practice it, the easier it becomes.

Is it possible to have too much empathy?

Treating empathy as an intellectual exercise instead of an innate skill or an emotional experience opens up a lot of doors. It allows for those who are short on natural intuition about others to develop it with practice. But, it also gives forgiveness and space for needing to distance your personal emotional processing from the understanding that others are suffering. We already talked about how empathy can be the fuel that drives compassionate action, and that's even easier when empathy doesn't require an emotional response.

You might remember our brief mention of compassion fatigue way up in the soup section when we were talking about the 24-hour news cycle, and we'd like to expand on that a little bit now.

What we've been calling compassion fatigue, like burnout, is an exhaustion of our ability to maintain a peak or heightened emotional response for an extended period of time. So, just like we broke things down above, let's use feelings, understanding, and action as the framework to reconsider compassion fatigue.

First of all, with our new definition of empathy, it's impossible to experience "empathy fatigue." Cultivating understanding is certainly hard work, but by disconnecting it from the emotional response and from the stress cycle, it no longer needs to push us up towards the burnout point or stretch us so thin that it becomes no longer possible. Sure, some days we might be too irritated or too tired or too frustrated to truly dig in to practicing empathy, but just like the days we miss our Duolingo practice, it's a streak we can pick up again tomorrow. Empathy does not need to lead to emotional exhaustion, because it does not require emotion.

Feelings, however, *can* push us into emotional exhaustion, and when we blend the concepts of sympathy and compassion together too much or when we operate on the belief that an emotional response is required in order to push us into compassionate action, we can absolutely exhaust ourselves. This is no better illustrated than with Americans' constant inundation with horrible, heartbreaking news stories.

Almost every article that references compassion fatigue uses Susan Sontag's 2003 quip from her short book *Regarding the Pain of Others*, where she argues that "flooded with images of the sort that once used to shock and arouse indignation, we are losing our capacity to react. Compassion, stretched to its limits, is going numb."[321]

The structure of a capitalist media is one that turns emotional responses into money. Emotional responses are what have you staying on one channel, even through commercial breaks.[322] They are what lead you to clicking on certain links over others or doomscrolling hours of your life away. When creating emotional responses equals money for companies that produce media, it doesn't matter if those responses are healthy for you or not. They're going to keep doing it, just like all the WIC ventures that make money off our ongoing discontent.

And, part of why this is such an easy area of our brains to exploit is because sympathy, empathy, and compassion are all tied to being a good person in our culture! It feels, deeply, like this kind of engagement is not just good, but also good for you. Virtuous people stay in the know. Kind people are concerned about others. These things are true, yes, but then, we make the leap to: a good, kind, virtuous person needs to know *everything* and needs to *feel* everything, too. Good people are also healthy, happy people, and that's all tied up in the Wellness Industrial Complex as well.

But, if compassionate action is a response to understanding instead of a response to feelings, then we can make choices such as where to donate our money and time, which causes to contact our representatives about, and who to vote for to create change *without an emotional response.*

Now, of course, most of the time we can't control our emotional responses. If you read a story about another school shooting and that causes you emotional pain, then that's normal and part of the way we connect to other humans. But, if that emotional pain is starting to turn into emotional exhaustion, then it's not serving you anymore. One of our body's self-protective measures is dulling or disengaging our emotional responses when they become too overwhelming to handle, and that can feel like running out of empathy and giving in to apathy instead:

> Most of the time, outrage itself feels largely useless. Stay mad, social media activists like to say. How hard is it to stay mad, I remember thinking last year—just watch 20 seconds of any news clip. But it did, in fact, get hard to stay mad. The news is still horrifying, at home and around the world; I know this intellectually, but the physical feeling of horror is gone.[323]

So, what if we stop making staying mad a requirement?

You can be informed without needing to be up-to-the-minute, from first opening your eyes in the morning to closing them again at night. Action can be driven by empathy instead of pain. Part of that empathy is an understanding that all of us—and self-empathy is critical here too—have limited resources, and what makes a successful community is everyone pitching in how and where they can. A culture of burnout means those resources get used up until there's nothing left. A culture of balance means those resources remain available and get replenished for the good of all who use them, like a perennial berry bush that fruits again each year.

So, can you have too much empathy? No, you really can't. But, that doesn't mean that caring can't be emotionally exhausting. Studies about compassion fatigue and burnout have been intertwined since the 90s. Carla Joinson identified among nurses "a unique form of burnout that affects people in the caregiving profession" that presented as a self-protective detachment from those they were caring for.[324]

Instead of looking for solutions to this problem, our current cultural approach seems hell-bent on making it worse. Social media demands emotional engagement, outrage—staying mad. Often, it values those feelings over actual action. Remember how Kristen calls phones "anger machines?" It's because most of what is fed to us through news alerts and social media is designed to make someone else money on our outrage. They can't make money on our actions, but they can on our outrage.

Besides, how do we even measure actual action? Can we possibly quantify help, support, compassion? We'd argue, no. But, a culture of accomplishment and productivity demands qualitative accountability. Helping your neighbor bring in their groceries isn't enough. No one's really sure what enough is, just that no one's doing it. The inundation of pain and suffering that we're exposed to, be it as a caregiver or as a social media activist, means nothing ever feels like enough because the amount of pain in the world never seems to go down.

The story we tell ourselves about these matters is that our participation in the world is measured by the times we post about Current Affairs on social media. Or, the number of dollars we've donated to certain causes. Or, the amount of hours we've spent volunteering, or watching documentaries, or, or, or. Are some of those good and useful and measurable ways to impact the state of the world? Absolutely! Are some of them performances driven by the anger machines? Yes.

This is only going to improve with a complete re-framing of what we expect from compassion and a new allowance for the self-protective measures that keep us from emotional exhaustion. Burnout care has to go beyond time off work and allow for time off from all emotional responses.

So, what's the take-away here?

When we first started writing this book, the one thing we knew we wanted it to talk about was empathy. Empathy is the core to everything we believe about how to human better, and that belief comes from over two decades of studying both people and organizations, and exploring the concept of empathy.

Empathy matters because it is the sun around which the solar system of relating to others revolves, and it's important to understand that empathy is a skill you can develop and not an innate superpower a select few have because empathy always asks: how can we ask more questions and how can we make fewer assumptions?

This is especially critical in a conversation about burnout, because as we explored in the last section, burnout changes the way you process *everything* that happens to you. When you're caught in a stress cycle that deep and that intense, you are *always* being chased by an invisible lion that others around you cannot see.

When a lion bursts into an office building, no one will harshly judge or be critical of their fellow employees screaming and running and throwing their staplers in their air. But, what if only one person could see the lion? Their reaction would seem completely out of place to their coworkers, an inexplicable outburst.

Burnout is that invisible persistence hunter, constantly tracking you, stalking you, and haunting you with the feeling that there is no such thing as rest, no opportunity for a break, no room even to breathe.

Some of us might give up and stop running, some might burst into tears, some might disconnect from reality entirely, and from the outside, from someone who can't see the threat of the lion at all, these reactions all seem odd and unnecessary. But, no one *wants* to be the person sitting on the sidelines, eating an ice cream, looking out at someone being hunted down and thinking, "Wow that person sure seems upset about nothing—it's a beautiful day in the jungle!"

Empathy is what lets us take:

> *This is not the reaction I would have in this situation. That person must be crazy/stupid/messed up/incompetent/ evil etc.*

And, turns it into:

> *This is not the reaction I would have in this situation. I should find out why it's theirs.*

As Patricia Moore says:

> Empathy is a constant awareness of the fact that your concerns are not everyone's concerns and that your needs are not everyone's needs, and that some compromise can be achieved moment by moment. I don't think empathy is charity, I don't think empathy is self-sacrifice, I don't

think empathy is prescriptive. I think empathy is an ever-evolving way of living as fully as possible, because it's pushing your envelope and pushing you into new experiences that you might not expect or appreciate until you're given the opportunity.[325]

We love the description of empathy as "an ever-evolving way of living as fully as possible" because that is our journey with redefining and recategorizing empathy. Empathy gives us the skills to see the whole picture—of ourselves and others. Empathy gives us the skills to question the stories we're told and the stories we tell ourselves and consider a different way of seeing, thinking, or living.

Practicing Empathy with Some 1990s Celebrity Women

One of the best ways to practice empathy is to listen to stories from people whose lived experiences are different from yours. We had this experience with four relatively recent documentaries: *"This is Paris," "Framing Britney Spears," "Miss Americana,"* and *"Pamela, A Love Story."*

Paris Hilton, Britney Spears, Taylor Swift, and Pamela Anderson—four women whose lives were shaped by fame at a young age and who had their personal and private lives splashed across tabloids, news media, and social media platforms for all to judge. For both of us, we had already decided who these women were and what we thought of them a long time ago. These films demanded that we form a new perspective.

It can be very confronting to realize that the way you perceive someone else was, first of all, not an opinion you truly formed yourself but one fed to you by the media you consumed, and, second of all, deeply unfair. It's easy to become defensive when that happens. Hearing these women tell their stories of exploitation, abuse, suffering, and then the added pain of the public perspective that they were deserving of all that because they were young, female, attractive, and talented is painful, and sometimes even difficult to accept.

These four films underscore the importance of asking more questions and making fewer assumptions. For both of us, we had to re-examine the assumptions we'd been handed and internalized, the SNL skits we'd laughed at, and the way we'd rolled our eyes when the seemingly rich and privileged were presented as whining about minor problems.

It's also important to have the reminder that these stories are not emblematic of outliers or anyone who fell through the cracks: *the system is designed to work this way*.

Our culture is built on an understanding that young women are to be exploited and that slut-shaming is an adequate defense against a woman who stands up for herself after suffering abuse. It's a difficult, painful thing to confront, not just that we are living in that system but that we have contributed to it.

But we didn't know these stories until these women felt empowered enough to share them with us, so many years later. It doesn't help that part of the messaging to consumers during the early years of fame for these women was that we *did* know these stories. Tabloids, entertainment news, talk shows, and now social media, encourage parasocial relationships that convince fans they're in the know and have a true connection with a celebrity. That makes it all the harder to confront the fact that these stories were biased, twisted, and designed primarily to make money for people who were largely unconnected to any of the celebrities they were discussing.

> We're grateful that all four of these women are sharing their stories and being supported in seeking new understanding from a public who was all too happy to provide mocking and revel in Schadenfreude when that was the message we were offered.
>
> What makes these documentaries a great empathy exercise — even if you didn't follow these stories or celebrities in the early years — is the reminder that we don't know what's truly going on in someone else's life and accepting the damage that making assumptions has done in the past and will continue to do if we don't make developing empathy a cultural priority.

We cannot move away from our culture of burnout and towards a culture of balance without practicing as much empathy as possible. We've given you all the stats to show how many Americans are suffering from burnout now and how many cultural barriers are blocking the way to real and lasting healing.

It may seem silly to talk about 1990s pop princesses in our empathy exercise, but if you take the time to watch those documentaries, then you will see how our culture of burnout was a huge factor in the lives and careers of these women.

We don't know what's going on in other people's lives. We don't know the individual and cultural challenges they are facing day-to-day. And, people don't know what we're going through, either. But, we do always have the power to get curious and to ask.

The next tool in our solutions toolbox is a natural transition from empathy. Empathy gives us the tools to understand ourselves so that we can evaluate our boundaries and how we do and don't use them. It also gives us the tools to understand the boundaries that others set, which goes a long way in building trust, managing relationships, and moving closer toward that lovely sounding culture of balance.

Chapter 15: Setting (and Keeping) Boundaries That Work

One of the most common pieces of advice handed out to those suffering from burnout is "you need to set more boundaries" or "you need better boundaries." But what does that actually *mean*?

And, once we know what it means, is it fair? Is setting boundaries the key to freeing yourself from your own burnout? And then, since, again, we're looking at this from a cultural perspective, how does that apply to a whole society that is burning out?

That's what we're going to explore in this chapter.

What are boundaries?

First off, let's dispel a myth about what boundary setting is and what it can't be. Boundary setting is *not* dictating what another person's behavior will or won't be, may or may not be. It *is* deciding what your response will be, given a certain circumstance.

Our definitions of boundaries is that they are the lines you define for what your behavior will be in response to someone else's words or actions.

Boundaries can be communicated in advance, but they don't have to be in order to be enforced. A boundary only controls you, yourself; you cannot control what other people choose to do. You can, however, inform people what your response will be to certain behavior, so they can choose their own actions accordingly.

Let's look at some examples.

Jamira is on a first date with a guy she met on an app. One boundary that she communicated ahead of time was that she will only meet for a first date in a public place. Her date, Seamus, respected that boundary and they agreed to meet at a bar for drinks and snacks.

Unfortunately, Seamus turned out to not be a very nice person. After he makes a rude comment about her appearance, Jamira decides to pay for her own drink and leave the bar. She blocks Seamus' number and deletes him from the app

Jamira can't control the fact that Seamus is a jerk, but she did establish and hold to her personal boundaries. Meeting in a public place was a boundary she communicated, and not staying in the bar to be insulted was one she hadn't communicated. She made choices about her own behavior based on her boundaries. If Seamus had pressed to meet at his place, despite enjoying their chats on the app, then she would have declined the date.

Daniel and Mark have just brought their brand new baby girl home from the hospital. The circumstances of her birth mean that her immune system is slightly compromised. They inform their close friends and family that visitors will be allowed after two weeks, but everyone must wear a mask in their house at all times to ensure their daughter's safety.

Daniel's sister-in-law, Jennifer, arrives at the house six days later, with no mask, and Daniel informs her she will not be allowed in or be able to see the baby except through the window. Despite her throwing a temper tantrum right there on the porch, Daniel will not let his sister-in-law inside.

Even though Daniel has no control over Jennifer's behavior—he cannot stop her from showing up at the house, nor can he stop her from throwing a temper tantrum—he can control who is and isn't allowed inside to spend time with his baby.

> Aracelli has been offered a new job and they are reviewing the proposed contract. In one section, their new workplace specifies that employees in this department are expected to have their phones on them between 6am and 9pm, even though paid working hours are between 9am and 5pm. At the next meeting, Aracelli explains that they are only willing to take on the extra on-call hours if their annual salary is bumped up by 5k.

Aracelli explained to the new company what their boundaries around extra hours are—in order to work more, they must be paid more. It's crucial to remember that this does not pass judgment on the company's choices. The company made it clear in the contract what the expectations for employees are, and Aracelli made it clear what their expectations are for compensation. If the company accepts the pay increase, then Aracelli may take the job. If the company does not, then Aracelli has set a boundary that they won't work those hours at that pay and, therefore, won't accept the position.

Boundaries are sometimes invisible, sometimes blatant. Every one we set has both benefits and consequences, and we all have them. Even if you've never considered that you have boundaries, you do. It's part of how we negotiate interpersonal relationships.

Can boundaries be flexible?

Yes. Look, this is something that most self-help and therapy-guiding books and workbooks don't want to get into too much. If you're someone who already struggles with setting and holding boundaries, then it can be helpful to think of them as immutable, impenetrable stone walls. But, in actuality, for most people, the boundaries we set with family, friends, and workplaces have quite a lot of flexibility, and more negotiation goes into them than we might think.

Let's explore the three main layers of boundaries.

Cultural Boundaries: these are the boundaries our culture has decided for us. They are the types of things where, if crossed, they can violate not only criminal and civil law but also the things which simply break "social law." They tend to be unspoken, except when they're being taught to children or debated politically. These are things we can assume in our interactions with others. Some will be specific to broader cultures, and some will be specific to small subsets of a cultural community. Some examples of cultural boundaries in the US are:

- Do not touch strangers intimately without their consent.
- Do not take things that don't belong to you.
- Certain topics are not appropriate to discuss in certain contexts, like telling your boss's boss about your foot rash.

Relationship Boundaries: these are the boundaries you discuss, negotiate, and manage with the people you maintain relationships of any kind with. These sorts of boundaries are usually best communicated very explicitly, and often morph and change as relationships grow and develop. Some examples of relationship boundaries are:

- I will not answer my phone after midnight. My friend Bernice knows if there is an emergency to text me first so I know to answer.
- I will only stay over at my boyfriend's house on weekends since I need to be up early for work, and he sleeps later.
- I will only visit my cousin Nestor if he has his dog on a leash as I'm quite fearful of her.
- My friend group always splits brunch bills evenly, and therefore, no one orders anything unusually expensive. If someone were to do so, I would ask them to cover the cost of the item separately.

Personal Boundaries: these are the boundaries that are core to who you are and do not tend to change much depending on who you're with. Often, very close personal, familial, or romantic relationships may have differing boundaries, but everyone has some hard lines that are unwavering for them. These boundaries are sometimes best communicated in advance, sometimes communicated in the moment, and sometimes not communicated at all. Some examples of personal boundaries are:

- I will not discuss my health or my body with strangers. If a stranger pushes the topic, I will exit the conversation.
- I do not go on blind dates, unless we have at least chatted online or spoken on the phone in advance.
- I do not eat fish or seafood of any kind.

The critical differences among these types of boundaries are the way they are negotiated with others. Cultural boundaries can shift and change, but that change comes with a cultural shift. It used to be considered inappropriate, or downright illegal, for women to show their legs in public and now, in most parts of the country, it's considered perfectly normal.

Cultural boundaries *should* shift and change. They reflect what our society thinks is important and worth protecting. Those who have had their rights denied can fight to push those cultural boundaries to be more inclusive, and those with privilege should be pushing right alongside them. Cultural shift can be slow, but it is also inevitable.

Relationship boundaries are likely the most complex to understand because there can be an enormous sea of nuance involved there. Negotiation is a key part of managing relationship boundaries.

Looking back at one of our examples, we can consider not answering the phone after midnight. This seems like an understandable boundary to have, especially if you frequently receive calls after midnight that are not emergencies but would impact your sleep anyway.

Imagine you work for an international company that has failed to recognize the breadth of timezones covered by their employees. Instead of checking to see where a colleague is located, workers will simply call at all hours and leave a message if no one answers. Because of the frequency of these calls, you set a boundary that you will not answer your phone after midnight, and you turn off your phone at night to prevent being disturbed.

However, you have one friend who is upset by this change. Bernice is the primary caregiver for her grandmother, whom she lives with, and she also has a medical condition of her own that makes her chances of needing to be temporarily hospitalized higher than average. You have volunteered to go and to stay with Bernice's grandmother if this happens, but she's concerned that by turning off your phone overnight, you will be unreachable in case of emergency.

So, you negotiate this boundary with Bernice. Your phone has a do not disturb setting that allows for certain contacts to be let through even when the ringer is off. You arrange it so that calls and texts from Bernice will go through no matter what time it is while everything else will be blocked. She knows to text you that it is an emergency, first, to wake you and then, to call. You know that if you see a text from Bernice after midnight, it's an emergency and you need to respond.

This arrangement might not be how everyone would handle this situation. Perhaps it's not how you would manage it at all. But, it's an example of a way that interpersonal boundaries can be: 1) person dependent, 2) flexible depending on context, and 3) negotiated when they cause conflict or concern with another person.

Let's also not let the example of burnout culture fly by! A company that doesn't enforce non-working time and expects employees to be available outside of their paid hours is contributing to a culture of burnout. International companies with teams operating in different timezones need to think harder about how to manage working hours than small, local teams, and the boundary set in this instance is one designed to protect you from work infiltrating personal time.

You can already see how setting boundaries can help prevent and recover from burnout, but also why we're stressing the importance of cultural shift. The company created the problem, your boundaries are a Band-Aid that might not be accessible to every employee.

What's the difference between boundaries, expectations, and consequences?

Boundaries, as we've discussed, are the choices you make for your own behavior in a given circumstance. Expectations are what we assume or hope other people will do in a given circumstance. Consequences are the results of the behavior we, or they, choose.

It's important to consider and to understand all these concepts holistically—the way they interact and how key each aspect is to managing interpersonal relationships. We can have expectations of another person that are either communicated explicitly, implied, or not communicated at all. If the other person does not meet those expectations, then we consider how that interacts with our boundaries and what the consequences will be.

People are not mind readers! Remember everything we talked about in the empathy section? This is a place where it is absolutely critical to employ those empathy skills. Both parties have boundaries and expectations, and consequences can come from either side.

> Andie manages a team of four at a small marketing firm. She expects her team to all be at their desks and working every day by 9am. One of her newest team members, Lena, doesn't show up until 10am most days.

Consider this situation. Your gut instinct may be that the employee should be written up for being late; however, while Andie's expectations may be that her whole team arrives by nine, what are Lena's expectations? Perhaps the employment contract stipulates that core hours for the company are 10-4, and otherwise flexible. Did Andie indicate during the interview process or during training that she has differing expectations for her team? Does HR allow for individual teams to reject core hours?

Lena can't read Andie's mind and know what the expectations for her are, so consequences such as being written up might come as a shock. The consequence for Andie, then, of having un- or under-communicated expectations is that Lena will lose trust and respect for her boss and may begin looking for alternative employment.

There are times when it's difficult to think about consequences logically and judge what's appropriate. When we are hurt or surprised or scared, we may lash out or cut someone off abruptly and later regret the choice. There are also times when we feel someone else has overreacted and the consequences we received are harsher than is deserved.

The keys to managing boundaries, setting expectations, and evaluating consequences are empathy and self-awareness. We need to be intentional about these things, partially so we can make rational, appropriate decisions in times of stress, and also, so we can recognize that the people we have relationships with cannot read our minds and will not always assume or guess accurately what our boundaries are. Cultivating healthy relationships also involves some flexibility, some willingness to negotiate and make exceptions for people you love and people you need to work with.

When is negotiation not the right answer?

As we mentioned above, negotiation is not a word most self-help books like to use when it comes to boundaries. But, you can recognize when negotiation is serving both parties and when it is not. At its core, negotiation requires that both parties are at the negotiating table in good faith.

Good faith looks like both parties being willing to bend on something. It doesn't have to be everything, and it doesn't have to be all the way. But, if neither party is willing to bend at all, then negotiation is not possible. That's not to say that it's bad or wrong to be unwilling to bend. You can refuse to negotiate and so can the other party. You can also come to the negotiation table with a willingness to bend but be unable to come to a satisfactory compromise. But, if you claim a willingness to negotiate without any intention to allow yourself to bend, then that's not negotiating in good faith.

There are also circumstances and boundaries that we'd argue it's not healthy or helpful to negotiate. You *should* have uncrossable lines about the ways you are comfortable being touched and not touched by strangers. There are things a partner or parent might say to you that are non-negotiable. These are decisions each person has to make for themselves, sometimes even with the help of a therapist.

What does "having your boundaries violated" mean?

It's gotten messy, we can't lie. Most people use the phrase to mean when a boundary line you have set is crossed. For some, it's limited to boundaries that have been communicated and even repeated. For others, any time a behavior crosses the boundary, it's been violated. There's a lot of emotional weight on that word, however, and it carries an implication of maliciousness or desire to cause harm from the other party.

It's important to remember that what may feel like a violation to you may not have been intended to be so by the other person. That doesn't mean you shouldn't enact your consequences or that you don't have the right to be hurt, but we need to maintain empathy even for people who are crossing our boundaries. They are a person, too, with their own wants and needs, and just because someone else's actions are hurtful doesn't mean we can assume the motivations behind those actions.

What do you do if someone crosses your boundaries?

That means it's time to enact the consequences you previously decided on. A boundary can usually be stated as an *if...then* statement. If my aunt brings up my grades at this party, then I will go talk to someone else.

So, your aunt brings up your grades at the party, and you excuse yourself from the conversation and go talk to someone else.

You set a boundary. The line was crossed by your aunt's behavior. So, you enacted the consequence of exiting the conversation.

Sometimes, what plays out is more like a bad faith negotiation. Someone tries to press against one of your boundary lines, hoping they can shift it, bit by bit, until it makes space for what they want instead of what you want.

We can go back to our list of examples of personal boundaries to show how this happens. Perhaps you have a personal boundary where you don't eat seafood. It's not an allergy or intolerance, but it's an intense dislike. Perhaps the last time you tried seafood you were very ill with food poisoning, which created a trauma response, or perhaps it simply repulsed you. Either way, it's your decision to cut those foods out of your diet.

A therapist or doctor might press against this boundary in a healthy way, in a space where you've established that you are open to having this boundary pressed. This is a good faith negotiation. If your aversion to seafood is born out of trauma, then a medical professional might feel it would be a good idea to explore exposure therapy to help you recover from the fear that prevents you from eating foods you like, but the recovery has to start with your desire for therapy.

If someone else, however—a friend, a date, a family member—pushes on your boundary in a way you haven't welcomed, then this is not a good faith negotiation. "Just try a little bit," "How about white fish?" "What if it's covered in sauce?" Maybe you cave, eventually, maybe you don't. Either way, these repeated nudges of your boundary line—especially when you have clearly communicated both your boundary and the consequences—can be exhausting.

The more frequently your aunt asks about your grades, it is likely the more hurt you will become. Perhaps, if it continues to escalate, then you'll choose to end the relationship. But, that wouldn't be true, necessarily, for someone else. A friend in the same situation may laugh it off. They may retain a relationship with their aunt, but simply end the conversation every time their grades come up. And, that works fine for them.

It can be really hard to separate out the reasons why our boundaries protect us, which also makes it hard to evaluate what's an "appropriate" way to feel or to act when a boundary line is crossed. Boundaries born out of resentment or vindictiveness may not serve us very well. Boundaries born out of fear may be so restrictive they're causing us pain in new ways. Some boundaries may seem extreme to others, but keep us alive.

It's not fair for us to say what would and wouldn't be an overreaction to someone crossing someone else's boundaries, but it is important to remember the empathy concepts we just discussed.

In every interaction, the other person is a person, too. They have their own boundaries and will enact their own consequences. They have their own fears, traumas, and generational perspectives. Your desires and your boundaries do not automatically trump the other person's simply because they're yours, and *yes*, that can cause conflict!

That's why it's so important to remember that boundary setting is about dictating your own behavior and not the other person's. Because, sometimes, your boundaries will be in conflict—it will not be possible for both parties' boundaries to be fully respected—and in these cases, the only possible outcomes are continued conflict (which we hope everyone reading this wants to avoid!), negotiation (which, don't forget, involves bending on both sides), or a parting of the ways, whether that means a break-up, a resignation, or an unfollowing on social media.

Speaking of social media...the internet has a complex relationship with boundaries!

How does social media stop us from setting boundaries?

First off, let's start with the fact that the average smartphone user checks their phone over 150 times a day.[326] It would be pretty hard to set any form of boundary when we're on our phones, using our apps, and managing our online relationships and interactions that many times a day.

Before we talk about how you set boundaries online, we want to spend a few words explaining *why* you need to set boundaries online. When we talk to people about the impact that social media and smartphones have on our brains and bodies, we find a lot of people don't even understand how these apps and platforms work.

A quick Google search will give you thousands of results on whether social media and smartphones are good or bad for us and our mental health. It's been an ongoing debate for years, mostly because there's a big information gap between the people who designed the software and the people who use it.

A 2017 research survey outlined six different addictive software design strategies that are built to prevent us from setting and keeping boundaries online.[327] We're going to go through each of these addictive design strategies with the hope that if we all understand the tech a bit better, then we can all find more effective ways to set boundaries.

1. Variable-reward system: Humans naturally operate on a reward system and social media applications have adapted the variable-reward system perfected by slot machines. The rewards on these apps (notifications, algorithms, viral posts, engagement) are random and unpredictable, which keeps us constantly coming back for more rewards, hoping to figure out the right time/text/story to get us those precious rewards.

2. Social reciprocity: Humans connect on and with social media because there is a "mutual exchange" that takes place with each social interaction. We are wired to feel we need to reciprocate others' social gestures, and we also receive chemical satisfaction in our brains and bodies when we get social gratification. In this way, we become attached not only to the social aspect of the application but the way it makes us feel good about ourselves.

3. Infinite scrolling: Most social media apps use the infinite scrolling appearance, where all the content loads on a single "page." This creates an interface where we continuously consume media because the "page" never ends. This feature makes it much harder to limit your time on an application and also makes it much easier to doomscroll.[328]

4. Illusion of choice: Though most of these applications give the illusion that the user is in control of the appearance and operation, that is far from the truth. Software designers often have the ultimate control, but the illusion of choice keeps us engaged and ignorant to the real operation of the application.

5. User investment: This is a rather basic principle that means humans tend to be more invested and more

engaged in things that we have created or built—or that we feel we have had some role in creating or building or customizing.

6. Gamification: We already mentioned gamification in our chapter on toxic productivity but it's worth spending a little more time on it here. Gamification is the process of using game mechanics to reward the completion of tasks. If these features do their jobs, then we get sucked into reading books we don't really like to earn badges on Goodreads or fixated on logging our food intake on our weight loss app. Turning ordinary activities into a "game" is a big part of the variable-reward system.

With these six design features, it's no surprise that we are so dependent on interacting with applications, and with others, through our smartphones and social media apps. These devices and applications do not want us to set boundaries; because, if we limit our interaction, then they don't increase their brand awareness, advertising reach, and profits.

Social media also creates distorted and inflated realities that give us unrealistic expectations for our ability to influence others, go viral, or achieve some level of social status.[329] We get stuck in a constant cycle of checking for updates, scrolling for information, or obsessing over the wording of a post or how many likes it gets. This cycle can then force us to change our expectations for what our own personal and relationship boundaries are and what they are for others. We end up online at all times of day, we accept friend requests and follows from people we don't know, and more and more of our boundaries disappear.[330]

So, what happens when we have almost no boundaries online? One of the consequences of these porous boundaries is the infamous concept of "cancel culture."

We do not have the time (or the energy) to get into a debate about cancel culture in this book.[331] But, it's worth noting what happens when people feel like they "know" everyone online. This belief of knowledge is also referred to as "parasocial relationships," which is another subcategory we don't have space for in this book. This all happens when users are tricked by software designs and algorithms to believe they should always be sharing their thoughts, feelings, and opinions when they are rewarded for their sharp witted thoughts with likes, follows, shares, and more social reciprocity.

Therefore, when they observe someone else online who has violated a cultural, relationship, or personal boundary, they are compelled to engage and pass judgment. Social media has convinced us that our opinions always matter, that we should share them no matter the circumstance, and that we're operating on all the information we need to make a decision.[332] Additionally, this dynamic often feeds into the false belief that online choices do not have offline consequences. Spoiler alert: they usually do.

In reality, life is way more complicated than a 140 character Tweet or Instagram Story or TikTok video. We're not at *Terminator* levels yet, but we do need to talk about how we can fight back against these technologies.

How do I set boundaries online?

There are so many wonderful results from the 21st-century tech boom. Friends that we lost touch with are only a message or video chat away. Online communities formed around entire spectrums of interests make safe spaces for people to express themselves. We've been given these remarkable tools to help us reimagine how people form relationships, share ideas, and yes, sell products.

Faced with the addictive strategies we outlined in the last section, it can be hard to imagine how we could set boundaries on our online interactions.

The first place to start is understanding. It's why we outlined the addictive elements of social media design. It's also why we wanted to spend so much time explaining the Wellness Industrial Complex in Section Three. You might have read this far and think that the WIC doesn't directly impact you. But, if you're on social media and you don't understand the manipulative nature of the algorithm, then you're not really in control of the information you are seeing and the elements of the WIC you are being exposed to.

The next step we recommend is spending some time figuring out how much time you spend online, and in what capacity. You could start a diary to keep track of your time spent, engagements, and feelings about each entry. How does being on Twitter make you feel? How easy is it for you to get sucked into scrolling on Instagram? How much pressure do you feel to open your Facebook app multiple times a day? Are your BeReal notifications causing minor cardiac events?

With the insanely rapid pace of technological development over the last 30 years, most of us haven't had the time or the energy to understand the full implications of each new device, feature, app, or trend. However, with the benefit of all this time and oodles of research, we've been able to better understand the potential impact of our online lives. Now that we know more, we can do better.

Social media is a tool, and it is neither inherently good nor bad. It can be altered and manipulated to suit both good and bad purposes, and for many of us, we cannot control or influence these purposes. However, we can control how we use it, how we choose to engage with it, and how we form relationships with others through those platforms.

It's going to take work, of that we are sure, but setting healthy boundaries always does.

How can I improve my boundary setting and respecting skills?

There are two keys to powering up these skills: self-awareness and (you guessed it!) empathy. You need to be aware of the ones you're setting, aware of the ones you haven't set yet but probably should, aware of the consequences you'll need to enact if your boundary lines are crossed, and aware if you're only setting those boundaries because Instagram told you to.

If you think you don't have any boundaries or someone you are in a relationship with doesn't have any boundaries, then what you may have is actually a failure of communication. They exist, and you will hold people accountable to yours whether you recognize it consciously or not. And, you need to communicate the boundaries that should be communicated, most importantly, the relationship boundaries. And, remember, it's not a boundary if it's about controlling someone else's choices or behavior or if the consequences are something you know you won't feel comfortable enacting.

For a lot of people, work is one of the hardest places to set boundaries. All the wonderful technological advances we just talked about have also drastically changed how and when and how long we work, too. Any research into burnout or boundary setting is full of horror stories about bosses calling at 3am, employees expected to work 14-hour days to finish a project, and emails requiring an answer during childbirth or a wedding ceremony.

Too many of us have allowed, or been forced, to dissolve many of our boundaries between our work life and our non-work life. But, we're here to tell you that we can, and must, push back against these flimsy and barely functioning boundaries. So many parts of American society that we've outlined in this book do *not* want us to make and keep boundaries. From America's obsession with toxic productivity, to restrictive gender roles and the WIC.

We know that setting boundaries at work can be extra hard, especially with the complicated power dynamics and varying relationships. If you feel your workplace or personal boundaries need a refresh, then here's where we suggest you start.

Different People are Different

We had a whole chapter on this for a reason. Start with asking more questions and making fewer assumptions. This goes for your own personal boundaries and the ones that other people set. Learn more about the folks you work with and why they might need some of those boundaries, especially ones that are different from yours. Consider those pesky intersections, because, we bet, they have some influence as well. And, be sure to consider the contextual privilege you have, too, either as a person in a position of authority at work or due to inherent, systemic biases in our culture like the ones we discussed around intersections.

Clear Communication is Kind Communication

Where would The Good Doctors be without Brené Brown? We shudder to think. As a reminder, this is one of our mottos that we've adapted from her work in *Dare to Lead* and other publications.[333] None of us are mind readers, and we all operate on assumptions and stereotypes when we don't have the information we need. Help yourself, your loved ones, and your co-workers out by clearly (and kindly) communicating your boundaries. If you are in a leadership position, then develop and implement a way for your folks to communicate their boundaries as well.

Set and Manage Expectations

This is similar to clear communication, but different enough to earn its own place. Boundaries are necessary, but there are also times that they have to be flexible. In your boundary evaluation, you will need to decide which boundaries can be flexible and which can't. Clearly communicate with your friends, family, co-workers, bosses, and underlings what your expectations are, and help them do the same.

Be Gentle with Yourself and Others

Dismantling centuries old systems is hard, y'all. Unlearning behaviors and thought patterns we've had our whole life, or even just the last decade, is really challenging, especially with systems that don't want to be dismantled and those invested in American capitalism and the WIC who don't want your behaviors to change. We use the word practice for a reason. Give yourself grace and space to make mistakes, to backtrack, to be a human being. And, then, try to do the same for the folks you work with.

Allowing staff to set boundaries, setting boundaries in employment and volunteer contracts, and sitting down with family and setting boundaries for all parties is healthy for everyone, not just the boundary setter. As a leader, knowing exactly what to expect from people makes evaluating, delegating, guiding, mentoring, and supporting all 100% easier. And, when you come to all of that from a place of empathy, you'll find that those around you are more willing to share, more willing to collaborate, and more willing to respect your boundaries in return.

How does privilege affect boundary setting?

You caught that mention, did you? Good question. The answer is: a lot. So, we want to go into it just a little deeper. It's also something far too many conversations about boundary setting, particularly in workplaces, gloss over. Generally, the amount of privilege and power you have in a certain circumstance is what enables your boundaries to slide along the scale from "wishes" to "absolutes."

An employee who relies on their job to put food on the table may not have the power or authority to enforce boundaries or enact consequences with their boss that they would really like to. A CEO of a big company may have the kind of authoritative power that means she never needs to come to the negotiation table as her boundaries are always seen as the most important.

As you may remember from Section Two, privilege creates unbalance, and the only way to restore balance is for those with privilege to actively and consciously acknowledge that power in ways that make space for those who have less. If you are in a leadership position at an organization, then you need to work extra hard to understand, acknowledge, and communicate about your employees' boundaries—the ones they feel safe maintaining and the ones they wish they could set but don't feel they have the power to—and the more you put in the work and use your privilege to protect those boundaries, the more respected you will be as a leader and the safer your staff will feel.

So what are all these boundaries even protecting?

A fair point! You might be wondering how boundary setting helps prevent burnout. Having solid boundaries helps you in three ways:

1) Your boundaries protect you from experiencing circumstances that continually activate your stress cycle or prevent you from breaking your stress cycle.
2) Your boundaries allow you to set limits on the amount of emotional responding you do when it comes to others' stories (remember doomscrolling, the 24-hour news cycle, and compassion fatigue).
3) Your boundaries keep safe the time and space you need to practice your Four R's.

We know what your next question is going to be, so let's just get right into it…

Chapter 16: The Four R's

If you've ever read or heard anything about how to combat burnout, then you've probably heard the advice, "You need to get more rest." If burnout is a "workplace phenomena" and the opposite of work is rest, then it's easy to see why "getting enough rest" is the go-to advice for burnout sufferers, but that's easy to say and difficult to do.

We also don't talk enough about what "rest" truly means. Rest includes sleep, but it is not *just* sleep. But, since our common understanding of rest is mainly physical rest, we're going to divide the idea of holistic rest up into four pieces: physical rest, rejuvenation, realignment, and reconnection—The Four R's.

The Four R's are all key pieces to a balanced life, and prioritizing them, promoting them, and investing in them for everyone is key to moving from a culture of burnout to a culture of balance.

What is physical rest?

Physical rest includes sleep and sleep-adjacent activities that stop the movement of our bodies and give them time to heal. Sleep is an incredibly important and deeply fascinating physiological process, and obviously, it is a big part of ensuring you get enough rest. But, it's not the only part.

Hopefully, by this point in the book, you're already jumping to this conclusion, but we have to recognize that just like experiences of burnout, trauma, and health look different for everyone, prioritizing physical rest looks different for everyone, too. For some people, it's mission critical to have a strict bedtime. For some, it's all about the arrangement of pillows. Some people need to nap midday. Some people need medication, CPAP machines, or other interventions to manage conditions such as insomnia and sleep apnea.

A friend of ours suffered from very severe sleep onset insomnia for over twenty years before beginning a two-year sleep hygiene overhaul, and it worked! She's still not a great sleeper, but she was able to get the sleep she needed most of the time simply by making lifestyle changes.

Our team at the office is a perfect example of a group of people who need wildly different sleep environments. We all need different room temperatures, different blankets, different levels and types of background noise, different equipment, and different medications and supplements.

And, that might seem crazy—sleep is a basic, biological need—how is it so complicated? But, just because something is a basic, biological need doesn't mean it's inherently easy for us to do. Eating is as well, and humans struggle with everything from breastfeeding to severe food allergies to disordered eating conditions.[334]

Another part is that we, as a culture, do not prioritize rest. And, we need to. A study in Seattle in 2016/2017 looked at teenagers' sleep times and grade performance before and after a school start-time shift. The school district moved high school start time from 7:50am to 8:45am, and a group of sophomore students in the same science class wore tracking watches for a period before the change and for a period after the change. Sleep onset (when they fell asleep) only shifted a tiny bit later, but sleep offset (when they woke) shifted quite a bit later with the result that, on average, the students were sleeping for 34 more minutes per night on school nights.

Let's be clear: it still wasn't enough sleep. The teens were getting, on average, seven hours and 24 minutes instead of six hours and fifty minutes, when the CDC, and nearly every global expert, recommends teenagers get a whopping 8-10 hours of sleep at night,[335] but it was still an improvement. This pattern of sleep better aligned with teenagers' natural, biological sleep clock, which pushes them to start going to sleep later but requires them to sleep longer. Teenagers sleep in late for a reason, and it's not laziness!

And, guess what? The later start time improved other things, too. Grades went up, the feelings of sleepiness among the teens went down, and for some schools, tardiness and absences also decreased.[336]

Teenagers have different sleep needs from children and from adults. Those with chronic health issues—both sleep related and not—often have different sleep needs than from those without. And, simply person to person, we all have slightly varying preferences, rhythms, and lifestyles.

Currently, our work and school culture expects everyone to adhere to a standard. Most offices are 9-5. Schools vary more, especially post-secondary schools, but start times pre-college tend to range from 7:30-9am and end around 2:15-3:30. Non-office work often operates in shifts, some of which go overnight.

The gut reaction to proposing change in these areas is often "but it *needs* to work that way." And, sure, there are some things that can't change. But what we're proposing here isn't a sweeping generalization. Obviously, there are industries where certain structures are critical, but when the result of imposing those structures is suffering for the people in those industries, how can we not investigate possible change?

Let's take hospitals as a quick example. It's so well known that residents are perpetually exhausted that *Grey's Anatomy* has gotten a decade's worth of stories out of the fact. Yet, we also know that exhausted humans make mistakes, and who wants mistakes made in terms of our health? No one. But, we need doctors and nurses to be available to us basically all the time because our bodies don't check the clock when they decide to spring a leak.

So, how do we balance the necessities of the profession with the necessities of their bodies? We're actually not sure, but we do know that the best place to start is to acknowledge that something has to change. In the U.S., Canada, and New Zealand, residents work between 60-90 hours per week, whereas in Australia and the European Union, they're limited to approximately 50. International governing bodies are acknowledging that the health of the caregivers is just as important as the health of the patients. Fabulous! We doubt the solutions on the table now are the ones that will fully work, but this kind of stuff has to start somewhere.

In some ways, our entire Section Four could be subtitled "you have to start somewhere." Because, as simple as it sounds, you do.

What is rejuvenation?

Just like all the aspects of holistic well-being, rejuvenation is very personal. These are things that answer the question: what brings you joy? For some people, this might involve movement—going for a hike, doing pilates, having a dance party in your kitchen. For others, this may involve stillness—watching TV in your Snuggie, meditating, reading a book in the sun—or even creativity—writing a novel, painting your dog's portrait, or redesigning your bedroom.

These are the things that make it feel like when you draw a breath it goes a little deeper, like the daylight is a little brighter, and your biggest smile comes a little easier. It's crucial to remember that what might be rejuvenating for some may be taxing or even deeply uncomfortable for others. You can almost certainly think of a friend who has a hobby or passion that you dislike. To truly engage with rejuvenation, you need to find the things that work for *you*.

A culture of balance makes space for everyone's rejuvenation, not just certain kinds.You may think gardening is boring, hard work for no reason, but it might be your best friend's greatest joy, or your mom's, or your coworker's. On a broader level, social judgment for different types of rejuvenation contributes to a culture of burnout because it tries to box people into the "right" or "acceptable" ways to find rest and pleasure.

A boss who approves one employee's request for time off to go to baseball spring training but denies another's request to go to a knitting convention because it's "for grandmas" isn't just being unfair, he's contributing to his employee's likelihood of burning out. And, we already know that leads to worse performance and more need for time off in the future. Similarly, a boss who finds her joy at the gym, buying a gym membership for each of her employees as a burnout prevention measure, is not leading with empathy.

This isn't to say that the solution is to give time off for everything no matter what, but it does mean that human beings need some kind of time that is fully safe from their workplaces—in all the many forms those can take—to pursue their own joy-giving activities, discrimination free.

What is realignment?

The third R is realignment. In some theological circles, this can also be called "keeping sabbath." Kristen has a story that captures it perfectly:

> I had the honor of growing up with several friends who were practicing Jews, and one of them once asked me what Sundays looked like for Christians. I remember shrugging and saying "church, homework, maybe naps." He looked a little surprised. "But I thought it was your Sabbath." "It is," I assured him. "Why are you so confused?"
>
> He went on to explain what the concept of sabbath meant to him and it's something I've never gotten out of my head. Sabbath, he informed me, was a 24-hour period where he created nothing. Not food, not crafts, not work, nothing. He created nothing so he would remember that he was a created being, and, in turn, would remember his place in the universe. He was created, not creator, and he needed to remember that once per week, or he'd get off kilter again.
>
> We are created, not creators.

Whatever your theology, however you see the world, consider this: very little is within your control. You do not have power over the actions or emotions of others. You cannot determine how things will truly pan out—you can only control you.The universe is vast and unknowable, and while you are deeply valued by your fellow humans, the harsh truth is that the planet will keep spinning without you.

To quote Eliza Doolittle, "Without you pulling it the tide comes in," after all.

In order to fulfill this R, you've got to carve time out each week to remember who you are and to align yourself in the grander scheme of things. For some people, this is going to church or observing a Sabbath, but for others, it might look like meditation, mindfulness practice, donating time or money to charity (though don't forget that volunteering can constitute another workplace), or writing in a personal reflection journal.

It's very common for those suffering from burnout to find "practice gratitude" as a recommendation for moving towards healing. We don't disagree. There's science to back up gratitude as a way to increase positive feelings and rewire the mind to be more resilient,[337] but there's also a ton of science to back up why yoga makes so many people feel good and we don't blanket recommend that to everyone either.

If there's one thing we hope you take away from this section of the book, it's that there is no one-size-fits-all solution to burnout, and anyone who says otherwise is not only probably trying to sell you something but is also perpetuating a culture of burnout. A culture of balance promotes finding your own way to realignment. It might be practicing gratitude, or it might not be.

What is reconnection?

> Our team was all together in the winter of 2023, dreaming and plotting about this book. Kristen had just given a talk that served as our starting point and was sharing an expanded vision of the R's — which at the time did not include reconnection.
>
> As she was talking, she slowed down and began to laugh. "Y'all, we're missing the people piece."

The irony of this is that Kristen is always the one who reminds us that we do need people, who encourages us to think about community connections, and who provides the neuroscience evidence that we thrive in healthy, covenantal relationships. It still took her three years of teaching about the R's to see this hole.

Thank goodness she got there before we published this, eh?

As much as some folks may think they should or they have to, one simply cannot do life alone. Reconnection is about forming and strengthening bonds with others. Burnout can be very isolating, and often, the first R that gets set aside is reconnection, especially for introverts.

In short, introverts are those who find being social costs them energy and extroverts are those who find being social gives them energy. For most people, it's actually a little more complex than this—and the current state of your mental health can play a huge role in energy levels and sociability—but as a broad generalization, for some people the calculation of "is it worth it" to reconnect with the people around them is going to vary.

Reconnection can be one of the hardest R's to make time for. Someone who is currently in burnout probably feels too emotionally exhausted to be social, and the very activities that could help them move towards healing, they're unable to do. It can also be difficult to maintain social circles as friends move and change and grow. Reconnection requires a true investment, but it pays back major dividends, we promise.

The key takeaways for this R are: reconnection isn't just worth it, it's necessary, and just like every other aspect of holistic health, it looks different for everyone.

Maybe for you reconnection looks like lunch twice a month with your best friend. Or, maybe it looks like attending a massive stadium concert with your twelve closest buds. It probably looks like both at different times, as we just went to Taylor Swift's Eras Tour and adored it, but then, we also needed quiet time with (and without) each other afterwards. Perhaps reconnection is something you only need to tend to once a month, or maybe you need to take time for it multiple times a day. It can include chatting with a new coworker around the coffeemaker and staying up late discussing the ins and outs of parenting with your partner.

What do all Four R's look like together?

When you stick them all together, balancing all Four R's contributes to a lifestyle that gives you peace, finds you joy, and doesn't feel like every day is a struggle against the perpetual quicksand.

That's the good news. You might have guessed the bad news already. Figuring out what feeds The Four R's for *you* is hard work, and it's never ending work. People grow and change. Painting watercolors might be rejuvenating for you in your 30s but was boring in your 20s. Perhaps you ran marathons for years, but a knee injury meant reevaluating and switching to pilates instead. It even changes from day to day. One day, you feel like going to a party with your partner and reconnecting with old friends. Another day, you feel like finding a book that opens you up to new perspectives, feeding rejuvenation and alignment at the same time.

Here's the other bad news that you also already know: the people you love, work with, care for, and interact with on a daily basis are all going to have different ways of feeding these Four R's. You might find some of those things hard to be around, hard to participate in, hard to respect, even. Perhaps you are not someone who finds power and comfort in crystals, but your aunt has a house covered in them. Maybe alcohol makes you feel dizzy but your partner likes a few beers on the weekend. We must find space in our lives for the things that fuel us and allow space in others' lives for the things that fuel them. You do not need to see the benefit in someone else's R-practice to respect that it works for them.

How can a workplace respect everyone's different R's?

If a workplace tries to create a one-size-fits-all formula, usually by outsourcing their wellness initiatives to apps and service providers, for helping their employees with the R's they need to cultivate holistic well-being, it will suit, maybe, a few people. But, since different people are different, there will be many people for whom it will be neutral or uninteresting, and they will simply not participate. And, there may even be people for whom it is actively harmful. Anyone who is struggling with a mental health issue should be seeking personal healthcare solutions from trained medical professionals. And, that isn't even the only concern with these sorts of services. Online therapy platform BetterHelp got in trouble with the FTC for selling medical data about its users, and has come under fire for the ethics of its advertising approaches.[338] [339]

We hope you agree, after everything we've explored here, that there is no one single solution to everyone's burnout and no one single right way to support a given individual's thriving and coping skills. What we can do is make sure everyone has the best opportunity possible to engage in everything we've established, and there are actually three simple things that can help level the playing field:

- Access to healthcare
- Time
- Financial security

That's really all people need to make this happen. Access to healthcare allows us to get appropriate treatment for mental health struggles, including preventative treatment. Time gives us an opportunity, uninterrupted, to engage in all Four R's, whatever that means for us, without "stealing" from other responsibilities like childcare or housework, or the R's needing to steal from each other (giving up sleep to engage in a hobby). And, financial security allows us the freedom to spend money *and* time on The Four R's.

We'll discuss a bit later some of the ways other countries handle providing these things and the outcomes they've seen, and we're certainly not going to claim that we know how to get these three things into the hands of every American. But, if you want to lower burnout rates at your organization, or do the work to prevent it in the first place, then ask yourself how you might improve your employee's access to these three things.

Can hours be reduced and staff increased to cover the gap? Can more PTO be offered? If your organization offers wellness programs already, how much do those cost? Can that money be distributed to other options instead, like a Four R's Stipend or better health benefits?

Keep in mind that fairness matters. All too often, companies provide these supports for administrative or executive level employees while hourly or manual labor departments remain unsupported.

If you're not in leadership, then perhaps you can open the door to negotiation with higher-ups who seem open to it. When it comes time for performance reviews, express how you prefer to be rewarded for good work, give your feedback on the benefits offered, including any workplace wellness programs, and offer alternative options. Discuss it with your coworkers.

And, be counter-cultural by setting boundaries that let you engage in your Four R's as much as you can.

If taking a bubble bath is your way to realign, amazing. If you find rest in meditation, fantastic. Rabid self-care advocates often forget that the most important piece of the puzzle of taking care of yourself is what works for *you*. So, explore, play, and find your joy, and then, do the work to make it a priority.

And, as you do what works for you, as you reclaim your time, and your personhood, as you draw boundaries around activities, as you choose to spend time with those who bring you joy and rest...others around you will notice and begin to do the same. Then, they will feel more grounded and inspire others, and so on and so forth, and by taking care of ourselves, we're all doing the small work of dismantling the system that treats us like interchangeable cogs in a profit machine.

Chapter 17: Cultivating Holistic Well-being

In Section Three, we introduced (or maybe re-introduced) you to the idea of the Wellness Industrial Complex and how harmful capitalizing on our health can be. Now, we want to offer an alternative. We cannot achieve this alternative position without the tools of empathy, boundaries, and The Four R's. But now that we're armed with those support mechanisms, we can look at the larger goal, the cultural big picture: cultivating holistic well-being.

If that sounds a bit woo-woo, we get it, but bear with us on this one.

Our good friend the WHO tells us that wellness is "complete physical, mental and social well-being and not merely the absence of disease or infirmity." The WIC thrives on splitting our focus on our well-being, by getting us to focus on our physical health, or our mental health, possibly at the expense of ignoring other factors. So many facets of the WIC are the complete opposite of practicing holistic well-being.

As per usual, we like to start with the basics.

What does "holistic" even mean?

We know that the word holistic is used a lot by wellness influencers within the WIC to talk about a more comprehensive approach to health. Even though it can have negative connotations within the WIC, the buzzword is a big part of reaching a culture of balance.

The term "holistic" is an adjective derived from the concept of "holism." Merriam-Webster defines "holistic" as, "Relating to or concerned with wholes or with complete systems rather than with the analysis of, treatment of, or dissection into parts."[340] Basically, when you apply holistic as a description for another term, such as medicine or well-being, it means you are interested in all the parts of that system or structure or concept, and how well those parts all work together.[341] Therefore, it's used within the WIC to talk about "holistic wellness" or wellness that is concerned with the whole person or system.

However, even though the WIC uses "holistic" a lot, many scholars argue that the whole industry (see what we did there?) has a hyperfixation on physical health and bodily appearance. From our perspective, that is how the influencers, companies, and practitioners who dominate the space know they can make the most money. We've already talked about Lizzie Braicks-Rinker's TEDx-UofW talk. Aside from explaining the core parts of the WIC, she also does a superb job of explaining how we, as a society, focus too much on improving physical health.

Chasing citations in TEDx talks can be a bit of work, but from the digging we've done, Braicks-Rinker's "8 Pillars of Holistic Wellness" appears to be based on the Substance Abuse and Mental Health Services Administration's (SAMHSA) "8 Dimensions of Wellness."[342] This talk was the first time we all had come across the 8 dimensions (or pillars). As we soon found, a quick Google search will give you lots of options for learning more about them—from "veterinary medicine" articles listed on the National Library of Medicine's website to a whole range of wellness influencers, activists, and practitioners.[343]

The frequency with which people are talking about holistic health and well-being—a marriage between traditional medicine and other wellness practices—is all further evidence that we are in the Fusion Phase of the 4 Phases of Wellness.[344]

Why are there 8 Dimensions of Wellness?

According to SAMHSA, the 8 Dimensions of Wellness are these forms of well-being:[345]

1. Emotional
2. Spiritual
3. Intellectual
4. Physical
5. Environmental
6. Financial
7. Occupational
8. Social

There are a lot of definitions for these dimensions, but we're more interested in what they mean to you.

Braicks-Rinker's TEDx contends that the WIC puts the most emphasis and weight behind the importance of physical well-being, at a direct cost to the other dimensions. In your Google search for the 8 Dimensions of Wellness, you will find a cornucopia of images and graphics of the dimensions—usually incorporating some form of Venn diagram to show their equal importance within the broader scope of holistic well-being.

After looking through and discussing these graphics as a team, we decided to represent the 8 dimensions in a slightly different way. While we love a good Venn diagram as much as anyone—especially when it shows all the parts of the whole—we wanted to go a step further by showing that the dimensions are connected *and* interdependent. They are not static or fixed sizes based on their importance because they do not have equal weight or equal space in our lives. We knew that had to be clear in our vision of the 8 dimensions.

Thus, we present to you (drum roll, please) The Good Doctors Wheel of Well-being:

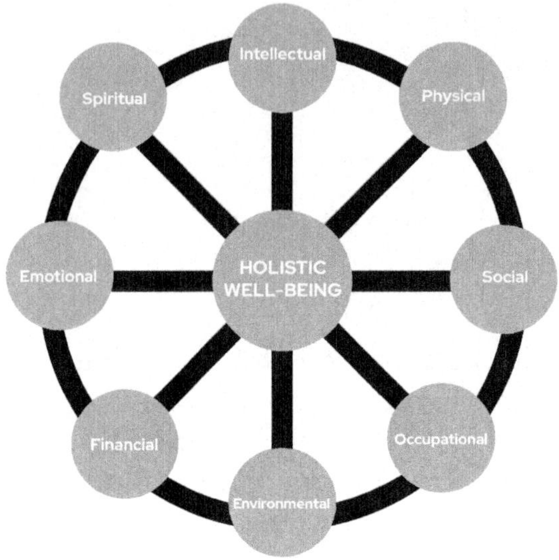

As you can see on our wheel, each of the dimensions is connected to each other and to the central hub through the rim and the spokes. To explore further the impact of the dimensions, we have three key points to address:

1. To cultivate holistic well-being and to move toward creating a culture of balance, we have to recognize that everyone has all 8 dimensions of well-being. The dimensions are all needed and they are all important—without each of them functioning in their role, the wheel is broken.

2. We have to learn to differentiate between the holistic importance of each dimension and its significance to an individual person. For example, if you are a marathon runner and that activity contributes to your physical, emotional, and spiritual health, then you might have a greater emphasis on those dimensions at certain times in your life.

Two of the three Abbey Research team members practice yoga. For Erin, the social dimension is a big part of her yoga practice since she has a vibrant community at her studio whereas Eleanor prefers to practice at home, and the social dimension is not a part of her practice. If you are a person of deep faith who is deeply involved in your local religious community, then your spiritual and social dimensions might take on more individual significance than other dimensions.

At different points in your life, or at different times during your burnout, you will need to give more specific attention to one or more dimensions over the others. However, as you can see from the graphic, when we provide equal *consideration*, not weight, for the dimensions, the wheel is balanced.

3. But, what happens when we spend too much time and energy only pursuing one of the dimensions? This is a big reason why parts of the Wellness Industrial Complex can be toxic, and even harmful. Though it is entirely possible, and necessary, for an individual to shift among different dimensions based on their personal needs, the toxicity and harm happens when the WIC argues/sells that focusing exclusively on one dimension will fix *all* your problems.

   Throughout the many cycles of the wellness industry—from the late 19th century to today—the WIC continuously shifts its emphasis among different dimensions of well-being—usually for the purpose of marketing a new product in order to participate in the capitalist economy.

How does the wheel become unbalanced?

Whenever we talk to folks, specifically about the toxicity of the WIC, we often use a reference to one of our favorite films, *The Princess Bride*. If you will indulge us now, we promise to connect all the dots.

When Westley (as the Man in Black) and Princess Buttercup are reunited after he bests Inigo, Fezzik, and Vizzini, they argue over her supposed lack of loyalty, and she tells him, "You mock my pain." The Man in Black replies, "Life is pain, Highness. Anyone who says differently is selling something."[346] As two cynical and pragmatic Elder Millennials, this line continues to resonate with both of us the older we get and the more of this world we experience.

So, how does this random movie quote relate to the WIC and our perceptions of wellness?

One of the greatest harms of the WIC is that it continues to sell us the idea that: 1) We are able to fully control our health and 2) By controlling our health we can control our lives.[347] Just one year after the release of *The Princess Bride*, Arthur Barsky argued that the current health situation (in the late 1980s) was a series of paradoxes. For Barsky, the final paradox is that "it is only when we accept the fact that some of our ailments are inescapable, that some afflictions are unavoidable, that we can learn how to put up with them and get on with the business of living."[348] Basically, what he is arguing is that "life is pain," and "anyone who says differently is selling something."

Our physical bodies—and minds—are always growing, changing, and yeah, breaking down—that's what living and aging means. But, we've constructed a Wellness Industrial Complex with a primary sales model that tells us we *can* control our lives by controlling our *health*—whether that means our physical, emotional, spiritual, or financial health, or any other single dimension on the Wheel of Well-Being.

Let's go back to our earlier question: what happens when we spend too much time and energy only pursuing one of the dimensions? In order to further illustrate our point, we're going to examine three times when the WIC and its participants exclusively marketed one dimension of well-being, for the purpose of increasing profits, influence, and cultural importance.

In our chapter on the WIC, we outlined the history of wellness. By and large, the wellness movements of the 20th century, including Workplace Wellness Programs, primarily and almost exclusively focused on improving physical well-being. Remember *The Biggest Loser* competitions we mentioned?

Returning to our Wheel of Well-being, take a look at what happens when the physical dimension is the primary focus of a person's well-being.

An Unbalanced Wheel: The Physical Dimension

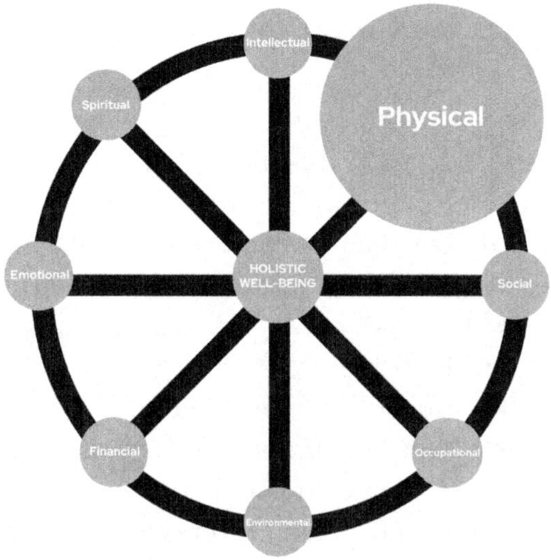

When we expend too much time, energy, and resources pursuing our physical well-being, or in other words, looking exclusively for physical health solutions to our larger well-being issues, the wheel becomes unbalanced because we put too much pressure on those particular spokes and that part of the rim. The physical dimension of our wheel might be strong, but the longer we spend working only on that part of the wheel, the weaker the other parts get. It seems rather obvious that if you're only working on one of the parts of the wheel and the other parts get neglected—then the wheel starts to wobble, the parts start to rust, and eventually, the wheel breaks.

This hyper focus on physical health is a popular feature of the WIC. From the emphasis on walking and other physical activities during the Life Reform movement of the late 19th century, to Jazzercise in the 1980s and CrossFit, SoulCycle, or Peloton now, we have a laundry list of movements, products, and influencers who profited off the marketing of the next great exercise craze. Each of these products are sold as the *right* and, usually, the *only* product you need to fix your problems and support your well-being.

One of the reasons it is easier for people to focus on, and then sell, physical health solutions is that physical problems are often ones we can see—we see an overweight person and assume that they are unhealthy. Physical problems are also the ones that are easiest to test—we can develop a new non-stick yoga mat or new lightweight running shoes, and we can test them to measure their efficacy.

Physical health and well-being is also a deeply embedded cultural value. Hundreds of thousands of products sold within the WIC are marketed as selling peak physical health and appearance. Skinny, well-toned, confident women sell yoga leggings, supplements, essential oils, and juice cleanses *while* also selling the idea that this magic product will make you the skinnier, more beautiful, more confident, and healthier version of yourself.

In order to cultivate holistic well-being, we have to train ourselves to recognize when our dimensions are unbalanced and when we're being sold a single solution to our problems. Though the trend in the WIC is toward overemphasizing physical well-being, there have been other movements and moments when other dimensions have also been overemphasized.

An Unbalanced Wheel: The Financial Dimension

Since the WIC cannot survive without capitalism, it is clear that the financial dimension has a tendency to take on too much weight and collapse the structure of the wheel. In fact, many of the MLMs and other businesses that sell crystals, essential oils, diet supplements, and exercise methods or machines, recruit new employees on the promise of financial security and even wealth.

As Kristen introduced in our first section on the WIC, women's participation in MLMs is highly gendered, and therefore, many of these women are hurtling toward burnout because of this hyperfocus on the need to be financially well, on the need to have a successful "side hustle."[349]

Similarly to the previous image, the image below shows the problem of hyper fixating on the financial dimension of well-being.

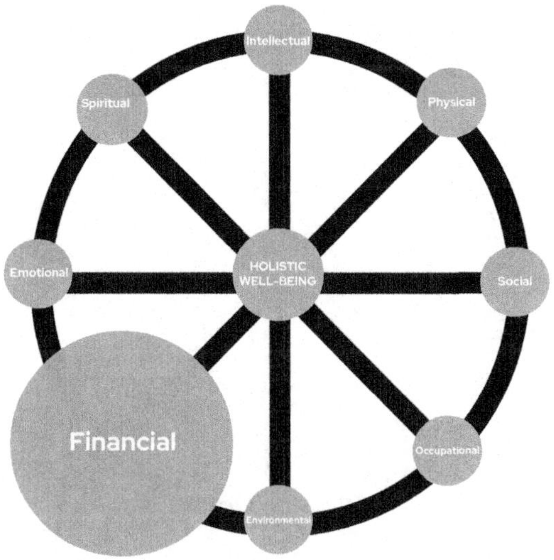

Personal finance gurus have long dominated the financial dimension of well-being, selling the best methods to establish your own personal wealth and stability. From the Suze Ormans and Dave Ramseys to the Warren Buffets and Instagram financial advisors, many folks are attempting to sell a version of well-being that starts with, and sometimes ends with, financial wealth.

But, the same thing happens to our Wheel of Well-being when we focus all our time and attention (and resources) on a different dimension.

An Unbalanced Wheel: The Spiritual Dimension

Since we already talked a bit about MLMs and hinted at their close relationship with the formation of cults,[350] we wanted to make sure and discuss the overemphasis on the spiritual dimension that is a common feature within the WIC.

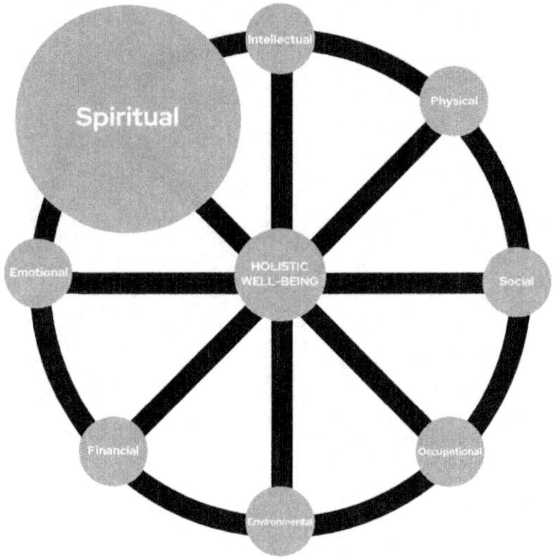

There are two elements of this: that 1) Mormon housewives are the largest percentage of MLM consultants,[351] and 2) some of the products themselves involve spiritual undertones.

MLMs target stay-at-home-mothers who are looking for a sense of freedom away from their children. They gravitate towards not only the promise of extra cash, but the concept of a purpose outside of motherhood. For many conservative Christians—including members of the Church of Jesus Christ of Latter Day Saints (LDS)—this is *incredibly* intoxicating. Many may not be permitted to work outside the home, by their culture or their husbands, and many have been raised since childhood to believe their primary role in the world is one of mother.

When someone who looks like them, thinks like them, and appears to be exactly like them, says they, too, can have a taste of freedom from the cycle of laundry, food prep, childcare, and homework...well, let's just say hundreds of thousands haven't been able to pass that up.[352]

Additionally, many MLMs use religious language to encourage their consultants that participating in the MLM is God's will.[353] This is addressed both in the *LuLaRich* documentary on Amazon Prime and in *Hey, Hun*, Emily Lynn Paulson's book on the lure and lies of the direct sales industry.

Finally, some products do carry implications that use of the product will enhance someone's spiritual journey. This may be true for some people, and candles and oils certainly have a long history of being integrated parts of religious practices, but the way MLM consultants are taught to sell through emotional manipulation can lead people to believe that these specific modern products are *mandatory* to said person's spiritual growth. The selling of any monetary element as mandatory to someone's life is capitalism and, in the realm of wellness, that means it's part of the WIC.

What does this mean? A few things. Using any products sold by an MLM for your practice of holistic well-being should come with an intention to use them in your own practice and not to automatically adopt the process they're selling. Does dabbing your temples with peppermint essential oils help your wind-down routine at night? Fabulous. But, you can continue this practice with conscientiousness; investigate where your products come from, what the company structures are like, and who profits from sales. Look out for the traps that tell you that the peppermint oil *needs* to be on your corn flakes, in your makeup, and in your shower diffuser (only $64.99) to solve *all* your problems.

It's easy to get caught up in the community language—these women believe in you and your well-being! This is a *tribe* of women supporting each other and isn't that beautiful?—without analyzing if that community is the right fit for you.

It's worth noting that this is the same for every single community. Humans are desperate for connection, and with our increasingly fragmented society, many are tempted to dive fully into any community that feels like it could be "the one." Soul Cycle, CrossFit, and their ilk also fall into this category, as do many traditional religious movements. Belonging is part of well-being, but so is making sure that belonging isn't facilitated entirely by your financial participation in said community.

Sometimes these things are exactly what people need! We have many friends who have found belonging in CrossFit, for example, and even in various MLMs (for a time). Kristen finds a lot of belonging in online communities that revolve around reading and writing Marvel fanfiction. We all have our things, and we all need to belong. Our caution for you, here, is to find belonging in an informed way.

What does it mean to truly cultivate holistic well-being?

We hope we've shown you how harmful it can be when we believe we can control our lives through focusing on one dimension of well-being. Holistic well-being means recognizing the impact that gravity has on our bodies and that we can't outrun aging. It means learning how to balance our wheel by unlearning a lot of the ways we understand our own physical, mental, and emotional health.

Lest you think we're not walking our own walk, Erin has returned to share her journey of understanding what holistic well-being can look like in her life.

Holistic Well-being (Erin's Version)

As long as I can remember, I've always been physically active. For most of my life, I would imagine my Wheel of Well-being looked a lot like the second image we shared, with the overemphasis on the physical dimension, to the detriment of others. When I reflect on it now, I think I always believed that if I was in good physical health, I would have control over my life.

While this led to periods of great physical health, it also led to toxic thoughts about my body shape, how I looked in workout clothes or bathing suits, and ever present thoughts about how I "should" look to be considered healthy. As I began to experience more of the world throughout my 20s, I slowly realized how important it was to be able to connect my physical health with my mental, emotional, and social dimensions.

In my late 20s, I started practicing yoga and started to change my relationship with my body. I was always told that yoga would be good for me since I'm so flexible, and at first, I found even some of the more advanced poses much easier than friends and classmates. However, I didn't do any of the work to understand the history and philosophy of yoga. I bought into the Western appropriation of it that focused more on getting a good sweat on and hitting some of those harder poses.

Eventually, after I returned to Pittsburgh, I was introduced to my current yoga teacher, who teaches a style of yoga called Iyengar. I've been practicing Iyengar yoga for 5 years now, and in no small way, it has changed my entire perspective about my own holistic well-being. Iyengar yoga differs from other styles, and is perhaps less popular, because it does not emphasize a cardio workout, moving quickly through poses, or promise super flexibility to people of all body shapes and sizes. Instead, Iyengar focuses more on spending time in each pose, working through a series of very detailed instructions and minute adjustments.

My teacher often says that the difference between beginner and intermediate practitioners is not the list of "hard" poses you can achieve, but the level of sensitivity you have to your own body. The style is taught for the individual to learn about their own specific body and needs. There are poses we don't do, or adjustments we all make, based on our own bodies. There is no "one size fits all model" in Iyengar, and the more time I spend as a practitioner, the more I realize how kind of toxic those models can be.

For example, for years I threw myself into a version of eka pada rajakapotasana or pigeon pose (just Google it, it's hard) without any support, because I could and because it was a "good stretch." However, I have since learned that because I learned the pose via an online, pre-recorded video, where the instructor could not see nor did not know me personally, I actually caused way more damage to my hips and pelvis that far outweighed any stretching benefits. I didn't do the research, didn't think about my own engagement with the practice, and I bought into the idea that this pose was for everybody. When in fact, this pose was certainly *not* for me and my hips.

One of the main philosophies in my current studio has actually become a guiding principle in this book. I remember sometime during one of our lockdown Zoom classes, my teacher was instructing us through a series of balance poses and said that "balance doesn't mean you are without movement. Balance means wobbling without falling over."

Yet, every picture of any person I've ever seen in vrksasana or tree pose is in "perfect" form—serenely balancing on one foot, hands in prayer position, like a gloriously poised statue. No one ever shows themselves wobbling, or even falling out of the pose. But it's the wobble that teaches us about our bodies and means that we're building strength and unlearning bad habits. It's the falling that teaches us to have fun and reminds us that it is a practice.

Other nuggets I've gleaned over the years have built up into a pretty solid foundation for my holistic well-being:

1. Yoga is a practice, which means there is no end point.
2. There is also no perfect achievement.
3. Every day is different because every day my body is different, and it needs different things.
4. The best practice for me is when I understand my own limitations and when I understand that I will never fully fix all of my physical problems.

Borrowing from Arthur Barsky's phrasing, one of the hardest things I've had to work on learning over the last 5 years has been that some of my "ailments are inescapable" and that some of my "afflictions are unavoidable." The athlete in me continues to want to "master" poses and judges myself when I don't. It's all a work in progress.

However, yoga is not the only part of my Wheel of Well-being. I have spent the years of COVID cultivating a collection of different practices that help keep me well. My gardening practice gives me a sense of accomplishment and care while also getting me fresh air and sunshine—it is my rejuvenation and my realignment. My cross-stitch practice keeps me off my phone at night and I find great value in creating and producing something for others—it is my reconnection. I have always loved music and travel and trying new foods. Those things also feed my soul and help me find my Four R's when I need them. Throughout the 30+ years of my wellness journey, I have never felt more balanced or more realistic about what balance means.

But, as we have argued throughout this book, and will continue to argue, this is *my* story. These practices work for me, but they might not work for you, and that's okay. It doesn't mean you've failed at well-being, or that you're doing a bad job of taking care of yourself. It doesn't mean I never have a mental (or physical) wobble, feel sorry for myself, or self-conscious about my body, or never succumb to road rage. It doesn't mean I never fall over. In fact, I do that a lot—in and out of the yoga studio. It just means I'm human and I'm trying. And trying to cultivate my own holistic well-being is way better for me than accepting the fate of living in an inescapable culture of burnout.

These are the best methods I've found for *me*, for *right now*. It took me a good few years of experimenting and adjusting to get here. I am so very far from the perfectly fit and perfectly calm yogi selling any means of props and treatments online. I am myself, imperfections, wobbles and all. And I'm pretty happy with how my wheel looks.

Holistic Well-being (Kristen's Version)

I'm still completely figuring mine out. Erin has been incredibly inspirational to me over the past few years as she's worked out her current practice, but I still struggle. I'm on mental health medications and in therapy, and those are huge helps, but... it's all a controlled wobble, right?

One of the lessons I'd love to pass on to all of you is that, just like Erin, the things that work for me work *right now*. If pilates works this week to calm my brain and help me focus on my breath, but it doesn't work next week, that's okay. I have a tendency to hyperfixate on things: foods, activities, lists. Sometimes I read books one after the other like popcorn, sometimes I only feel like playing video games. I'll go through stretches where I walk every day, others where I am simply one with my couch. Whatever my body and soul needs that day is okay. Maybe in another season of my life, I'll have a more regular practice. What I have right now is things I know will fit each of the Four R's and I do them as often as I find myself able.

Whatever your answers to these questions are, as long as you aren't harming yourself or others, then it's okay.

How do you practice holistic well-being for yourself?

For us, a big part of the process of figuring out your own path to holistic well-being is learning how to separate yourself from the pressure of your participation in the Wellness Industrial Complex. You have to see the toxicity of the culture of burnout and know how deep it goes into American life before you can find the combination of modalities that will work for you.

You have to start doing the work to understand that nothing is automatically right for you, nothing will fix all your problems, and nothing will give you immediate and lasting results without some experimentation and work first.

But, this is the solutions section, so let's talk solutions.

Our three main solutions to cultivating holistic well-being are basically the three previous chapters: learn and practice empathy, set and respect boundaries, and figure out what The Four R's look like for you.

Kristen has very different R's than Erin, and the keys to helping each other work on our well-being are empathy and communication. We know that different people are different, and so, Erin doesn't try to convince Kristen that gardening will help with her anxiety and Kristen doesn't try to sell the benefits of video games to Erin. We talk about what we need, and we talk about what our boundaries need to look like in order to meet those needs.

We cannot practice our holistic well-being in isolation. The point is that we need community, even if the activities or hobbies or practices that make up our well-being are done in isolation. Speaking in a virtual TED talk about their burnout philosophy, Amelia Nagoski said, "The cure for burnout is not self-care. It is all of us caring for each other. We can't do it alone. We need each other."[354]

The Good Doctors could not agree more. We have to understand that each of us is on our own journey toward holistic well-being. Each of those journey's will take time, patience, and experimentation, until we find out what works for us. While we are on those journeys, we will need the support of the people in our lives.

They can help us practice empathy with ourselves and others, they can support and respect the boundaries that we set, and they can encourage us to take the time we need to practice our Four R's.

We need this community of humans to help us dismantle the culture of burnout that exists in all of us. We need this support in order to be able to bring our best and most authentic selves to all parts of our lives, especially if we are involved in paid work.

What can you do to support holistic well-being at work?

The most popular answer to this question is to immediately jump to a four-day work week. There is, admittedly, lots of evidence that it works for a lot of people.[355] It may work in your work culture! But, we're extremely hesitant to recommend it wholesale to the American workforce.

First of all, there are some industries for whom it is simply not feasible. Manufacturing, medicine, and K-12 education are just a few off the top of our heads. Athletics, fast food restaurants, and public utilities are some others. So if we're only recommending four-day work weeks as the pangea solution to restoring balance, how do we address these industries?

By starting the conversation differently. Instead of jumping to a conclusion and seeing how our culture could fit that conclusion, start with what your culture needs and can sustain and start conversations from there.

As we've discussed throughout the book, Kristen and her brother own a manufacturing company. They make life-critical products, and moving to a four-day week is not feasible for their industry or their culture. That doesn't mean that they aren't concerned with employee care. Instead, they throw cookouts for employees throughout the summer. They make sure to thank everyone for their hard work as often as possible. They provide flexibility for child care. They support employees through illnesses and make ways for their team to pursue higher education if they choose.

They support *the whole employee*, who all work Monday through Friday, 8:00-4:30.

What would supporting the whole employee look like for you?

Maybe it means reevaluating your bereavement policy. Maybe it means setting up a GED finishing program for your entry-level workers. Maybe it means adding some introvert-friendly activities to your corporate social calendar. Or, maybe it does mean a four-day work week. There are lots of places that offer that option—most business services such as marketing could shift to this, as many already do in the summer.

Whatever you do, don't start with a solution. Start with learning more about yourself and the folks you work with. Ask more questions about what they need, make fewer assumptions about who they are. Seek understanding and practice empathy. Set boundaries and try to keep them, and do the same for others.

Start with The Four R's. Ask your folks what those R's mean to them and how you can help support them. We've given you a lot of tools and a good starting point.

So where do we go from here?

We don't want to tip our hat too much before the final chapter, but we hope it's rather obvious by now that cultivating your own holistic well-being and helping others do the same is a *huge* part of how we move from a culture of burnout to a culture of balance.

For us, holistic well-being is understanding why we have a culture of burnout, taking all the good parts of the WIC (of which there are many), and leaving the toxic parts behind. Holistic well-being means we understand that different people are different and that we don't know what others are carrying or what stories they tell themselves.

It means that we work as hard as we can to see and to understand how all the parts of a person—their unique constellation of attributes—make up the complicated human in front of you. Remember, understanding does not mean agreeing with or condoning any behaviors or actions. But, we firmly believe that if we start to take these steps, then we can start to dismantle the culture of burnout that has trapped us all in toxic and unhealthy relationships with our bodies, with our health, with our planet, and with each other.

What happens when we start to do that? We move toward creating a true culture of balance.

Chapter 18: A Culture of Balance

We've set up this idea of a culture of balance, but we have yet to talk about what *balance* really means. We wanted to make sure we built up all the foundational understanding necessary to finish off with a conversation about what a culture of balance actually looks like.

A culture of balance prioritizes, as the Nagoski sisters would say, the human-being and not the human-doing. It recognizes that everyone is different: personally, intellectually, spiritually, religiously, physically, socially, and culturally. It starts with an understanding that all humans have fundamental worth. It gives space to everyone to build a comfortable, joy-filled life without stressors for the sake of stressors.

A culture of balance respects that: 1) we are built on a culture of burnout and that takes time to shift, 2) different people and different generations and different genders are different, 3) we all have our traumas, and 4) health can't be bought and paid for. It prioritizes empathy, respects boundaries, and cultivates holistic well-being. And, it gives everyone a chance to find the rest that's right for them.

When you picture balance, you might, like Erin mentioned in her story about her cultivation of holistic well-being, imagine a woman in expensive, perfectly fitted athleisure wear on a rock-rimmed beach with highlights in her hair, one leg up in a perfect tree pose, her eyes serenely closed. This is the Wellness Industrial Complex view of balance.

You might also think about a seesaw with Work on one side and

Life on the other. That's burnout culture's view of balance.

Life balance is a lot more like our wheel of well-being, lying perched on a ball that's settled at the center. Each spoke of the wheel has a basket that carries an aspect of your life in it. The wheel spins and it wobbles and you fill up some baskets some days and other baskets other days. And, burnout is one of those baskets feeling so heavy that it's dragging on the ground, slowing down the whole wheel, and leaving a divot in the dirt.

It's hard to get the wheel spinning again. You need to pile up a lot more in the off-setting baskets to outweigh how tilted it's become. But, it is possible, and once it's going, it's easier to maintain when you're being mindful about your baskets.

Erin's yoga instructor was right. Balance is not stagnant. If you've ever done a yoga or pilates class yourself (or even tried to balance a basketball on your finger), then you know that finding balance actually involves constant movement. It's key. There's a never-ending gentle fluctuation back and forth, a willingness to bend a little more this way and then a little more that way to keep from tumbling down to the ground. Doing a balancing position with your body involves tiny clenches and releases from a whole slew of muscles from your core to your arms to your legs, and balancing your life is the same way.

Balance also isn't binary. You're not either balanced or not balanced. There's no point at which we can say, "Ah, the wheel is perfectly balanced, and therefore, you are Done Balancing." The true "adulting" (yes, we're Millennials) is recognizing that this balancing act is something we always need to do to stay healthy—not just physically, but holistically—and when one basket starts to overfill, other baskets need to balance out.

What does overfilling a basket look like?

Overfilling your own baskets looks like saying yes too often, ignoring The Four R's, and failing to keep boundaries in your interpersonal relationships. Part of this comes from you, and part of this comes from the cultural expectations you're swimming in.

We talked about how setting boundaries is often touted as one of the sure-fire ways to help prevent and treat burnout, and here's where you can see why. Boundaries are about more than just saying no to things that upset you or that you don't want to do. The boundaries that are critical to preventing and treating burnout are the ones that protect your need for balanced baskets. If one basket is getting too heavy, putting on blinders and pretending it's not is never going to solve the problem.

Short-term, stress can be pushed through, a lack of balance can be survived. But, there will be an expiry date where that divot is too deep, and pulling that wheel through the dirt will be too hard. And, by then, it takes so much weight to bring down the baskets that were ignored for so long that it can feel impossible to do so. You might ask yourself, "Is it not easier to dig the divot deeper? Make more space for the heaviest basket?"

It isn't—and that kind of thinking is a symptom of the cultural problem. "Can't you just lean in? Try harder? Hang on until..." But, until comes, and there's another "until" after that, over and over.

And, when the basket tips all the way over? Well, sometimes people end up in the hospital, like our friend Mark, back in Section Three. Or, there are a staggering number of people who end up injured, sick, or even dead, from overwork and workplace incidents. Burnout isn't something we can just push through and hope for the best. The only solution is balance.

So, if each person has their own balance to maintain, what does that have to do with a cultural shift?

Being counter-cultural is expensive—in time and energy, if not in actual money. It takes guts and dedication and often societal privilege to stand up to cultural norms and say, "This is unhealthy; we need to stop this."

If your work and your partner and your friends and your parents all expect you to take more and more and more for only one or two baskets, leaving you no time or space for the others, what are you supposed to do? Pushing back is hard. For some people, it's downright dangerous.

In his very first paper on burnout, Freudenberger proposed ways we might prevent burnout.

Because he believed that burnout is particularly linked to specific working environments and organizational contexts, he proposed intervening at an organizational rather than just an individual level. His recommendations included shorter working hours, regular job rotation, and frequent supervision and staff training.[356]

He saw burnout as a cultural problem right from day one, and yet, American society cannot step away from the notion that exhaustion is a personal failure. And, it's hurting, even killing, us.

Remember the Puritans? And all the other soup ingredients we talked about? The soup we swim in can either support taking the time and energy to fill a basket, or it can push back against it. We can change the recipe. The Puritans believed that only the work basket was worth your time, regardless of how slow the wheel was spinning or how deep a divot it was grinding into the dirt. That divot was a badge of honor instead of a cry for help, and *that's* what we need to change.

Burnout is a cultural problem. Changing our culture can prevent it and mitigate it, but whenever that's not possible, or while we're in the process of creating change, stress, and burnout, we need personal solutions and coping skills. The more we each demand our right to individual, holistic well-being, the more others will feel empowered to do the same and the more our cultural expectations will shift, until an expectation of balance becomes the norm.

We can leave the Puritans in the past, where they belong.

What does a culture of balance look like?

The culture of burnout is all around us. It's the soup we swim in, seasoned with our own personal experiences, perspectives, and context.

What is a culture of balance? For our money? Denmark.

We joke, but really, there are a few elements of Danish culture that we think are aspirational when it comes to dismantling the culture of burnout. They are routinely ranked as one of happiest countries on Earth, after all.[357] This does not mean that Denmark is perfect, or that no one in Denmark is burned out. No society or culture is perfect or appropriate for all of its citizens—but we should keep trying.

Kristen's paternal family tree branch hails from this tiny nation, and she's had the privilege of visiting relatives over there several times. As she's curious and extroverted, she's also started conversations with strangers while there about what makes Danish culture so unique. Between answers she's gleaned on the ground and other research she's done, she's been using Denmark as an example for a while of some lessons we can all learn in order to create cultures of balance.

Just like the Puritans are at our core, Vikings are at theirs. The difference is that while Vikings were also self-sufficient, they were self-sufficient as entire tribes. It was fundamentally communal and interdependent within the tribe. You were not only encouraged to ask for help, but it certainly sounds like it would never occur to you not to.

This leads to a few things that experts believe contributes to their "happiest country" rankings.[358] First, they do not tie economic success or status to a persons' morality. As we've talked about *at length* in this book, America does. Second, they are highly social, with the average Dane belonging to at least three social groups at one time. This could mean a sports team, a book club, a religious group, a cooking club—anything that requires people to socialize in an organized way with people they're not related to. How many Americans do you know who can claim regular participation in three such groups at a time?

All of this leads to the third element: "remarkable social cohesion."[359] Now, this particular point is a chicken or the egg one. Do they have this level of cohesion because the governmental welfare state has created it, or the other way around? Experts are split, but for our money, it doesn't matter.

In general, Danes trust their government, and each other, to do what they're supposed to do at higher levels than many other countries.[360] We haven't talked about trust too much in this book, but it's a primary factor in creating a culture that doesn't foster burnout. Can the people around me be trusted to take care of me, to honor my work, to accept my needs without judgment?

Now, let's acknowledge some issues that we don't want to replicate. The Danes are very homogenous as a country in terms of both race and culture. There are disproportionately high rates of hate crimes against immigrants. Despite the social safety net, there are citizens who fall through the cracks.[361] Like we said, no country is perfect, and we're not here to deify Denmark. We simply want to explore another way to be.

Journalist Michael Booth sums this all up nicely when he concludes that Danes are, largely, content. They're not caught in the hamster wheel of keeping up with the Joneses (or Christensens, if you will). The welfare state keeps them, by and large, equal (exceptions of course), so there is room for striving, but also the safety net to relax and stop panicking about achieving the next rung of success. In his argument, a key to the culture of balance is contentment.

We don't disagree.

Now, Denmark is certainly not the only culture that is significantly more balanced than the United States. While the United Nations produces the World Happiness Report every year—in which the U.S. ranked 16 in 2021, which definitely made us quirk our eyebrows up[362]—there are other individual cultures that we'd like to recognize as well. While we were researching Inuit peoples and other Indigenous cultures in Alaska, we learned so much about the importance of balance within a culture. Balance with each other, with the lands, and with both the spirits and their ancestors.

The Yakutat Tlingit Nation of Southeastern Alaska[363] are one of our favorite examples. In their tradition, the people are divided between the raven and the eagle tribes. In order to maintain balance within the Nation, no one born a raven is allowed to marry another raven—they must marry an eagle, and vice versa. To them, this maintains both power balance and energy balance within their people.

So, while you may not live in a country with a robust social safety net and a culture of mutual support, nor one that values balance with ancestors and land, there are small ways that everyone can build practices which foster balance in their own lives.

What can I do to cultivate a culture of balance?

When you're given a new perspective on things, it can create an immense amount of motivation that makes you want to get up and reorganize your entire life in one fell swoop. We really hope this book hasn't given you the feeling that you need to do that, but that's exactly how Kristen would react if she read this book.

First, a small note about how your brain handles change: not well. Bless its cotton socks, our brain's *modus operandi* is to keep us safe at all times. Introduce some sort of big new plan—like going to the gym every day after multiple years of never going—and your brain will shut that down *so fast*. This is why most folks cannot keep their New Year's resolutions. They pick big scale goals and swing for the fences when, instead, they should pick big dreams and create small, achievable goals to reach that dream with baby steps.

Basically, if we want to change anything about our habits, we have to trick our brains into thinking nothing is happening. Therefore, our best recommendation is to do something tiny. Pick *one thing* that allows you to exhale a little bit more, sleep a little bit deeper, connect back to yourself a little bit quicker. Pick *one thing*. And, for the next six weeks, do that *one thing*.

Then, maybe add another. And, another. Maybe tweak the ones you've already added because they need an adjustment. Maybe dump one because it's not working at all and try something else. No matter what combination of ideas you want to try—keep them tiny and keep them secret from the security officers who live in your amygdala and want things to stay unchanged.

The process of cultivating your rest, rejuvenation, realignment, and reconnection is *a lot*. A workbook accompanies this book for that reason; we want to give you space to work through our recommendations at your own pace.

However, for those of you for whom a workbook isn't your favorite, here's a handy summary of some questions we've encouraged you to ask yourself or tips we've given throughout the book.

Cultivating Empathy

Our five tips for creating your own empathetic practice. (Page 217 to 218)

1. Get Curious
2. Consume More Stories
3. Push Your Social Media Feeds Outside Your Comfort Zone
4. Seek Understanding Instead of Condoning
5. Look Inside as Well as Outside

Boundary Setting

Tips for Setting Boundaries. (Page 241 to 244). Whether you're looking to set stronger boundaries with friends, family, work, or online, these evaluation steps work for every type of relationship.

1. Different People Are Different
2. Clear Communication is Kind Communication
3. Set and Manage Expectations
4. Be Gentle With Yourself

One of the best ways to evaluate your own boundary setting is to pick a relationship where you think you need different boundaries and go through each of these tips like an inventory. Are you remembering that this person is different from you? Have you communicated your boundaries clearly, and have you managed your expectations about their reactions? Do you remember to be gentle with yourself when you push a boundary or give in to a boundary being pushed?

As for social media boundary setting—which we also cover on page 240—the questions are pretty similar. How much time do you spend on each app or device? Is that how much you want to be spending?

The Four R's

Tips for Physical Rest

1. Take a sleep study to make sure you do or don't need a CPAP machine or other medical intervention
2. Earplugs, pillow, eye mask, mattress—do whatever your body needs to create the ideal environment for sleep for you. Research sleep hygiene concepts to find the approaches that suit you best.
3. Experiment with teas, aromatherapy elements, or supplements if your brain needs some help shutting off

Tips for Rejuvenation

1. What is fun for you to do? Do more of it. (Yes, it can be that simple.)
2. Is there a hobby you currently enjoy but don't do because you feel pressured to monetize it or create for others instead of yourself? Wipe those expectations off the board and re-start with something just for you.
3. Which physical activities or places make you happy? Add it to your schedule so that the time doesn't get eaten by other things.

Tips for Realignment

1. Do a quick inventory of your activities and responsibilities. When you think of stopping any of them, do you feel panicked? Is your immediate response, "I could never do that"? Start there and poke at those assumptions.
2. Think of one task where you'd really like help but don't feel like you can ask for it. Take a deep breath, summon five seconds of bravery, and ask someone.
3. Find a crevice of your time on a regular basis to do something that reminds you that you are important but not imperative.

Tips for Reconnection

1. Who is it joyful for you to spend time with? Intentionally make time to see them.
2. Is there a loved one you struggle to stay in touch with? Reach out and see if there's another way you can keep in contact. If email doesn't work, maybe schedule a regular call or use an instant messaging platform.
3. Consider which types of social interaction fill your basket (Big parties? Paint night? A sport's team? Tea with your bestie?)—Hot Tip: they don't have to be the same ways as your loved ones; you can compromise!

Our Four R's

To give you some examples of how different people find their Four R's, we've both written out some of the ways we find each of these things, and we also reached out to a friend of ours who is very different from us in many ways and asked him about his Four R's as well. As always with our examples, they're meant to serve as inspiration, not prescription, so feel free to pick and choose from our experiences if you're looking for more ideas to expand your thriving toolkit.

The Four R's (Erin's Version)

I already talked a little bit about some of my R's in the previous chapter, but here is my approach in a more comprehensive way:

1. Rest:
   a. A big part of my rest is getting regular chiropractic adjustments, because I can really disrupt my alignment while I'm sleeping.
   b. I've been a big fan of setting my Do Not Disturb for years.

c. Ever since my anxiety peaked during COVID, I've used low dose melatonin to help me fall asleep and stay asleep.
d. Finally—I communicate with our team when I don't get enough rest, and we are flexible enough that if what I really need more than anything is a nap, then I take a nap.

2. **Rejuvenation:**
   a. Shocking none of you by now, my biggest piece of rejuvenation is my yoga practice, which includes both the asana (poses) and pranayama (breathing) branches.
   b. Being in nature is big for me, so my gardening is very important.
   c. Getting to travel to new places has always been rejuvenating and something I actively make time for every year (when possible).
3. **Realignment:**
   a. Again with the yoga—it serves so many roles.
   b. Listening to music is a solitary activity that really grounds me and relaxes me. As an introvert, I need to be very intentional about giving myself and my nervous system time to recharge and recover.
   c. I come from a massive family and spending time with them is one of my favorite ways to be reminded of who I am and where I come from and what matters most.
4. **Reconnection:**
   a. Because I'm an introvert, I reconnect to humanity in different ways. For me, it's important to read a book from a different perspective or cultural group, to watch a movie or documentary that in some way

expands my understanding.

b. I enjoy volunteering at smaller events or donating my time in other ways (helping with graphic design).

c. My cross stitch is really about reconnection for me—aside from one piece, I only do projects for others. I've done birth announcements and wedding gifts, as well as fun feminist slogans. I enjoy the process of figuring out what to make the person as much as the process of creating it.

The Four R's (Kristen's Version)

1. Rest
   a. I have pretty severe sleep apnea, so me and my CPAP are absolutely best friends. My husband and I sleep in separate rooms when we're at home because we both disturb each other's sleep, and when we're traveling together we both wear headphones. I have searched *long* and *hard* for noise-canceling headphones I can sleep in, and I think I may have actually found a pair.
   b. I have a chronic pain disorder, so part of rest for me is making sure I get regular massage and acupuncture treatments so that I can rest.
   c. Erin *taught* me the value of Do Not Disturb, and it has shifted my phone usage completely.
2. Rejuvenation
   a. As our resident extrovert, you'll be shocked to know that time with my

friends is *extremely* rejuvenating to me. Preferably, this happens while eating excellent food together, but over cups of tea on couches is also an A+ experience.

b. When I think of things that feed my soul, I'm blessed to have cultivated quite a few. Live theater, being a Disney Adult, singing loudly in my car. I'd be remiss if I didn't mention baseball here. All live sports, really, but primarily baseball. I can't not be romantic about it.

c. Reading provides both rest and rejuvenation — especially romance novels, so I would like to take this opportunity to thank every single human who has ever written one so that I could take care of myself effectively.

3. **Realignment**

a. I grew up in church, and my favorite part was always singing together. Now that I don't attend a congregation regularly, I mostly practice this through concerts. The power of singing the same words with an entire group of people I will never actually know nearly knocks me to my knees whenever I get to do it. Yes, this includes Taylor Swift and Mumford & Sons concerts. Truth is truth, whatever it sounds like.

b. My plumb line is my personal faith, and while I am not particularly excellent at keeping Sabbath, the knowledge that I need to drives me to try. I stand at the ocean and sing the hymns of my childhood. I sit outside and breathe. As best I can, I do something every day to remind myself that I am created and beloved, I am not Creator.

4. Reconnection
    a. I am a wild extrovert and being with people generally fills my energy tank. Only specific people fill my reconnection R, though, and I am fierce about making sure I stay in contact with them as much as possible. Erin and Eleanor are two of my anchors in this way—I have to be connected to them to feel connected to myself. (They know this, I'm not creepy with it, I promise.)
    b. Volunteering is essential to my reconnection which is essential to my realignment and my rejuvenation and my rest. Whether it be in Marvel fandom, or in international education and equity, I need to give my time to help others to fulfill this R.
    c. Allow me to be sappy on main for a few seconds: a big piece of this one for me is my marriage. We both live chaotic travel lives and don't always get the time we need to really connect. After a specifically tough season where we just kinda let things happen, we've become much more intentional about how we communicate, what kind of time we spend together, and how often we do it. If I'm not connected to my covenant that I made with John over ten years ago, I am not my full self.

The Four R's (Jason's Version)

(A friend of the team, we thought it was time to let a dude speak)

1. Rest:
    a. I am a big napper and sometimes take a few naps a day. If that means napping on my lunch break and eating while I work, then that's what I need to do.
    b. I'm still figuring out if there are medications or interventions that can help me get more restful sleep, so I'm working with my doctor to explore those options.
    c. I like sound when I sleep, so I usually put podcasts, white noise, or thunderstorm sounds on in the background.
2. Rejuvenation:
    a. I love working with my hands, so painting miniatures and building stuff always bring me joy. I have two 3D printers, a CNC machine, workshop tools, and an entire painting desk.
    b. I also like doing similar things with mouse and keyboard; I design 3D models and PCBs which I then construct in my workshop. My favorite recent project was a lightsaber that really lights up and makes a bunch of cool sounds when you swing it!
    c. I am a huge video game fan. I collect games, all of which I play, and I engage with new tech and news in the video game world. I love recommending games to other people based on what they already know they like and supporting indie devs and creators.
    d. I recently got into mixing cocktails, and

I like playing with flavor combinations, making syrups, and learning about how alcohol is made and used.

3. **Realignment:**
   a. I volunteer to moderate, run, and organize communities around some of my hobbies and passions. It's hard work, but I believe I have a duty to spread positivity and cultivate safe spaces.
   b. I'm an intensely curious person, and I always let myself fall down research rabbit holes. I like to explore content from people I don't agree with to help me understand other perspectives and points of view.
4. **Reconnection:**
   a. It's important to me to stay in touch with my dad, so I call him once or twice a week to chat.
   b. I love card and board games, and whenever possible, I meet up with my friends to play.
   c. I'm a moderate extrovert and really interested in VR games and technology, so playing immersive, multiplayer, VR games lets me meet new people, make friends, and rejuvenate as well.
   d. My wife is my best friend in the whole world, and nothing makes me feel reconnected as quickly or as easily as time spent with her—doing pretty much anything—does. Even though we spend a lot of time apart, we make sure to reconnect each day to fill each other in on pretty much every thought that goes through our minds!

Cultivating Holistic Wellness

Be skeptical of trading money for well-being. Research the companies and products you want to use, and remember that if something doesn't work for you, it's not because you failed or there's anything wrong with you. There is no magic cure, as much as we may want there to be. Put yourself first over marketing.

Keep searching and re-evaluating until you find the thing that works for you. Find a few things. Don't be afraid to quit things that stop working. Kristen used to love writing book reviews and found that incredibly rejuvenating. Then, it became a chore, and she no longer does it. Find things that work, stop things that don't, and make sure to laugh a little along the way.

Living a Life of Balance

We'd encourage you to draw your own Wheel of Well-being and write in some ways that you fill your baskets. How balanced does it look? Is any one basket in a rut? If it is, then one of the above tips might help you lift that one back into balance with the rest of them.

In Conclusion...

...we are hopeful.

Maybe it hasn't sounded that way to you. There are a lot of statistics and concepts presented in this book that are scary, hard to confront, or heartbreaking. We definitely went through all of that while researching for this project, and sometimes the amount of work we need to do culturally feels utterly overwhelming.

But, we are hopeful.

Just as finding your own path to holistic well-being involves baby steps, so does changing our culture. We can re-flavor the soup we swim in one ingredient at a time, until the parts that cause hurt and suffering are diluted away.

There is no perfectly right or wrong way to enact change, only people who care, trying their best, and you're already doing that by asking more questions and making fewer assumptions.

We said this book was about how to human better, and in writing it, we also think we've become better humans. If it inspires anyone to join us on that path, then it will be well worth it. Because we are truly hopeful that we can do better, and we can do it together.

Acknowledgements

It's cliche, but true — no book is written alone (or with two people). It would be rude of us to pretend otherwise. We have some joint thanks and then a few solo words as well.

From Both of Us:

To Josh and Sharyl at Kardia House — thanks for taking a risk on us and believing that these recovering academics could write a book that people understand! For all the late night WhatsApp messages and Google Doc comments — we're so sorry we forgot what tense we were writing in. To Maggie for the cover design, Christine for the typesetting, and Laura for the editing. Laura, especially, helped us make some key moments make sense, and also deserves an award for putting up with our flexible relationship with commas.

To Taylor Swift, Gregory Alan Isakov, Lin Manuel Miranda, and the Vitamin String Quartet for providing the soundtrack to so much of our typing. To *American Ninja Warrior* and *Below Deck* for the relaxation provided, and to the oodles of romance authors who penned books that remind us to never settle for less than joy.

To Roger Nielsen for forcing our hand to write this, and to Brian Nielsen for creating the financial space for us to do just that.

To everyone in our Buccaneers family — you have no idea how much we love you. Emory, Beth, Clarisse, the Costins, the Palmers, the Baggs, the Barbers...on and on and on. The home we have found in North Charleston is such a gift. Plus, sweet tea.

To the Irish Framily: Ciara, Mark, Fred, Brittany, Richard, Éabha, Maggie – you are all in this book in all the ways you've held us and fed us and loved us in the last decade. Except maybe Mark.

To Eleanor: What the hell do we say that could *possibly* touch who you are to us? The English language is inadequate. Plus, we'd rather make you uncomfortable by heaping praise on you in person.

And to every sports team who has broken our hearts in the last four decades: we hate you, we love you, we can't wait for you to do it again. Right, Jeh?

From Kristen:

If I could make a wish right now, it would be that my nieces and nephews never know the crushing weights we describe in here. They probably will, though, so I'll be at the ready with auntie hugs and plenty of snacks. Sophia, Chase, Oliver, Fred, Cahair, Evelyn, Quinn, Cormac, Caoláin, Connor – you are all so loved.

To everyone who has loved me, made me laugh, held me when I cried, broke bread with, adventured with – thank you. From Yardley to Wilmore to Waco to Belfast to Discord and everywhere in between. Special shout outs to Katie for helping with the rough edges, Joell for being glitter, and Marie, Ashy, Ferret, Jeh, Moody, Des et al for superheroes. To everyone else who has made sure I remember who I am when I've forgotten, you have no idea how much I am who I am because of you.

To Mike Stroope, who taught me how to write, and John Brewer, who made sure I know how to research. To Gaynor Yancey and Jon Singletary for giving me the gift of being a social worker. I know they'll never read this, but they're all over these pages.

My family is ridiculous and I'm grateful to be theirs. Mom, Dad, Brian – the core four, as Beth calls us. How did I get so lucky? Dad—thanks for teaching me to fight my own battles, but always taking up the sword when I needed you to. Mom—you gave me reading, kindness, and a safe place to land. Brian—no words. Glad we get to fling rings into Mordor together, whatever they may be. My aunts, uncles, and cousins – thanks for the LBI-centric memories. To my various in-laws, thanks for making my life richer.

John. I mean…what? Thanks for choosing me and forcing me to play *Lego: Harry Potter* all those years ago. I'm sorry it led to having to use your words. I love you 3000 for as long as we both shall live.

In 2011, I stood on a sidewalk in Belfast and asked a new friend if she wanted to walk into town with me to buy a phone. 12 years later, you're holding her answer in your hands. Erin, I will never want to do this life without you. Thanks for choosing me, too.

From Erin:

I am beyond blessed to have friends and family around the world who challenge me, support me, and help me balance grounding with growing. To all the folks in my favorite places – Pittsburgh, Colorado Springs, Belfast, Roundstone, Clonmel, and Charleston – thanks for the laughs, the hugs, the bitch-fests and gin marathons, the cups of tea, and the belief in me and our work.

To my blood relations, the Hinson Clan and McDonough Nation, I love you all to the moon and back. I am grateful every day I was born into our wacky and wonderful families and that you all continue to walk this "one road" with me.

The three people that ground me the most are my parents and my brother. Momma, you are my OG Best Friend (I'll explain what that means) and I am a better person for every day I know you. Daddy, you are such a great cheerleader, and your belief in my success and happiness is such a comfort on the hard days. Will, you are a great human and my favorite brother, and I couldn't do this job without your support.

Kristen – there is literally no one else I would want to do this work with. Cheers to starting our Authors Era, to kicking off our 40s with a bang, and to all our adventures yet to come!

Endnotes

For our list of specific burnout resources, please visit https://bit.ly/ARburnoutlist

Section One: What Is Burnout?

1. World Health Organization (WHO), 2019. "Burn-out an "occupational phenomenon": International Classification of Diseases."
2. American Psychiatric Association (APA), 2013. *Diagnostic and statistical manual of mental disorders* (5th ed.).
3. Nagoski, Emily & Nagoski, Amelia, 2019. *Burnout: The Secret to Unlocking the Stress Cycle*, pg 79-81.
4. Heinemann, Linda & Heinemann, Torsten, 2017. "Burnout Research: Emergence and Scientific Investigation of a Contested Diagnosis," *SAGE Open*.
5. Ibid.
6. Ibid.
7. Makin, Gregg, 2005. Unpublished PhD Thesis. "Understanding the turnover intentions of youth pastors." Regent University. Accessed through ProQuest June 6, 2023.
8. Taniguchi, Hiromi & Thomas, Leonard, 2010. "The Influences of Religious Attitudes on Volunteering." *International Society for Third Sector Research*, pg 351.
9. Abramson, Ashley, 2021. "The impact of parental burnout: What psychological research suggests about how to recognize and overcome it." *APA*.

10. Mayo Clinic, 2021. "Job burnout: How to spot it and take action."; Canadian Centre for Occupational Health and Safety, 2023. "Workplace Stress—General."
11. Godwin, Richard, 2022. "More People than Ever Are Experiencing Burnout, but What Can We Do about It?" *Men's Health.*
12. Chopra, Deepta & Zambelli, Elena, 2017. "No Time to Rest: Women's Lived Experiences of Balancing Paid Work and Unpaid Care Work." I*nstitute of Development Studies*, pg 30.
13. Malesic, Jonathan, 2022. "How Men Burn Out." *The New York Times.*
14. Canadian Centre for Occupational Health and Safety, 2023. "Workplace Stress—General."
15. Michel, Alexandra, 2016. "Burnout and the Brain." *Association for Psychological Science.*
16. Ibid.
17. Hart, Gemma, 2020. "A detailed look at why employee burnout can be so detrimental to businesses." *ALM | Benefits Pro.*
18. Michel, Alexandra, 2016. "Burnout and the Brain." *Association for Psychological Science.*
19. Oswald, Andrew et al, 2015. "Happiness and Productivity." *Journal of Labor Economics.*
20. Headspace, 2021. "Rising work stress and burnout."
21. Pazzanese, Christina, 2016. "The high price of workplace stress." *The Harvard Gazette.*
22. We have yet to speak to a business owner who isn't concerned about profit and loss statements. If you are one, please get in touch because we legitimately have some questions.
23. Ferguson, Jacquelyn. "Workplace Stress Strains Organizations' Bottom Lines." *Corporate Wellness Magazine.*
24. UMass Lowell. "Financial Costs of Job Stress."
25. Shoshan, Hadar Nesher & Sonnentag, Sabine, 2020. "The effects of employee burnout on customers: An experimental approach." *Work & Stress: An International Journal of Work, Health & Organizations.*
26. For our complete list of burnout resources and recommendations: Burnout Resource List.
27. Heinemann, Linda & Heinemann, Torsten, 2017. "Burnout

Research: Emergence and Scientific Investigation of a Contested Diagnosis," *SAGE Open*.

Section Two: The Soup We Swim In

28. Hall, David G., 2019. *The Puritans: A Transatlantic History*, pg 10.
29. Constitutional Rights Foundation, 2013. "Puritan Massachusetts: Theocracy or Democracy?"
30. For more information on the specifics of separation of church and state, google "BJC Separation of Church and State," and they'll be able to help.
31. Brief note on these points: the Puritans had "Calvinistic theology," which is named for John Calvin, a dude who had a lot of thoughts about Christianity and wrote quite a lot of them down. However, there is RAGING DEBATE as to whether the faith practiced as "Calvinism" would be something John Calvin might even approve of, in the same way that a lot of people don't know if Martin Luther would be all that thrilled with how Protestantism, as a whole, has turned out. All that being said, there are a lot of elements of Calvinist theology, and even the specific subset of Puritanical theology, that don't matter to our discussion today. So, before anyone reading says, "You guys, that's a real oversimplification of a complex theological system"—we know. It totally is. It's not wrong, though.
32. We should say, here, that this connection between Calvinist theology and Capitalism was first made by sociologist Max Weber in his work *Protestant Work Ethic and the Spirit of Capitalism*. His specific conclusions have been proven wrong since his writing in the early 20th century, but the foundational vibes are accurate.
33. ChangeFactory. "Working with cultural differences." ; Maricopa Community Colleges. "Hofstede's Cultural Dimensions."
34. Rosenbaum, Ava, 2018. "Personal Space and American Individualism." *Brown Political Review*.
35. Andre, Claire & Velasquez, Manuel, 1992. "Creating the Good Society." *Santa Clara University*.

36. Ibid.
37. Zakaras, Alex, 2022. "Alex Zakaras on The Roots of American Individualism." *Princeton University Press.*
38. Ibid.
39. Ibid.
40. Ibid.
41. Robinson, Quentin. "The Birth, Life and Death of the American Porch." *Tippecanoe County Historical Association.*
42. Craven, Jackie, 2019. "Influences on American Home Styles, 1600 to Today." *ThoughtCo.*
43. University of Virginia Miller Center. "McCarthyism and The Red Scare."
44. Posner, Gerald, 2020. *Pharma: Greed, Lies, and the Poisoning of America*, pg 131.
45. Ibid.
46. Prior to the big push for a drug to treat infections and viruses, the pharmaceutical industry had only focused on developing pain treatments. We had phenobarbital on the market by 1912, and the infamous oxycodone joined the fray by 1916. Ibid, pg 28.
47. Ibid, pg 35.
48. Ibid.
49. Abbey Research "Dopesick" YouTube Playlist.
50. *Pharma: Greed, Lies, and the Poisoning of America*, pg 62.
51. We don't have the time, or the mental health bandwidth, to get into all the damage done by Arthur and the Sacklers (what a shit boy band name), but we do have some recommendations on where to start: Gerald Posner's book *Pharma: Greed, Lies, and the Poisoning of America*, Patrick Radden Keefe's masterpiece *Empire of Pain: The Secret History of the Sackler Dynasty*, and Beth Macy's seminal work *Dopesick: Dealers, Doctors, and the Drug Company that Addicted America.*
52. *Pharma: Greed, Lies, and the Poisoning of America*, pg 93.
53. Stewart, Ellie, 2018. "The Trial of OJ Simpson and the Rise of 24-hour News Media." *Medium.*
54. It is important to note that 24-hour news channels were not the only contributors to our current state of information overload. The 1980s also brought us MTV and ESPN 24 hours

a day, helping to train all Americans to expect constant updates about our favorite musicians and sports teams, as well as news stories. If you don't know, or in case you forgot what happened in Waco, see: Monroe, Rachel, 2023. "What Really Happened at Waco." *The New Yorker*.

55. Zorthian, Julia, 2015. "How the O.J. Simpson Verdict Changed the Way We All Watch TV." *TIME*.
56. Ibid.
57. Spector, Nicole, 2017. "'Headline stress disorder': Hope to cope with the anxiety caused by the 24/7 news cycle." *NBC News*.
58. APA, 2017. "Many Americans Stressed about Future of Our Nation, New APA *Stress in America*™ Survey Reveals."
59. Spector, Nicole, 2017. "'Headline stress disorder': Hope to cope with the anxiety caused by the 24/7 news cycle." *NBC News*.
60. Gabbert, Elisa, 2018. "Is compassion fatigue inevitable in an age of 24-hour news?" *The Guardian*.
61. Ibid.
62. To read more about understanding generational categories with a healthy dose of skepticism here, see Dimock, Michael, 2023. "5 things to keep in mind when you hear about Gen Z, Millennials, Boomers and other generations." *Pew Research Center*.
63. From both of us: *Eye-roll emoji* Levin, Sam, 2017. "Millionaire tells millennials: if you want a house, stop buying avocado toast." *The Guardian*
64. Cambridge Dictionary. "lawnmower parent."
65. We Are Teachers (online teacher's blog), 2018. "Lawnmower Parents Are the New Helicopter Parents & We Are Not Here for It." and also Hopegood, Rose, 2020. "The perils of 'sharenting': The parents who share too much." *Al Jazeera*.
66. From Erin: I guess we really have to cite *Must Love Dogs* here, and I'm not sad about it. *Must Love Dogs* (2005).
67. Fry, Richard, 2018. "Millennials are the largest generation in the U.S. labor force." *Pew Research Center*.
68. Monahan, Kelly, et al, 2018. "Decoding millennials in the gig economy: Six trends to watch in alternative work." *Deloitte*.

69. Parker, Kim, *et al*, 2022. "COVID-19 Pandemic Continues To Reshape Work in America." *Pew Research Center* ; McKinsey & Company, 2021. "The future of work after COVID-19." *McKinsey Global Institute.*
70. This may be a surprise to some of you, but we're seeing consistent data that The Youths are over being isolated into Zoom rooms. See: Bruner, Raisa, 2021. "Remote Work Is All Gen Z Knows. But Are They Satisfied?" *TIME.* ; Williams, Trey, 2023. "Gen Z is leading the growing pack of workers who want to go to the office more, and they say they're more productive for it." *Fortune.*
71. Parker, Kim & Igielnik, Ruth, 2020. "On the Cusp of Adulthood and Facing an Uncertain Future: What We Know About Gen Z So Far." *Pew Research Center.*
72. One of our favorite parts of our lives! The CRI is run in collaboration between ourselves and Charleston Southern University Hans A. Nielsen College of Business. We provide internships in emotional intelligence and marketing, and they provide us with an entire university in which to do research about how to prepare Gen Z for the workforce and the workforce for Gen Z. Honestly, we love it and can gush about the folks there for, conservatively, ten years.
73. Cassady, Kim, 2017. "3 Ways Technology Influences Generational Divides at Work." *Entrepreneur.*
74. Milmo, Dan & Packham, Alfie, 2023. "'They're 25, they don't do emails': is instant chat replacing the inbox?" *The Guardian.* ; Gilpin Faust, Drew, 2022. "Gen Z Never Learned To Read Cursive: How will they interpret the past?" *The Atlantic.*
75. Fares, Omar H., 2023. "Gen Z goes retro: Why the younger generation is ditching smartphones for 'dumb phones'." *The Conversation.*
76. Aguas, M. Jake, 2019. "Millennial and Generation Z's Perspectives on Leadership Effectiveness." *Emerging Leadership Journeys Journal.*
77. Nguyen, Terry, 2022. "Gen Z does not dream of labor." *Vox.*
78. We need to thank the incomparable Stanley Tucci for that last phrase, which he uses in the truly underrated movie *Easy A.*

Spell it with your peas!

79. You will have seen from the Table of Contents that we're devoting a whole chapter to the Wellness Industrial Complex in Section Three. It is a huge part of how we live and work in American burnout culture, so stay tuned for all the juicy gossip later on.
80. For deeper dives see: Pessoa, Luiz, 2010. "Emotion and Cognition and the Amygdala: From "what is it?" to "what's to be done?"" *Neuropsychologia.* ; Boyer, Pascal, 2020. *Minds Make Societies: How Cognition Explains the World Humans Create.*
81. Ssentongo, Paddy & McCall-Hosenfield, Jennifer, 2021. "Gun violence soared during the COVID-19 pandemic, a new study finds—but the reasons why are complex." *The Conversation.*
82. Perlman, Merrill, 2018. "The origin of the term 'intersectionality'." *Columbia Journalism Review.*
83. The best explanation we've come across to explain this default assumption is Caroline Criado Perez's "default male" description. Criado Perez, Caroline, 2019. *Invisible Women: Data Bias in a World Designed for Men*, pg 1-25.
84. Henderson, Felicia A. & Kinias, Zoe, 2020. "Unearthing the Roots of Systemic Racism." *INSEAD Knowledge.*
85. Cheyenne, Yasmin, 2022, *The Sugar Jar: Create Boundaries, Embrace Self-Healing, Enjoy the Sweet Things in Life*; Hemingway, Kristin, 2018, *The Black Girl's Guide to Self-Care*; Hersey, Tricia, 2022. *Rest is Resistance: A Manifesto*
86. Fusaro, Roberta & Rahilly, Lucia, 2021. "The state of burnout for women in the workplace." *The McKinsey Podcast.*
87. Irvin, Lanaya & Kulkarni, Manjusha, 2023. "Hate incidents are creating a burnout crisis among Asian and Asian American professionals, new research reveals. Here's what we need to do next." *Fortune.*
88. Ibid.
89. Cheng, Lisa. "Burnout, Rest, and the Asian-American Experience." *Asian Mental Health Collective.*
90. Ibid.
91. Byrne-Haber, Sheri, 2019. "Disability Burnout is Real: Left unchecked, disability burnout can completely take over your

life." *Medium.*

92. Ibid.
93. Ibid.
94. Jain-Link, Pooja & Taylor Kennedy, Julia, 2019. "Why People Hide Their Disabilities at Work." *Harvard Business Review.*
95. Ibid.
96. Neff, Megan Anna. "Autism and ADHD Burnout Recovery." *Neurodivergent insights.*
97. Ibid.
98. Ibid.
99. Winegarner, Beth, 2021. "'The Battery's Dead': Burnout Looks Different in Autistic Adults." *The New York Times.*
100. Clarity Clinic, 2022. "Not Just a Language Barrier: Anxiety and Stress in Immigrants."
101. Noe-Bustamente, Luis et al, 2022. "In Their Own Words: Asian Immigrants' Experiences Navigating Language Barriers in the United States." *Pew Research Center.*
102. APA, 2022. "Work, Stress, and Health & Socioeconomic Status."
103. Ibid.
104. Ibid.
105. Brown, Brené, 2018. *Dare to Lead*, pg 258.
106. Harper, Faith, 2017. *Unf*ck Your Brain: Using Science to Get Over Anxiety, Depression, Anger, Freak-Outs, and Triggers.*
107. Burton, Robert A., 2008. *On Being Certain: Believing You Are Right Even When You're Not*, pg 258-259.
108. Harper, Faith, 2017. *Unf*ck Your Brain: Using Science to Get Over Anxiety, Depression, Anger, Freak-Outs, and Triggers*, pg 17.
109. U.S. Department of Agriculture Economic Research Service, 2011. "Where are the food deserts in the U.S?"
110. For more information on this topic and to get involved, check out any of the following organizations: Move for Hunger, D.C. Central Kitchen, Philabundance, 412 Food Rescue, and Food for Thought Foundation.
111. Everytown For Gun Safety, 2022. "MONUMENTAL VICTORY FOR GUN SAFETY: Everytown, Moms Demand Action, Students Demand Action Celebrate Gun Sense Champi-

on President Joe Biden Signing Bipartisan Safer Communities Act Into Law."

112. National Institute of Mental Health, 2023. "Coping With Traumatic Events." ; *Unf*ck Your Brain: Using Science to Get Over Anxiety, Depression, Anger, Freak-Outs, and Triggers.* ; Boland, Matthew et al (eds.), 2022. "How Intergenerational Trauma Impacts Families." *PsychCentral.*
113. Kristen has no idea how to be brief about trauma, and this was a real fight for her to get the word count down. She can talk about epigenetic markers for *hours*, but we know not everyone knows what they are. Thanks to Dr. Nadine Burke Harris for this analogy: if your DNA is the music notes on a page, epigenomes are the markings which tell you how to play the notes. Epigenomes select certain pieces of your DNA over others to tell your brain how to react to life happening around you. Those epigenomes are programmed by our ancestral trauma. So, sometimes, it really is your parents' fault.
114. Marken, Stephanie & Agrawal, Sangeeta, 2022. "K-12 Workers Have Highest Burnout Rate in U.S." *Gallup.*
115. Rosenkrantz, Holly, 2021. "Pandemic-Related Rise in Unionization Means Managers Need to Watch Workplace Dynamics." *SHRM.*
116. Wong, Brittany, 2021. "What Is Toxic Productivity? Here's How To Spot The Damaging Behavior." *HuffPost.*
117. Ssentongo, Paddy & McCall-Hosenfield, Jennifer, 2021. "Gun violence soared during the COVID-19 pandemic, a new study finds—but the reasons why are complex." *The Conversation.* ; UN Women. "The Shadow Pandemic: Violence against women during COVID-19."
118. Lluch, Cristina et al, 2022. "The Impact of COVID-19 Pandemic on Burnout, Compassion Fatigue, and Compassion Satisfaction in Healthcare Personnel: A Systematic Review of the Literature Published during the First Year of the Pandemic." *Healthcare (Basel).*
119. We thank TEDxFarmingdale 2021 for the opportunity for Kristen to present some of these ideas. Parts of this section were first spoken at that event.
120. Conflict Archive on the Internet (CAIN). "Fact Sheet on the

conflict in and about Northern Ireland." *Ulster University.*
121. Channel 4 News YouTube Channel, 2014. "Seamus Heaney reads 'Whatever You Say, Say Nothing'" ; Ustungdag, Ezgi, 2022. "Expressing Humanity During 'The Troubles:' The Poetry of Seamus Heaney." *Duke University Blog.* ; Beiner, Guy, 2018. "Opinion: Whatever you say, say nothing." *Belfast Telegraph.*
122. Cohen, Arianne, 2021. "How to Quit Your Job in the Great Post-Pandemic Resignation Boom." *Bloomberg Businessweek.*
123. Barrero, Jose Maria et al, 2021. "Don't Force People to Come Back to the Office Full Time." *Harvard Business Review.*
124. Gonzales, Matt, 2022. "Nearly 2 Million Fewer Women in Labor Force." *SHRM.*
125. York, Joanna, 2022. "The immunocompromised workers being left behind." *BBC Worklife.*
126. Fuller, Joseph & Kerr, William, 2022. "The Great Resignation Didn't Start with the Pandemic." *Harvard Business Review.*
127. Ibid.
128. Iacurci, Greg, 2023. "2022 was the 'real year of the Great Resignation,' says economist." *CNBC News.*
129. Marsden, Harriet, 2022. "TikTok is credited with coining the term 'quiet quitting.' Now it's turned against it." *Insider.*
130. Ibid.
131. Ibid.
132. Newport, Cal, 2022. "The Year in Quiet Quitting." *The New Yorker.*
133. Marsden, Harriet, 2022. "TikTok is credited with coining the term 'quiet quitting.' Now it's turned against it." *Insider.*
134. Harter, Jim, 2023. "Is Quiet Quitting Real?" *Gallup Workplace.*
135. Newport, Cal, 2022. "The Year in Quiet Quitting." *The New Yorker.*
136. Ibid.
137. Ibid.
138. Morss, Sidney, 2023. "Who's bringing napkins? Generation-Gap Pt. 59." *TikTok.*
139. Simms, Kalia, 2021. "What We Know About Gen Z in the

Workplace." *Great Place To Work.*
140. Rosenberg, Michael, 2021. "Simone Biles, Naomi Osaka Signal New Era of Prioritizing Mental Health." *Sports Illustrated.* ; Gonzales, Matt, 2022. "Naomi Osaka, Other Athletes Work to Destigmatize Mental Illness." *SHRM.*

Section Three: Our Culture of Burnout

141. Aflac, 2023. "Workplace benefits trends." *Aflac WorkForces Report.*
142. Sreenivasan, Hari, 2019. "The true story behind the 'welfare queen' stereotype." *PBS News Weekend.*
143. To be clear: this is a lie. It looks good on Instagram, but it's a lie. We don't all have staff to cook, clean, and mind our children. We do not all have financial resources to travel on our own time schedule. We do not all have bodies that work the way we want them to. We simply do not all have the same 24 hours in a day. Kristen's started leaving thumbs down emojis on every post that claims this—we invite you to join her should you feel so called.
144. Bologna, Caroline, 2018. "Why The Phrase 'Pull Yourself Up by Your Bootstraps' Is Nonsense." *HuffPost.*
145. Swansburg, John, 2014. "The Self-Made Man." *Slate.*
146. Kristof, Nicholas, 2020. "Pull Yourself UP by Bootstraps? Go Ahead, Try It." *The New York Times.*
147. Ibid.
148. Hobsbawn, Eric, 2013. "The myth of the cowboy." *The Guardian.* ; CBC Radio, 2022. "How the idealized cowboy helped build an imagined America." *Canadian Broadcast Company.*
149. Kahneman, Daniel & Deaton, Angus, 2010. "High income improves evaluation of life but not emotional well-being." *Proceedings of the National Academy of Sciences of the United States of America.*
150. Stieg, Cory, 2021. "From the 'perfect' salary to keeping up with the Joneses, here's how money really affects your happiness." *CNBC Make It.*
151. APA, 2022. "Stress in America 2022."

152. Ibid.
153. Ibid.
154. Prendergast, Clementine, 2021. "Put Avoiding Toxic Productivity At The Top Of Your To-Do List." *British Vogue.*
155. Wong, Brittany, 2021. "What Is Toxic Productivity? Here's How To Spot The Damaging Behavior." *HuffPost.*
156. North, Anna, 2021. "Long hours make bad neighbors." *Vox.*
157. O'Connor, John, 2020. "It's time to rethink "success" in America." *The Georgetown Voice.*
158. Ibid.
159. How many of us have only practiced Duolingo because the Owl bullied us into doing it for an achievement? Just us?
160. Haynes, Trevor, 2018. "Dopamine, Smartphones & You: A battle for your time." *Harvard University Graduate School of Arts and Sciences.* ; Ricci, Jeanne, 2018. "The Growing Case for Social Media Addiction." *The California State University.* ; Neyman, Chauncey, 2017. "A Survey of Addictive Software Design." *California Polytechnic State University.*
161. Thompson, Derek, 2023. "Why Americans Care About Work So Much." *The Atlantic.*
162. Mikhail, Alexa, 2023. "Hustle culture is a dangerous myth, burnout expert says. Here are 6 ways to beat it." *Fortune.*
163. Lufkin, Bryan, 2021. "Why do we buy into the 'cult' of overwork?" *BBC Worklife.*
164. Mikhail, Alexa, 2023. "Hustle culture is a dangerous myth, burnout expert says. Here are 6 ways to beat it." *Fortune.*
165. Bondarenko, Veronika, 2023. "Beyond 'Quiet Quitting': Another Workplace Trend Is Making Employers Even Angrier." *TheStreet.*
166. Stinson, Jr., John F., 1990. "Multiple jobholding up sharply in the 1980's." *U.S. Bureau of Labor Statistics Monthly Labor Review.*
167. We'll talk more about Denmark later. But, this isn't the only thing about them we should be paying attention to: Organization For Economic Co-Operation and Development (OECD), 2023. "Average annual hours actually worked per worker."
168. Ibid.
169. Ibid.

170. Miller, G.E., 2023. "The U.S. is the Most Overworked Developed Nation in the World." *20 Something Finance.*
171. Ibid.
172. Ibid.
173. U.S. Bureau of Labor Statistics, 2022. "Average hours per day spent in selected activities on days worked by employment status and sex."
174. Jones, Jeffrey M., 2023. "Half in U.S. Say They Are Worse Off, Highest Since 2009." *Gallup News.*
175. Lee, Juhohn, 2022. "Why American wages haven't grown despite increases in productivity." *CNBC.*
176. Gould, Elise, 2020. "State of Working America Wages 2019." *Economic Policy Institute.*
177. De Visé, Daniel, 2023. "Recession or not, Americans feel like they're poorer." *The Hill.*
178. Ibid.
179. Mikhail, Alexa, 2023. "Hustle culture is a dangerous myth, burnout expert says. Here are 6 ways to beat it." *Fortune.*
180. Chappell, Bill, 2021. "Overwork Killed More Than 745,000 People In A Year, WHO Study Finds." *NPR.*
181. OECD, 2023. "Average annual hours actually worked per worker."
182. Ro, Christine, 2021. "How overwork is literally killing us." *BBC Worklife.*
183. Cha, Youngjoo & Weeden, Kim A., 2014. "Overwork and the Slow Convergence in the Gender Gap in Wages." *American Sociological Review*, pg 476.
184. Ibid, 478.
185. Lufkin, Bryan, 2021. "Why do we buy into the 'cult' of overwork?" *BBC Worklife.*
186. Ibid.
187. Prendergast, Clementine, 2021. "Put Avoiding Toxic Productivity At The Top Of Your To-Do List." *British Vogue.*
188. North, Anna, 2021. "Long hours make bad neighbors." *Vox.*
189. Ibid.
190. Deloitte, 2020. "Mental health and employers: refreshing the case for investment."
191. Lufkin, Bryan, 2021. "Why do we buy into the 'cult' of over-

work?" *BBC Worklife.*

192. If you're unfamiliar with its work, we recommend listening to this: If Books Could Kill Podcast, 2023. "Men Are From Mars, Women Are From Venus."
193. Canadian Institutes of Health Research, 2023. "What is gender? What is sex?"
194. Ibid. Also, for a much more comprehensive description of sex, gender, sexuality, and romantic categories, check out this poster: Wanna Learn More Network. "The Holistic Trans Body Poster."
195. Don't believe us? Not sure what we mean? Here's loads of other folks to back us up. On disproving the gender binary: Fuentes, Agustín, 2023. "Here's Why Human Sex Is Not Binary." *Scientific American.* ; Fuentes, Agustín, 2022. "Biological Science Rejects the Sex Binary, and That's Good for Humanity." *Sapiens.* ; Tate, Charlotte Chucky et al, 2020. *Undoing the Gender Binary.* Cambridge University Press. On gender expressions changing over time: Urquhart, Ianna, 2019. "Exploring the history of gender expression." *Link, University of California.* ; Klein, Jessica, 2022. "'Gender fluidity': the ever-shifting shape of identity." *BBC Worklife.*
196. European Institute for Gender Equality, 2023. "gender roles." ; UN Women Training Centre. "Gender Equality Glossary."
197. Grady, Constance, 2018. "The waves of feminism, and why people keep fighting over them, explained." *Vox.*
198. We would both like to thank them for their work to make sure we could do things like open credit cards in our own names without a male signature, which was not possible when our mothers were born.
199. Parker, Kim et al, 2017. "On Gender Differences, No Consensus on Nature vs. Nurture." *Pew Research Center.*
200. Walker, Kristi et al, 2018. "Strong Men, Caring Women: How Americans describe what society values (and doesn't) in each gender." *Pew Research Center.*
201. Parker, Kim & Stapler, Renee, 2017. "Americans see men as the financial providers, even as women's contributions grow." *Pew Research Center.*

202. Ibid.
203. Walker, Kristi et al, 2018. "Strong Men, Caring Women: How Americans describe what society values (and doesn't) in each gender." *Pew Research Center.*
204. Parker, Kim & Stapler, Renee, 2017. "Americans see men as the financial providers, even as women's contributions grow." *Pew Research Center.*
205. Malesic, Jonathan, 2022. "How Men Burn Out." *The New York Times.*
206. Ibid.
207. Criado Perez, Caroline, 2019. *Invisible Women: Data Bias in a World Designed for Men*, pg 70.
208. Miranda, Veerle, 2011. "Cooking, Caring and Volunteering: Unpaid Work Around the World." *OECD Social, Employment and Migration Working Papers*, pg. 7.
209. Gonzales, Matt, 2022. "Nearly 2 Million Fewer Women in Labor Force." *SHRM.*
210. Note from Kristen: Even post-Cabbage Patch and Rainbow Brite dolls, in church, I was asked to volunteer for nursery duty, and I spent my middle school years changing diapers, singing Veggie Tales tunes, and passing out Goldfish crackers. None of the boys were ever asked.
211. Walker, Kristi et al, 2018. "Strong Men, Caring Women: How Americans describe what society values (and doesn't) in each gender." *Pew Research Center.*
212. Godwin, Richard, 2022. "More People than Ever Are Experiencing Burnout, but What Can We Do about It?" *Men's Health.*
213. Ibid.
214. World Health Organization (WHO), 2019. "Burn-out an "occupational phenomenon": International Classification of Diseases."
215. HR News, 2022. "Women Are Suffering From Burnout More Than Men."
216. Lean In, 2020. "Women are making out and burning out during COVID-19."
217. Chopra, Deepta & Zambelli, Elena, 2017. "No Time to Rest: Women's Lived Experiences of Balancing Paid Work and Un-

paid Care Work." *Institute of Development Studies*, pg 30.
218. Malesic, Jonathan, 2022. "How Men Burn Out." *The New York Times.*
219. Ibid.
220. A 2020 academic publication that examined gender differences in parental burnout found that "escape and suicidal ideats as well as neglectful behaviors toward children were more common in burned-out fathers than in mothers." Roskam, Isabelle & Mikolajczak, Moïra, 2020. "Gender Differences in the Nature, Antecedents and Consequences of Parental Burnout." *Sex Roles.*
221. Malesic, Jonathan, 2022. "How Men Burn Out." *The New York Times.*
222. Ibid.
223. Priory Group. "Men's Mental Health: 40% Of Men Won't Talk About Their Mental Health."
224. Bipartisan Policy Center, 2022. "Paid Family Leave Across OECD Countries."
225. Because Google is our overlord, the only way we found to access Oxford Languages was actually the Google search. None of us own a copy of the OED, sadly. We promise that if you google "definition of wellness" you'll get the same result.
226. Callaghan, Shaun et al, 2021. "Feeling good: the future of the $1.5 trillion wellness market." *McKinsey & Company.*
227. Aflac, 2023. "Workplace benefits trends." *Aflac WorkForces Report.*
228. Ibid.
229. This isn't unlike how Corporate America tried to "solve" diversity for many years. Almost as though doing the actual leadership work is too much, but you have to report some progress to the shareholders.
230. Humphreys, Stephen, 2010. "The unethical use of BMI in contemporary general practice." *British Journal of General Practice.* ; Cleveland Clinic, 2022. "Is BMI an Accurate Measure of Health?" ; American Medical Association, 2023. "AMA adopts new policy clarifying role of BMI as a measure in medicine."
231. Cleveland Clinic, 2021. "Is It Bad to Lose Weight Too Quick-

ly?"
232. Foley, Joanna, 2023. "Health Debunked: Is Being Skinny Healthy?" *GoodRx Health*. For further reading see: Gaesser, Glenn A. 2002. *Big Fat Lies: The Truth about Your Weight and Your Health*. and Lavie, Carl J. 2014. *The Obesity Paradox: When Thinner Means Sicker and Heavier Means Healthier*.
233. Your Fat Friend, 2020. "'The Biggest Loser' Is One of the Most Harmful Reality Shows on Television." *Medium*.
234. Aflac, 2023. "Workplace benefits trends." *Aflac WorkForces Report*.
235. Global Wellness Institute. "What is Wellness?"
236. Stewart, Donna E. 1988. "Pursuing health with a vengeance. Book Review: *Worried Sick. Our Troubled Quest for Wellness*." *Canadian Medical Association Journal*, pg 973.
237. Ibid.
238. Ibid, pg 974.
239. Blei, Daniela, 2017. "The False Promises of Wellness Culture." *JSTOR Daily*.
240. Ibid.
241. Global Wellness Institute. "History of Wellness."
242. Ibid.
243. Blei, Daniela, 2017. "The False Promises of Wellness Culture." *JSTOR Daily*.
244. Ibid.
245. Global Wellness Institute. "History of Wellness."
246. Ibid.
247. Blei, Daniela, 2017. "The False Promises of Wellness Culture." *JSTOR Daily*.
248. Ibid.
249. Kensington Palace. "Queen Victoria. From Pampered Princess to Elderly Empress: Wife, Mother and Queen."
250. Kale, Sirin, 2021. "Chakras, crystals and conspiracy theories: how the wellness industry turned its back on Covid science." *The Guardian*.
251. McPeck, William, 2019. "The Forgotten History of Worksite Wellness Programs: Coming Back Around To Employee Wellbeing." *LinkedIn*.

252. Global Wellness Institute. "History of Wellness."
253. Peerfit, 2021. "The History of Corporate Wellness and Its Evolution to Today's Workforce." *Peerfit Pulse*.
254. Ibid.
255. McPeck, William, 2019. "The Forgotten History of Worksite Wellness Programs: Coming Back Around To Employee Well-being." *LinkedIn*.
256. Peerfit, 2021. "The History of Corporate Wellness and Its Evolution to Today's Workforce." *Peerfit Pulse*.
257. Mujtaba, Bahaudin G. & Cavico, Frank J. 2013. "Corporate Wellness Programs: Implementation Challenges in the Modern American Workplace" *International Journal of Health Policy and Management*, pg 193.
258. Zula, Ken et al, 2013. "An Evaluation of Workplace Wellness Programs: A Perspective from Rural Organizations." *The Journal of Applied Business Research*, pg 659.
259. "Corporate Wellness Programs: Implementation Challenges in the Modern American Workplace," pg 194. ; "An Evaluation of Workplace Wellness Programs: A Perspective from Rural Organizations," pg 659.
260. Mattke, Soeren et al, 2013. "Workplace Wellness Programs Study." *Rand Health Quarterly*.
261. "An Evaluation of Workplace Wellness Programs: A Perspective from Rural Organizations." pg 659.
262. "Corporate Wellness Programs: Implementation Challenges in the Modern American Workplace," pg 195.
263. "Workplace Wellness Programs Study," pg 4.
264. "Corporate Wellness Programs: Implementation Challenges in the Modern American Workplace," pg 195.
265. Ibid.
266. Brown, Elizabeth A. 2017. "Workplace Wellness: Social Injustice." *New Yorkers United for Justice Legislation and Public Policy*, pg 202.
267. She argues specifically that the Health Insurance Portability and Accountability Act (HIPAA) may not protect the kind of health and fitness data that wearable technology or fitness apps might collect. Also, the Americans with Disabilities Act (ADA) does not fully protect employees from discrimina-

tion based on the kind of data they could potentially access through WWPs. And, since Big Tech companies are so trustworthy with our data...maybe we don't do this? Ibid, pg 206 & 208.

268. Ibid, pg 208.
269. Peerfit, 2021. "The History of Corporate Wellness and Its Evolution to Today's Workforce." *Peerfit Pulse.*
270. Osilla, Karen Chan et al, 2012. "Systematic review of the impact of worksite wellness programs." *The American Journal of Managed Care.*
271. "Workplace Wellness: Social Injustice," pg 214.
272. "Workplace Wellness Programs Study," pg 3.
273. "Workplace Wellness: Social Injustice," pg 200.
274. Brown argues that another piece of legislation that also contributed to the increase in WWPs was the introduction of the "Cadillac tax" in 2018. This tax represented a 40% non-deductible excise tax on employer-sponsored health coverage that had high-cost benefits. You might be wondering how this would motivate employers to start WWPs, but according to Brown's research, a 2015 survey found that "70% of responding employers reported that they were expanding wellness programs to delay the impact of the tax." Ibid, pg 201.
275. Zula, Ken, 2014. "Workplace Wellness Programs: A Comparison Between Best Practice Guidelines and Implementation." *The Journal of Applied Business Research*, pg 783.
276. Brown also digs into the limitations on HIPAA and the ADA to impact WWPs, but we didn't want to spend too much time in the weeds. If you want to dig around in those weeds, have at it: "Workplace Wellness: Social Injustice," pg 198-199.
277. Ibid, pg 199.
278. "Corporate Wellness Programs: Implementation Challenges in the Modern American Workplace," pg 195.
279. Here's what we know about Long COVID: National Institutes of Health Care Management, 2023. "Long COVID: What We Know." ; Mazer, Benjamin, 2022. "Long COVID Could Be a 'Mass Deterioration' Event." *The Atlantic.* And here's an insurance perspective on the changes to healthcare coverage: BDO USA, 2022. "How COVID-19 Changed the Health In-

surance Industry."
280. Kelly, Kerri, 2022. *American Detox: The Myth of Wellness and How We Can Truly Heal*, pg 23.
281. Kale, Sirin, 2021. "Chakras, crystals and conspiracy theories: how the wellness industry turned its back on Covid science." *The Guardian.*
282. Stewart, Donna E. 1988. "Pursuing health with a vengeance. Book Review: *Worried Sick. Our Troubled Quest for Wellness.*" *Canadian Medical Association Journal*, pg 974.
283. Braicks-Rinker, Lizzie, 2023. "Your body is talking to you, are you listening?" *TEDxUofW YouTube Channel.*
284. Ibid.
285. Ibid.
286. Ibid.
287. Criado Perez, Caroline, 2019. *Invisible Women: Data Bias in a World Designed for Men*, pg 1-25.
288. Ibid, pg 196-197.
289. Jolly, Natalie, 2020. "Why are Women Buying GOOP? Women's Health and the Wellness Movement." *Birth: Issues in Perinatal Care*, pg 3-4.
290. We don't really have time to get into the larger conversation about women and healthcare, but here are a few resources if you'd like to take a deeper dive: *Invisible Women: Data Bias in a World Designed for Men* ; Cleghorn, Elinor, 2021. "Medical Myths About Gender Roles Go Back to Ancient Greece. Women Are Still Paying the Price Today." TIME. ; International Women's Day. "Power, privilege and priorities: Embrace equity in women's healthcare." ; Hamburg, Katarina, 2008. "Gender bias in medicine." *Women's Health.* ; Samulowitz, Anke et al, 2018. ""Brave Men and "Emotional Women": A Theory-Guided Literature Review on Gender Bias in Health Care and Gendered Norms towards Patients with Chronic Pain." *Pain Research and Management.*
291. Jolly, Natalie, 2020. "Why are Women Buying GOOP? Women's Health and the Wellness Movement." *Birth: Issues in Perinatal Care*, pg 4.
292. George, Jennifer, 2023. "Is Health Wealth? The Relentless Rise Of The Wellness Industry." *ELLE.*

293. Kale, Sirin, 2021. "Chakras, crystals and conspiracy theories: how the wellness industry turned its back on Covid science." *The Guardian.*
294. Jolly, Natalie, 2020. "Why are Women Buying GOOP? Women's Health and the Wellness Movement." *Birth: Issues in Perinatal Care.*
295. While Kristen has Thoughts on MLMs, she's, by far, not the only one. For more information, please see *LuLaRich* on Amazon Prime, the work of Roberta Blevins, or the new release *Hey, Hun: Sales, Sisterhood, Supremacy and the Other Lies Behind Multilevel Marketing* by Emily Lynn Paulson .
296. McGrath, Orla, 2023. "Expert explains why Mormon women embrace multi-level marketing." *University of Colorado Boulder.* ; Carter, Neil, 2021. "Why Evangelical Christians Love Multi-Level Marketing So Much." *Patheos.*
297. FTC, 2023. "FTC Takes Action Against doTERRA Distributors for False COVID-19 Health Claims."
298. FTC, 2020. "FTC Sends Warning Letters to Multi-Level Marketers Regarding Health and Earnings Claims They or Their Participants are Making Related to Coronavirus."
299. Also, we're all part of things that feel a *littttttle* culty sometimes. Check out Amanda Montell's *Cultish: The Language of Fanaticism* for a deeper understanding of what just feels like a cult and what is one. Then, DM us for our thoughts on sports fandoms.
300. O'Sullivan, Sadhbh, 2023. "Wellness Culture Won't Save Us. It's Only Making Us More Sick." *Refinery 29.*
301. Ibid.
302. Ibid.
303. Ibid.
304. Knoll, Jessica, 2019. "Opinion: Smash the Wellness Industry." *The New York Times.*
305. Ibid.
306. Kale, Sirin, 2021. "Chakras, crystals and conspiracy theories: how the wellness industry turned its back on Covid science." *The Guardian.*
307. Bell, Poorna, 2020. "From Palo Santo To Crystals, Millennial Wellness Damages The Communities it Borrows From."

Refinery 29.

308. Ibid.
309. Westbrook, Scarlett, 2022. "Wellness culture is destroying our bodies and the planet." *i-D Vice.* ; VICE News, 2022. "Inside the Wellness Industry's Controversial Supply Chains." *VICE News YouTube Channel.* ; DW Documentary, 2023. "The dirty business of beauty." *DW Documentary YouTube Channel.* ; McClure, Tess, 2019. "Dark crystals: the brutal reality behind a booming wellness craze." *The Guardian.*
310. Kale, Sirin, 2021. "Chakras, crystals and conspiracy theories: how the wellness industry turned its back on Covid science." *The Guardian.*
311. Ibid.
312. O'Sullivan, Sadhbh, 2023. "Wellness Culture Won't Save Us. It's Only Making Us More Sick." *Refinery 29.*
313. From Kristen: I winced when I read this line that Erin brilliantly wrote. I joked that she should just tag me next time. Suffice it to say, this is a piece I struggle with a lot.

Section Four: Solutions

314. Krznaric, Roman, 2015. *Empathy: Why It Matters, and How to Get It*, pg X.
315. Armstrong, Kim, 2017. "'I Feel Your Pain': The Neuroscience of Empathy." *Association for Psychological Science.*
316. Ibid.
317. Hough, Lauren, 2021. *Leaving Isn't the Hardest Thing*, pg 161.
318. Is this cadence a direct ode to *Hamilton*? Who's to say.
319. Krznaric, Roman, 2015. Empathy: Why It Matters, and How to Get It, pg XV.
320. Stanford University Marketing Professor, Jennifer Aaker, found, "Stories are up to 22 times more memorable than facts alone." VMware Women's Leadership Innovation Lab, Stanford University "Harnessing the Power of Stories." See also: Zak, Paul J., 2013. "How Stories Change the Brain." *Greater Good Magazine—UC Berkeley.*
321. Gabbert, Elisa, 2018. "Is compassion fatigue inevitable in an

age of 24-hour news?" *The Guardian.*

322. We could talk about this forever, but since we can't, here are a couple other folks if you're interested to learn more: Eder, Jens et al, 2019. "Media and emotion: an introduction." *NECSUS.* ; Nahon-Serfaty, Isaac, 2018. "The hypodermic effect: How propaganda manipulates our emotions." The Conversation. ; Hullinger, Jessica, 2015. "Why Social Media Deliberately Manipulates Your Emotions." *Fortune.*
323. Gabbert, Elisa, 2018. "Is compassion fatigue inevitable in an age of 24-hour news?" *The Guardian.*
324. Ibid.
325. Krznaric, Roman, 2015. E*mpathy: Why It Matters, and How to Get It*, pg XXI.
326. Neyman, Chauncey, 2017. "A Survey of Addictive Software Design." *California Polytechnic State University.*
327. Ibid.
328. Klein, Jessica, 2021. "The darkly soothing compulsion of 'doomscrolling'." *BBC Worklife.*
329. Kalligas, Kouris, 2017. "Social Media's Dark Side: Learning to Set Boundaries." *Entrepreneur.*
330. If you want to understand more about how toxic and addictive social media (and specifically influencer lifestyle) can be, then we highly recommend the 2021 HBO documentary *Fake Famous.*
331. If you'd like to read more about cancel culture, have at it: Vogels, Emily A. et al, 2021. "Americans and 'Cancel Culture': Where Some See Calls for Accountability, Others See Censorship, Punishment." *Pew Research Center.* ; Dudenhoefer, Nicole, 2020. "Is Cancel Culture Effective?" *PEGASUS—The Magazine of the University of Central Florida.*
332. As we write this chapter, the most recent example is the general public's *strong feelings* on Taylor Swift's dating life and threats to cancel her over it. By the time you read this, we're sure it will be something else.
333. Brown, Brené, 2018. "Clear Is Kind. Unclear Is Unkind." *Brené Brown.*
334. For a particularly American look at food culture, check out *The Eating Instinct* by Virginia Sole-Smith.

335. CDC, 2022. "How Much Sleep Do I Need?"
336. Dunster, Gideon P. et al, 2018. "Sleepmore in Seattle: Later school start times are associated with more sleep and better performance in high school students." *Science*.
337. Chowdhury, Madhuleena Roy, 2019. "The Neuroscience of Gratitude and Effects on the Brain." *Positive Psychology*.
338. Fair, Lesley, 2023. "FTC says online counseling service BetterHelp pushed people into handing over health information—and broke its privacy promises." FTC.
339. Maastricht University, 2021. "How the BetterHelp scandal changed our perspective on influencer responsibility."
340. Merriam-Webster Dictionary. "holistic."
341. More on holism from Merriam-Webster: "The whole is greater than the sum of its parts" expresses the essence of *holism*, a term coined by the great South African general and statesman Jan Smuts in 1926. Holism generally opposes the Western tendency toward analysis, the breaking down of wholes into parts, sometimes to the point that "you can't see the forest for the trees". Holism is an important concept in the sciences and social sciences, and especially in medicine. Holistic medicine tries to treat the "whole person" rather than focusing too narrowly on single symptoms. It emphasizes the connections between the mind and the body, avoids the overuse of drugs, and has borrowed such practices from Eastern traditions as acupuncture and yoga." Ibid.
342. SAMHSA is a part of the US Department of Health and Human Services. You can access their 2016 PDF describing their dimensions of wellness here: SAMHSA. "Learn The Eight Dimensions of Wellness."
343. For example: Stoewen, Debbie L., 2017. "Dimensions of wellness: Change your habits, change your life." *The Canadian Veterinary Journal.* ; Piedoux, Alexandra, 2018. "The 8 Pillars of Holistic Wellness—What It Truly Means to Be Well." *Medium*.
344. McPeck, William, 2019. "The Forgotten History of Worksite Wellness Programs: Coming Back Around To Employee Wellbeing." *LinkedIn*.
345. SAMHSA. "Learn The Eight Dimensions of Wellness."

346. The Princess Bride (1987)
347. "Pursuing health with a vengeance. Book Review: *Worried Sick. Our Troubled Quest for Wellness*," pg 974.
348. Ibid.
349. Paulson, Emily Lynn, 2023. *Hey, Hun: Sales, Sisterhood, Supremacy and the Other Lies Behind Multilevel Marketing*, pg 79.
350. Watch this, it's succinct and fabulous: Mina Le, 2023. "Let's Discuss MLMs, Pyramid Schemes, and Grindset Culture." *Mina Le YouTube Channel.*
351. *Hey, Hun: Sales, Sisterhood, Supremacy and the Other Lies Behind Multilevel Marketing*, pg 124.
352. Ibid, pg 71.
353. Lindsey, Daryl, 2016. "Follow the profit: How Mormon culture made Utah a hotbed for multi-level marketers." *KUTV.*
354. Nagoski, Emily & Nagoski, Amelia, 2021. "The cure for burnout (hint: it isn't self-care)." *TED YouTube Channel.*
355. Liu, Jennifer, 2023. "Workers report a 4-day workweek improves health, finances, and relationships: It 'simply makes you happy'." *CNBC make it.* ; Westfall, Austin, 2023. "Is the US ready for a four-day work week?" *FOXBusiness.* ; Bonnell, Courtney, 2023. "4-day work week trial yields overwhelming success in U.K., researchers say." *PBS NewsHour.*
356. Heinemann, Linda & Heinemann, Torsten, 2017. "Burnout Research: Emergence and Scientific Investigation of a Contested Diagnosis," *SAGE Open.*
357. Hunter, Marnie, 2022. "The world's happiest countries for 2022." *CNN Travel.* ; Kahneman, Daniel & Deaton, Angus, 2010. "High income improves evaluation of life but not emotional well-being." *Proceedings of the National Academy of Sciences of the United States of America.*
358. Danish Government. "Why are Danish people so happy?"
359. We thank Mr. Booth for helping us synthesize a lot of what Kristen has learned over the years into this handy couple of paragraphs. Booth, Michael, 2012. *The Almost Nearly Perfect People: Behind the Myth of the Scandinavian Utopia*, pg 23.
360. Danes pay between 58% and 72% income tax, and Kristen's

family often tell her they'd never trade it for anything. By and large, the country works for the majority of its citizens, and when they compare their healthcare experiences to the ones of us over here, they shudder. Whether or not it's sustainable in the long term is a wildly long debate that we don't have space to get into here, nor do we think that piece disrupts the rest of the puzzle we're arguing for here.

361. *The Almost Nearly Perfect People: Behind the Myth of the Scandinavian Utopia.*
362. Hunter, Marnie, 2022. "The world's happiest countries for 2022." *CNN Travel.*
363. *Yakutat Tlingit Tribe Official Website.*

Books Cited

This is the list of each and every book we cited in The Culture of Burnout. But…it is far from all our citations, so to access a comprehensive list of every single citation, scan the QR code below the list. We didn't want to clutter up the book with endless pages of references, but we still wanted y'all to have access if you wanted to learn more. Scan away and have at it!

Booth, M. 2012. *The Almost Nearly Perfect People: Behind the Myth of the Scandinavian Utopia*. Picador USA.

Boyer, P. 2020. *Minds Make Societies: How Cognition Explains the World Humans Create*. Yale University Press.

Brown, B. 2018. *Dare to Lead*. Random House.

Burton, R. A. 2008. *On Being Certain: Believing You Are Right Even When You're Not*. St. Martin's Press.

Cheyenne, Y. 2022. *The Sugar Jar: Create Boundaries, Embrace Self-Healing, Enjoy the Sweet Things in Life*. HarperOne.

Criado Perez, C. 2019. *Invisible Women: Data Bias in a World Designed for Men*. Abrams Press.

Gaesser, G.A. 2002. *Big Fat lies: The Truth about Your Weight and Your Health*. Gurze Books.

Hall, D. 2019. *The Puritans: A Transatlantic History*. Princeton University Press.

Harper, F. 2017. *Unf*ck Your Brain: Using Science to Get Over Anxiety, Depression, Anger, Freak-Outs, and Triggers*. Microcosm Publishing.

Hemingway, K. D. 2018. *The Black Girl's Guide To Self-Care:*

A 30-Day Self-Care Workbook. Independently Published.

Hersey, T. 2022. *Rest is Resistance: A Manifesto*. Little, Brown Spark.

Hough, L. 2021. *Leaving Isn't the Hardest Thing*. Vintage.

Kelly, K. 2022. *American Detox: The Myth of Wellness and How We Can Truly Heal*. North Atlantic Books.

Krznaric, R. 2015. *Empathy: Why It Matters, and How to Get It*. Tarcherperigee.

Lavie, C.J. 2014. *The Obesity Paradox: When Thinner Means Sicker and Heavier Means Healthier*. Gildan Media Corporation.

Macy, B. 2018. *Dopesick: Dealers, Doctors, and the Drug Company that Addicted America*. Little, Brown and Company.

Montell, A. 2021. *Cultish: The Language of Fanaticism*. Harper Wave.

Nagoski, E. & Nagoski, A. 2019. *Burnout: The Secret to Unlocking the Stress Cycle*. Ballantine Books.

Paulson, E. L. 2023. *Hey, Hun: Sales, Sisterhood, Supremacy, and the Other Lies Behind Multilevel Marketing*. Row House Publishing.

Posner, G. 2020. *Pharma: Greed, Lies, and the Poisoning of America*. Avid Press Readers.

Radden Keefe, P. 2021. *Empire of Pain: The Secret History of the Sackler Dynasty*. Anchor.

Sole-Smith, V. 2020. *The Eating Instinct: Food Culture, Body Image, and Guilt in America*. St. Martins Press.

Full citation list:

Printed in Dunstable, United Kingdom

64165396R00188